NOTES ON THE PORO IN LIBERIA

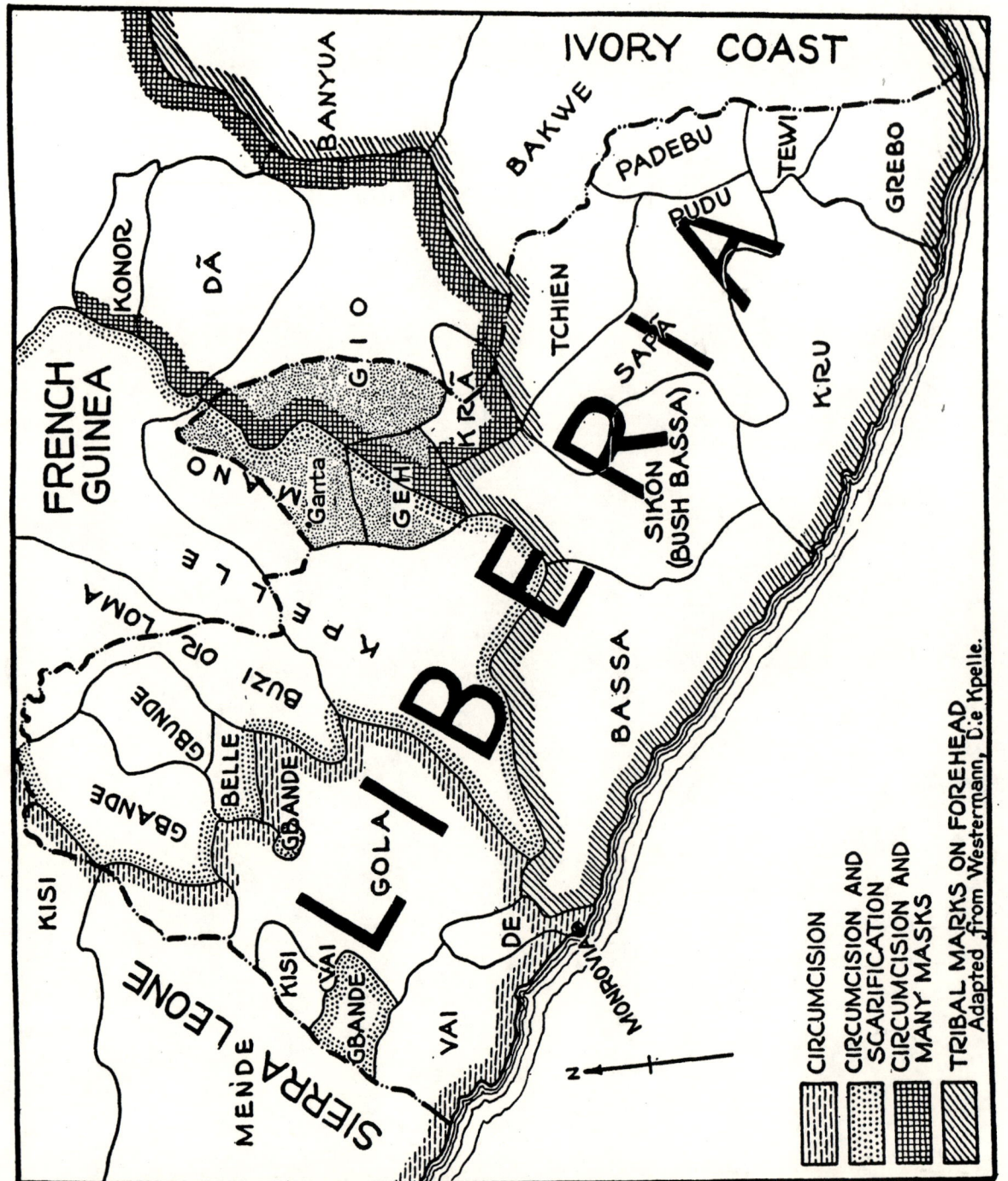

Fig. 1. Map of Liberia showing distribution of the Poro.

PAPERS
OF THE
PEABODY MUSEUM OF AMERICAN ARCHAEOLOGY
AND ETHNOLOGY, HARVARD UNIVERSITY

Vol. XIX—No. 2

NOTES ON
THE PORO IN LIBERIA

BY

GEORGE W. HARLEY

CAMBRIDGE, MASSACHUSETTS, U.S.A.
PUBLISHED BY THE MUSEUM
1941

This Facsimile
of the
Original 1941 Edition
Published by the
Peabody Museum of American Archaeology
Is Strictly Limited to
200 Copies
of Which This Is

Number 105

ISBN 1-57898-266-9

Martino Publishing
P.O. Box 373
Mansfield Centre, CT

Ethnographic Arts Publications
1040 Erica Road
Mill Valley, CA

Ethnos Inc.
Las Vegas, NV

CONTENTS

INTRODUCTION 3	The Poro of the Gio Tribe 24
THE PORO IN LIBERIA 5	The Poro in Other Tribes 26
Tribal Distribution 6	The Sande Society for Girls . . . 27
Some Details of Operation of the Poro in	The Powerful Inner Circle of the Poro . 31
the Mano Tribe 13	BIBLIOGRAPHY 35
The Poro Among the Gɛh People . . 19	CATALOGUE NUMBERS FOR
Entertainers and Special Spirits . . . 22	SPECIMENS 39

LIST OF ILLUSTRATIONS

FIGURES

1. Map of Liberia showing distribution of the Poro. ii
2. Dandai 28
3. Chart of social authority trends showing dominance of the Poro over all of society 30

PLATES

I. Masks from the Mandingo, Gio and Mano-Konor tribes.
II. Masks from the Mano tribe.
III. Masks from the Mano tribe.
IV. Masks from the Mano tribe.
V. Masks from the Gɛh tribe.
VI. Masks from the Gɛh tribe.
VII. Masks from the Gɛh tribe.
VIII. Masks from the Gɛh tribe.
IX. Masks from the Gio tribe.
X. Masks from the Gio tribe.
XI. Masks from the Krā, Konor and Gio tribes.
XII. a. Sande mask, Krā tribe; b, Janus mask, Gola tribe.
XIII. a. Janus staff; Krā tribe; b, headdress worn by god of war, Konor tribe; c, mask worn by dancers and entertainers, Mano tribe.
XIV. a, Masked dancer from Monrovia; b, entrance to Poro; c, d, Masked dancers on stilts; e, g, scarifying knife and razor; f, whistle used in making "voice of the spirit."

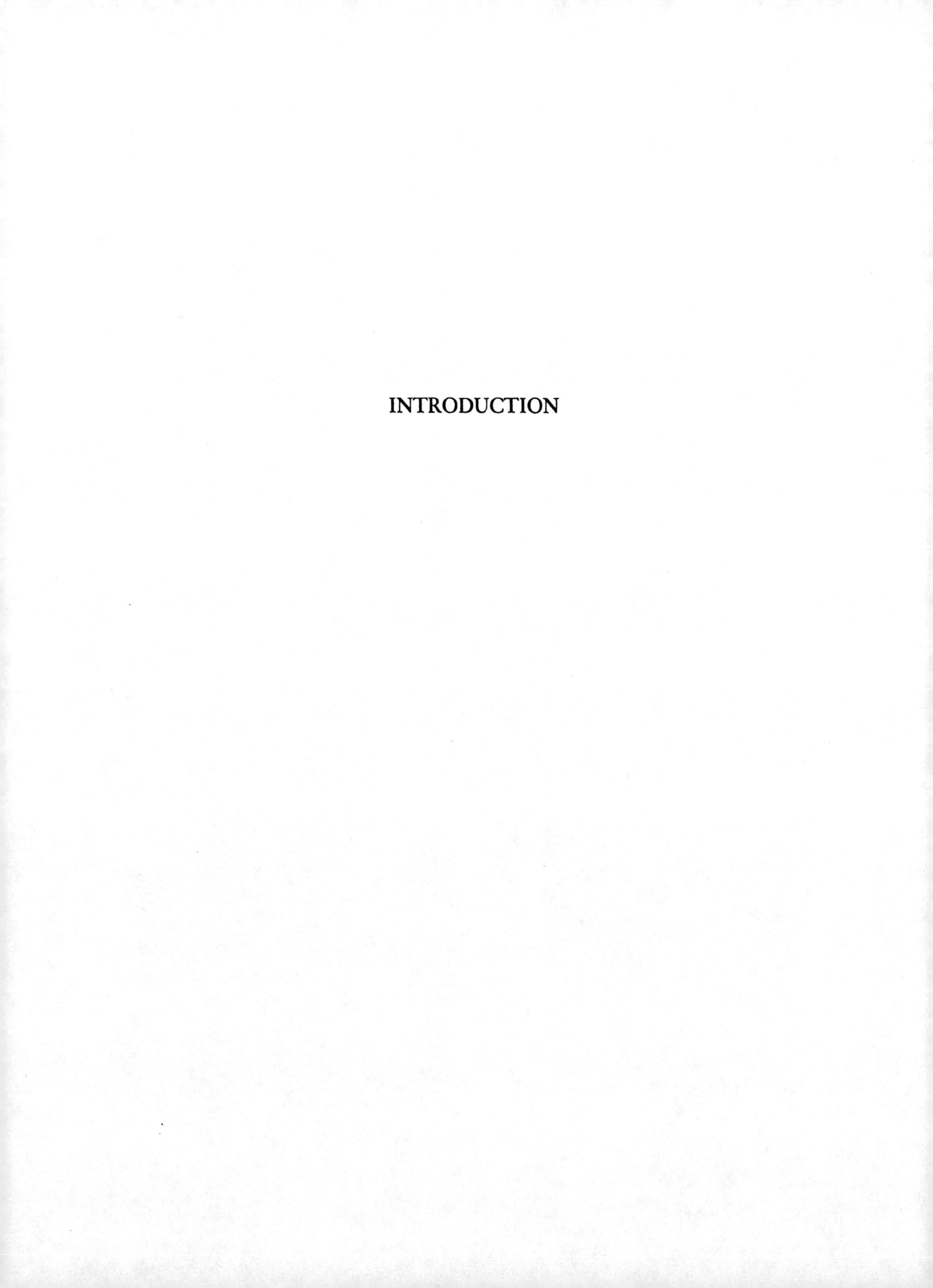

INTRODUCTION

INTRODUCTION

AMONG those customs and institutions which belong to Africa as a whole, tribal initiation ceremonies are perhaps the most universal. Although these ceremonies vary in detail, the underlying principle is everywhere the same. No boy or young man is considered a member of the tribe until he has been initiated by suitable rites into the company of his elders. The adolescent must undergo certain ordeals to prove that he is ready and worthy to take on the responsibilities of citizenship—until then, he does not count. The boys who pass through this initiation together form an age group which acts as a social unit in after life, both in peace and war.

These initiatory rituals are conducted more or less in secret in a secluded part of the forest, though in some tribes the ceremonies are not only public, but even witnessed nowadays by the women. In the old days the usual custom was probably universal, viz. that boys were initiated in secret, so far as the women were concerned. Circumcision was part of the initiatory rite, and sexual continence was enforced during the period of segregation.

In many tribes a corresponding initiation ceremony was held for the girls, and the operation of clitoridectomy paralleled the circumcision of the boys. Both boys and girls were given sex instruction and prepared for the responsibilities of parenthood. They were also taught tribal lore and custom. This educational phase of tribal initiation is emphasized in some places more than others, and is especially prominent in West Africa, where this institution is commonly referred to as the bush school.

The idea of rebirth into a new life is clearly brought out at the end of the ritual. There is usually a ceremony more or less closely simulating death for the initiate as he enters the period of initiation, with a ceremony of rebirth as he returns to the community ready to face life on his own responsibility.

In addition to circumcision, there are in many tribes various mutilating operations frequently misunderstood by observers who describe them as peculiar modes of adornment of the skin, ears, nose, lips etc. They are usually more in the nature of tribal marks, easily so recognized when they take the form of tattooing, or scarification of geometrical designs upon the body. These marks may also denote a man's standing in the community or membership in a secret society.

Tribal initiation everywhere contains, along with the idea of instruction in tribal lore, a supposed contact with the ancestral spirits. The noise of the bull-roarer is everywhere supposed to be the voice of the ancestral spirits, and is used to intimidate the women who are denied any direct contact with the spirit world.

In West Africa especially, the boys in the bush school are supposed to be in close contact with the spirits during the entire period of segregation, if not actually residing in the realm of the unseen. At any rate, they must not be seen by women. The discipline on this point is absolute in many tribes. It is the emphasis upon this point that makes the tribal initiation also a secret society.

In Liberia and adjacent countries the bush school has reached a very high stage of development, resembling in many important details the secret initiation schools of Melanesia and Australia more closely than those of Bantu Africa. Called by different names in different tribes, this complex organization in the extreme western part of Africa seems destined to be known to literature as the Poro, the term applied to it by the Mende of Sierra Leone.

The function and influence of the Poro does not stop after the puberty rites are performed and the class of boys is graduated. On the contrary it forms a very powerful and secret organ to control all its members, and this means all the adult male members of the tribe. The leaders of the society hold sway over the common men, impose laws upon them and keep them in check by the fear of the supernatural power with which they are believed to be endowed. This fear lies behind all chiefs and political leaders, behind all heads of families and men of standing. It has an enormous influence in regulating the social and economic life of the people.

So strong is this power that it is felt even outside tribal limits, and many details of the organization are intertribal, so that a man of high standing will be so recognized even in a distant tribe whose language he cannot speak. An elaborate secret language of signs has thus developed, which is said to be similar to that of freemasonry.

The religious significance of the Poro should be emphasized. Not only are the men supposed to meet the ancestral spirits in the sacred grove; but they conduct rites and sacrifices of a type suggesting the worship of high gods. Though these high gods do not form a pantheon as they do among the semi-Bantu of Nigeria, there is evidence that traces of them appear in the secret ritual within the Poro, perhaps visibly as masked figures. At any rate the Kpelle and Mano names for the grand master of the Poro—*Namu* and *Nyamu* or *Nangma*—may be forms of the name of the supreme being of the true Negro tribes called variously *Nyam*, *Nzambe*, *Anyambe*, etc. The information concerning the secret ritual of the Poro is at present so scanty that little or nothing can be said about the high gods of the people where this organization is still strong.

THE PORO IN LIBERIA

ALTHOUGH the Poro is still alive in Liberia, it is undergoing rapid changes, of which the most important have already been completed; especially the suppression of cruelties, such as human sacrifice. These, of course, no longer occur. The original political power of the Poro is also gone, though there is some remnant of respect for it even among the government officials.

It is for this reason that I prefer to speak of the Poro as in the past. Much of the information that has come to me concerns those practices which have been modified or done away with. I shall attempt to describe the Poro as it was, so far as my information makes this possible, rather than try to disclose what it is today. In some tribes it has been almost completely suppressed for a generation. There are Mano men now grown and in position of chiefs who have never had the opportunity to be initiated. Moreover some of them do not want to be initiated. An excellent evidence of the breaking down of the old order is the simple fact that I, an outsider in every sense of the word, have been able to collect this information which has been so sacredly guarded for untold generations. Most of this information came to me with the ceremonial masks which I have collected for the Peabody Museum of Harvard University.

This collection of three hundred and fourteen masks is by no means exhaustive and has a few duplicates; but it is enough to give a fair idea of their use in the Poro and a glimpse of the Poro itself. There are wide gaps in the information, especially as to the details of the three years training in the Poro school. These notes are most useful to show the contact of the Poro with the outsiders, especially the women, and to show some of the religious ideas of these people. Although the name Poro is not the name for this organization among the people with whom we worked for ten years, I use it because it has already been accepted as the most convenient name of the society by other writers in Liberia and adjacent countries.

The Poro was both a tribal initiation rite and a secret society. It had all four of Loeb's[1] criteria of a tribal initiation, *viz:*

[1] Loeb, 1929, p. 288.

1. The use of the bull-roarer to frighten the women.
2. The representation of spirits throughout the ritual.
3. The fundamental idea of death and resurrection of the initiates.
4. Mutilation, or the cutting of the tribal mark on the skin prior to admission into full tribal citizenship.

Furthermore, it was all-inclusive in tendency, anyone not willing to join being forced to do so eventually. This compulsion was evidently strong enough to create the necessity for a parallel organization for the women, best known under the name Sande. Both organizations had age groups and division between aristocracy and commoners.

Among the northern tribes the Poro had also the circumcision rites and sex instruction which accompany initiation in most African tribes.

As a secret society it had:

1. Absolute secrecy with the death penalty for both peepers and informers.
2. Entrance fees and further fees for each degree of advancement.
3. A pyramid of degrees, said to be ninety-nine in all, in which members of two or three families were eligible for initiation into the final secrets.
4. Ordeals of manhood, and training in warfare, tribal customs, and the various guilds and professions. Skill in the arts was secretly guarded.
5. The privilege of contact with the spirit world.
6. A sign language, songs and dances with a hidden meaning.

There are secret initiations of striking similarity in widely scattered parts of the world: the initiation of boys in Angola; the Galo ceremony of Zanzibar; the Porrang of the early Australians; the Crocodile initiation of New Guinea; Melanesian initiations, especially of the Dukduk of the Bismarck Archipelago; and secret society initiations of many of the American Indians such as the Hamatsa initiation of the Kwakiutl Indians of British Columbia. There is definite evidence from several sources that there were similarities between these Poro rites and those of freemasonry, so striking as to suggest a common origin.

TRIBAL DISTRIBUTION

The Mano, Gɛh and Gio masks which furnish the bulk of the material for this paper came from the northern tip of the central Province in an area constituting roughly five percent of the area of Liberia. They cannot be taken as completely representative of the Poro in other areas, but may well serve as a key for the study of the Poro in its various types. It was here that the spread of the true Poro with its intense frightfulness met the more conservative type characterized by a multitude of masks. The former type, practising both circumcision and scarification, spread from a center in the northernmost tip of Liberia occupied by the Buzi or Loma people. It spread to the adjacent Gbandɛ and Gbundɛ, and through the great Kpelle country to the Mano and half of the Gɛh tribes. It is from the Buzi center that all tribes now get their sacred fire. The conservative type featuring ancestral masks seemed to be most highly developed either among the Bush Bassa or the adjacent Gio tribes, including half of the Gɛh. Both these cultures are said to have come from the northeast. The highest degrees in the Poro, however, and the organization most closely resembling that of freemasonry is claimed by the Vai people whose history and migration has been preserved. They came from the Mandingo Plateau, also to the northeast, but they have entered Liberia from the northwest through Sierra Leone, or along the border country. Their form of Poro does not include scarification, but makes circumcision the main feature, combined, however, with the central idea of all Poro societies—intensive training for manhood and womanhood. Since these tribes are nominally Mohammedan it is difficult to reconcile the highly developed form of the Buzi group with the fact that the highest degrees are held by Vai families who say there are in all ninety-nine degrees in the Poro. In the fourth group of tribes called the Kru peoples, neither circumcision nor scarification is practised, but the tribal marks are tattooed on the forehead in bold black. The Poro with them exists in a somewhat modified form, yet it is said that the highest development of the "devil palaver" or ancestral masks is among the Bassas, one of the tribes in the Kru language group. These are questions that cannot be discussed adequately until more information comes to light.

Also paradoxical is the fact that the Mandingoes, who are also Mohammedans, have a very weak form of Poro scarcely more than a simple circumcision, and not called Poro by the other tribes. This is probably due to the degeneration of any idea linking them with the soil as the Poro definitely did, a degeneration due to their semi-nomadic life. The Mandingoes of Liberia seem to be most closely linked to the cattle culture of the Mandingo Plains to the north. I have a few masks from the Mandingoes (pl. I, a). They are distinctly different from those of other people, preserving the refinement of feature and characteristic expression of the Mandingo face. One of these, (pl. I, b) came to me with the story of its use, which shows also a different culture. It is a mask used formerly in preparing for war. The officiating individual was a woman. The sacrifice was a palm cabbage. The sacred meal was eaten with a ceremonial spoon by all the warriors. Then both spoon and mask were buried in the road and each warrior stepped over it saying: "Let us all return by this same road." They were supposed to be immune to spears and bullets. When the warriors returned, the mask and spoon were taken up. The priestess would wash the spoon, put medicines into it and give each warrior a sip before he returned home. If anyone had been killed in battle, a black cat had to be sacrificed to the mask by the oldest warriors assembled in the secret place in the bush. They danced and sang, asking for renewed protection.

We have evidence of the spread of the secret society with scarification and frightfulness from the Buzi area in the northwest into the Mano country, meeting there a highly developed use of the ancestral mask as an object of worship coming in from the northeast, and swinging around into the Gɛh country to the south. The question arises of the possibility that the Mano people themselves originated from a combination of two peoples coming from these directions. There is some evidence in the language of these people that this may have happened. If it did, it was very long ago.

Though the Poro was primarily a secret society initiation school, the upper degrees and inner circles included duties which controlled government, politics, war, and inter-tribal relations. It was possible for the peers to meet and decide certain things without the common men knowing anything about it. Yet they could not declare war without the consent of a similar body of women meeting in the sacred house of the Sande. A general war was theoretically impossible if either Poro or Sande was in session.

A man of standing in the bush when traveling in a strange country could enter the Poro school and be immediately received according to his rank. The one in charge would put him through his paces, degree after degree, until one of the two dropped out. The person out-ranked would "throw" his cow's tail (carried by all big men as a sort of badge of seniority) to the other. If the visitor was senior he returned the cow's tail handle first, making two times a slight motion in his host's direction, then the third time actually handing it to him. This should be done with the left hand.

The Poro may be thought of as an attempt to reduce the all-pervading spirit world to an organization in which man may participate. It was the mechanism by which man might contact the spirit world and interpret it to the people, where men became spirits, and took on god-hood. But since this spirit world was largely man-made, the Poro was a place where human ambitions used spirit powers for selfish ends. The final secret of the Poro was frightfulness. The all-highest knew enough to say simply: "I am what I am." In the meantime old age among both women and men enjoyed a comfortable respect, and each man had his place in the community.

Under the old regime the chief was not the central power of the tribe. He was useful for ordinary matters, but cases could be appealed to the tribunal of the Poro, which was final. When a masked "spirit" or a gɛ came to town the chief stood in the corner. Certain matters the chief had to refer to the Sande. The old men called (in Mano) *ki la mi* were beyond his jurisdiction. They could be tried only by their peers. They could not fight. They could not be insulted or made the object of physical violence. But there was usually one chief in the community who was also a peer. He was something of a king, and had power of life and death over his subjects provided he worked through the Poro, never against it.

Before initiation the boys were called *gbɔlɔ*, which means an image, shadow, or imitation. While in the Poro they were *bɔ gie*, or little spirits in the bush. After graduation they were *kwɛa*, or citizens. As *gbɔlɔ* they were not held legally responsible for their acts. Any lawsuit or complaint must be directed toward the father or uncle. The boy could own no property. If he did, it would do him no good, because once he was initiated all the past was null and void. If he had married a wife before then and took her again afterward he would have been killed. Consequently, if a boy inherited a wife from his father, she would have to be held in trust by his uncle until he was initiated. Any other wealth could be held by an uncle for him. He was allowed to transact petty business with other boys, but he was careful to collect all such debts before he went into the bush.

To him, as to the women, the officials of the Poro were known only as masked figures called gɛ's, and supposed to be spirits. These gɛ's spoke a foreign language in a rolling falsetto voice with a peculiar quality attained by speaking through a "blowing-drum," or tube with holes at the sides covered with discs of membrane cut from the egg sacs of large spiders. The boy played with other boys, helped his mother on the farm, and ran errands for the chief and other men. He might go hunting with his father but he could never take part in any activity of the community as a whole. He was like a goat so far as the community was concerned, no matter how old he was.

There were three bushes or schools in the Mano tribes: (1) *K'lɛ bɔ̃*, or the circumcision school, which was of small importance if held separately. Graduation from this did not entitle him to any privilege, (2) *Di da bɔ̃*, the corresponding circumcision school for girls called Sande in other tribes, (3) *Gɛ bɔ̃*, the "devil bush," or Poro proper, where he was initiated into full manhood. Officials who wore masks and others who could not be seen but only heard by outsiders were called "devils" by the English-speaking Liberians from the time they first settled on the coast. It is better here to call them gɛ's, as they are called in Mano. Gɛ means spirit. They were supposed to be the spirits of the forest, or of the Poro. Poro means the earth, or the ground, and by association with the Poro school, the forest camp in which the school was held.

It is impossible to discuss the gɛ without saying something about the ceremonial masks, which are frequently referred to as gɛ's, though the proper name for them in Mano is *bai*. They were neither gods nor devils, but a little of both. Yet it is not quite fair to call them demons and let it go at that, because they were primarily portrait masks of tribal heroes, especially those who had helped to establish the Poro. The founder of a Poro was a holy person. "He never died." His actual death was kept secret. His body was secretly disposed of, and in some cases embalmed by smoking and kept in the loft of the sacred house in town where no one but the keeper of the secrets ever went, unless it was the man who was to succeed the holy leader. He was prepared by fasting without water for four days, then admitted first to one house then another until he came finally into the sacred house. When the hand of the dead leader rested on his head, he seemed to feel his spirit enter into him. Then he went out disguised in the portrait mask of the dead leader and carried on his work. In this way an occasional mask became symbolically the dwelling place of the spirit of the ancestor whose portrait it was (pl. I, d). Other masks were caricatures, or faces half-animal, half-human (pl. VIII, h). A few in time became conventionalized as ancestral gods; one, the god of the dance, was identified perhaps with the moon (pl. V, g). One with human breasts for horns became the god of childbirth and fertility (pl. XI, d). The function of these various masks and their indwelling spirits will be understood from details to be given later. That they were greatly feared in themselves is shown by the death penalty meted out to anyone desecrating one, or exposing it to public gaze when properly worn with its accompanying complete disguise. This consisted of a shirt covering even the tips of the fingers, called *gana*; a raffia skirt touching the ground, called *ga*; and some sort of headdress, one form of which was a tall headpiece called *kpɛa*. The wearer was usually a *zo*; that is, a man who belonged to a family of men of special talents in spiritual matters, and consecrated to that work. His work will be described later in detail. There were also women *zo*'s who worked in the girl's school or Sande. There were a few rare women who were consecrated as men, and went into the men's school, or Poro. Only one at a time reached official status, and as such was the consort of the *zo* who was the head of the Poro. She was called *wai*.

When the time came for the Poro, the town leaders might ask the proper officials to open a chapter in the community, but first the chief would sound out public opinion to be sure that they were ready, for it was a serious drain on the public wealth for the Poro to carry on its work for a period of three years or more. When the time was decided the chief called all the citizens to come home, no matter where they were. The men must be close to the home soil and help make everything go right. The people were in this way bound to their native soil. One did not leave home permanently unless exiled for witchcraft.

They usually waited until the chief's son was old enough so that he could be the leader of his age group, not only in the Poro, but afterward in other age groups. On graduation he would be leader of the young men or warriors organized into a subsidiary secret society called *Gaiyumbo*; later he would be chief; finally he would be a big man among the *ki la mi*, or peers. In the Poro there would be three classes: commoners; chiefs; and priests, or *zo*'s.[2]

The information that has come to me from the Mano includes many details of the property and procedure of the various officials in the Poro. Let us look first at the whole thing the way the *zo* saw it. He was very near the center of everything, because he knew by hereditary right the inner workings of the Poro and its *gɛ*'s. It was the duty of a *zo* to instruct his son privately in all these things before he went into the Poro. It was the right of the son to know all without learning it under the heavy discipline of the Poro school.

Among the *zo*'s themselves were several grades. A big *zo nangma*, or *namu*, was head of each Poro chapter. The *zo zɛ gɛ* (pl. I, d) was even higher, having power to kill a rival *zo* who was trying to make trouble for a *nangma*. There was a still higher *zo* who had the right to demand a fee from all other *zo*'s for the privilege of sharpening their ceremonial razors on his sacred whetstone. This whetstone was an ancient celt, passed down from father to son. It could never be bought or sold, but its transfer to the son was solemnized by a human sacrifice—the oldest son of the recipient—killed in the house of the great *zo*, cooked by his ceremonial consort *wai*, and eaten by *zo* aristocrats assembled for the occasion, the father of the sacrificed boy partaking of the sacrament, with the others. This celt, called *lai*, was as sacred as heaven itself. (*Lai* means heaven, or sky.) Its keeper, called *da da lai* the messenger of the sky, was the big commander of all *zo* palaver. When any *zo* wanted to conduct a Poro session he had to sharpen his razor for the sacred scarifying operations on this stone, edge to edge, paying three cloths, plus one bucket of rice, plus one white chicken, plus ten white colas—a small fee, in consideration of his being a *zo*. *Da da lai* could charge much more if he chose to do so. If the visiting *zo*

[2] The term *zo*, is roughly equivalent to our word "doctor," sometimes denoting one skilled in medicine, philosophy, or divinity, and sometimes—an honorary distinction. The term *zo* also connotes something similar to the English word "lord," as *zo*-ship is hereditary.

nicked the edge of the celt, he paid one cow as fine for his carelessness. The one which I saw had evidently been worn down to less than half its original length by repeated sharpenings long, long ago. It seems probable that this celt was originally used for the operations now performed with the razor. If so, this use preceded the discovery of iron by these tribes.

When the keeper wanted to go on a journey he asked the celt about it by casting lots. This was done with the split halves of two cola nuts, saying to the celt: "They have called me. I want to go there. If you agree let the cola sit down." Then he threw the cola on the ground. If all pieces fell face down or all face up, it was well. If some were up and some down, he would not go. To make sure he did this three or four times, the best three out of four being the final decision. If no cola was handy he could use four cowrie shells.

The celt had to pass on to some one else before the death of the keeper. He and his *wai* cooked and ate the sacred parts of the sacrifice—forehead, heart and larynx. The remainder of the body must be completely consumed by the other *zo*'s before leaving the house. During the ritual the "voice of *Gɛ*" was heard in the town so no one would venture into the quarters of the *zo*'s. The *gɛ* had many "voices," one of which was sweet music produced on a flute-like instrument.

The holder of the *lai* could also create other *zo*'s, and provide them with their fetishes and medicines and tricks of the profession. He could also superintend the carving of a mask for a *gɛ*, and make the sacred robe and skirt. Some of these powers he could pass on to the other *zo*'s, for suitable fees and sacrifices.

The greatest of these fetishes was *Dunuma*, for which the fee was the oldest son of the recipient sacrificed and eaten in the Poro. The symbols of *Dunuma* were a horn of medicine and a cone of black clay called *lai zo mba*. The holder was a law unto himself, and begged no man's pardon. With this power, however, came tremendous responsibilities, and the danger of poisoning at the hands of a jealous rival. He might call himself *Dunuma*, though never in public. The name itself was sacred and not to be uttered except when its power was to be used. He wore on occasion the mask of *Nangma*, or *gɛ nangma*, and was the grand master of the Poro chapter, which he conducted with the help of *Wai*. *Wai* could also have *Dunuma* on payment to him in like manner as he had paid, but her mask was different. It was also called *wai*. She could carry on in his absence as head of the Poro.

Dunuma even lorded it over the various *gɛ*'s. A waiting *gɛ* must apply to him for permission to dance in the town, presenting white cola to the *dunuma* mask[3] and smearing a bit of the contents of the *dunuma* horn on his left heel, on his forehead and over his heart. One visiting *gɛ* failing to do this tripped while dancing, fell and died. A "witch" can catch a *gɛ* only through the left heel.

Dunuma did not cut farm. All his needs were supplied by others. He went into the Poro only on special occasions, *Wai* carrying on for him in the meantime. His special duty there was to tell the members and initiates the laws which were to govern them. This happened after the scarification wounds of the initiates had practically healed. Wearing the mask of *nangma*, he walked in and said, "*Dunuma*," at which everyone present bowed down to the ground resting their heads on folded arms, remaining so until he touched each in turn on the back with a bundle of sticks,—his emblem of authority. He then told them the laws of the Poro. All addressed him as *Dunuma*. Any initiate previously reported to him as troublesome or stupid was left prone as long as thought necessary. If a very bad boy he was intermittently flogged by *Wai*; rarely, by *Dunuma* himself, using a bundle of fine switches. The boy might even be left all day, and if he was a hopeless case, flogged to death. He then was consumed as a sacrifice to the discipline of the school. There were no graves in the Poro. Everything there was supposed to be in the sacred realm of the spirits who leave no graves behind them for others to ask questions about. There was also the idea that consecrated substance must meet a consecrated end, as in any sacrament. The mask of *dunuma* never appeared outside the Poro. If a quarrel was brewing, he would appear, say "Dunuma," and leave them all face down to cool off.

To protect him from witch (poison) the big *zo* had a small tin of medicine of which he licked a little every day, probably itself a mixture of poisons to develop a tolerance. It was supposed to "catch" any person trying to bring "witch," throw him down, and make him confess. Then he would be killed and eaten. The big *zo* and *wai* ate the forehead, heart and larynx. The rest was eaten by the assembled Poro. Such protection was very necessary against other *zo*'s, jealous of his power.

---

[3] Probably the same as *gblɔ zɛ gɛ* (fig. 2) and worn only by a *dunumā zo* or *da da lai* acting as *nangma*.

One might say: "This head zo has too good a reputation. It is about time something happened to spoil his good luck. I will see what I can do." Such rivalry and poisoning was not unusual. One big zo became so famous he was deified as the zo killer (pl. I, d). He had seventeen rivals to his credit before he himself became no more than a mask. This mask was so feared that a dog was supposed to fall dead on seeing it. An uninitiated person, especially a woman, would also "fall dead." When it was worn into town, a messenger gave warning. All women gathered children and dogs and scuttled inside the houses, kneeling and clapping their hands behind fastened doors. Even the initiated men crawled around at their duties on hands and knees. So one's deeds lived after him, and one's reputation was perpetuated.

Any zo could have poison. A big zo admitted publicly that he had it, a small zo dared not mention the fact. For this poison there was no known antidote. It was composed of crocodile gall (or python gall) mixed with the bark and leaves of two plants *mene gbɔla* and *yeīn yidi*. A little smeared on the blade of a knife was enough—smeared on one side. The poisoner invited his rival to eat "meat" with him. This meant elephant meat, the proper food of zo's. It could not be refused. The host then had only to remember which side of the knife had poison on it, use the knife to cut the meat, and give the victim the half from that side of the knife. Zo's ate frequently together, one never knowing when the other might get the drop on him.

The popularity of a big zo depended largely on his skill with the scarifying razor. He might call other zo's in to help him with the scarifications if there were a large number of boys, but he would ordinarily do the cutting himself. Big scars were a disgrace, both to the operator and to the initiate. Every man was proud of fine dainty marks. If the razor slipped and made a deep cut the operator must pay a fine of one cow and ten cloths. He could not go and get these things himself. He stayed in the Poro, himself a prisoner, with his foot in a stick until his family was notified by his superior or some other big zo. If the fine was not paid that same day, the prisoner forfeited his own life as the same sort of a sacrifice that he had so often helped to eat. He was eaten by the other zo's, not by the neophytes. He was a sacrifice to efficiency.

To avoid such a calamity the operating zo wore an iron ring around his arm, just above the elbow, "so all his muscles would be careful." To make the skin soft he rubbed it with the juice of a succulent plant. To help the boy sit still he rubbed his skin with the juice of one of the *urticaceae*, producing an itching like that of poison ivy. The boy didn't dare scratch. The cutting really felt good. The marks were cut with the help of two tiny hooks like fish hooks, or hawk's talons made of iron. With these hooks set close together in a suitable handle, the operator picked up two tiny bits of skin and sliced them both off at the same time, cutting with the edge of the razor against the points, lest points and razor should go too deep. If he was clumsy he was called the "old woman making pots," i.e. his marks were like those on a pot. If he was skillful, boys would be sent to him from adjacent towns, and his prosperity would be assured.

To aid in this popularity he had a fetish—clay cone to which he prayed every new moon, sacrificing an egg or a chicken. If this was not convenient on the day the new moon was seen he must talk to it, spewing cold water on it from his mouth and saying: "I will owe you this month's sacrifice until next month" or "I will give you your part tomorrow." This cone, called *zang*, was supposed to be as intelligent as a person. In fact, it was supposed to turn into a person at night and go about saying good things about its owner. The ritual of sacrifice to this *zang* was quite elaborate.

He had also a bit of black magic with which to "tie" an enemy's name and so put a spell on him to cause bad luck, a certain sickness or even death. This fetish was a fearsome thing, not to be approached without due precaution. It could even turn on the owner if he did not wash the spell off of it after he was through. *Wai* also had something of the sort with which to tie her enemies.

All these properties the zo had to keep absolutely secret. The most sacred of them all were the two little hooks with which he lifted bits of skin. If he sold or revealed these he would be killed and eaten by all. Even his own son would partake, showing that the obligation in this respect was stronger than the clan taboos which forbade any eating of one's own family, though anyone else was good meat.

Any work he did in connection with fitting out a *gɛ* was also a high secret. The work must be done in a place as far away from his own village as practical, out in the forest. If anyone should stumble upon him while at work he must be sworn to secrecy. He usually made the outfit in pieces, each piece in a different place. When all was assembled, the gɛ-to-be was asked to pay as fee: "a white chicken," meaning a human sacrifice, to be eaten as usual except the heart, forehead and larynx. The larynx in this case was eaten by the gɛ-to-be so that his own voice might be fine and always disguised. He was given also the forehead to dry and keep so that he would not forget that he was a spirit—that his mask had the soul of the sacrifice to witness and tie him to the laws of the gɛ, especially the one that said he must die if he exposed himself to the public as a man with a mask. He must be merely a mask with a voice, acting in character, and always something more than human. The heart went to the zo who made the outfit. He had it dried and covered with leather by the blacksmith, and fitted with a cord so that it hung just over his own heart. One zo would exchange courtesies with another by asking: "How many zo's have come to you?" *Zo* means heart. He was sometimes vulgarly referred to as the "heart man."

Not every zo was a zo of the Poro. There were zo's in every one of the professions: warrior zo's, blacksmith zo's, diviner zo's, witch catching zo's, herbalist zo's, midwife zo's and others. A zo in any organization was the one who knew all the secrets with power to pass them on to others.

A zo may or may not be a gɛ. That is a different matter. A zo may even defy a gɛ publicly if it had been so arranged previously. For a big chief to refuse to allow a gɛ to settle a palaver would add to the chief's prestige tremendously. I have heard of a warrior zo, who was also a big chief, who did just that. Yet people say that this same chief met his death by exposing the gɛ's mask and property to profane eyes during a petty war.

Just what was a zo? He was first a member of the Poro. By heredity he knew many of its secrets from his father without being initiated. He was a sort of nobility. But a child, boy or girl, could become a zo if a diviner so decreed. Perhaps the child was sickly, or fretful. If the diviner said, "It is because he is a zo and has not been properly treated," the parents would hasten to the big zo and ask him to make for the child a *mæ̃*, which is a small mask about two inches long, not to be worn on the face. Then they presented it to the child, saying: "We did not know you were a zo. Now that we know, we will be good to you." Such a child was supposed to have easy access to the spirit world. Perhaps he or she had a tendency to epilepsy or hysteria, or seemed to have some uncanny power of intuition. These were the ones who became zo's. The diviner said: "the *mā* is behind him."

The *mæ̃* was a small portrait of the owner (pl. II, a-c, e-f). No one else was supposed to see it. For a young child it was covered with cotton string wound on it. It was worn hung around the neck, until he was old enough to be told the mysteries of the zo and assume some of the responsibilities. If there was an uncle who was a zo he would be the one to instruct the boy, or an aunt the girl. The child then passed into the other family. If they did not make a *mæ̃* for the child right away, they would be instructed, perhaps, to make three small *yinis* to hang on the child's neck. Or they might bring the fetish of the zo nearest in kin. This zo would take a chicken, show the child to the chicken, show the medicine to the child, and say: "This kind of medicine is your medicine. It was the medicine of our forefathers. We have asked the diviner about you. He says you are a zo. We know it now. You must get well. You will be a bigger zo than I am." Then they would kill the chicken, eat it with rice and palm oil, rub the zo fetish with some of the oil, and finally rub the child with some of the same oil.

The diviner might say of a girl, "She will be a man-zo." Then she would be sent to the men's bush school, never to the women's. She would be ritually a man. She would grow up to be *wai*, the consort of *nangma*, and the most interesting character in the Poro.

She alone of all women would have her *mæ̃*. *Mæ̃* was the mark of a man zo. The oath of a zo on the *mæ̃* was more binding than life itself. It was spoken of as the mother of all masks, and therefore the mother of all gɛ's. No woman was ever allowed to bear the name *mæ̃*. There was a large one made for each chapter of the Poro. It lay on a mat at the entrance of the sacred grove where all who entered must swear on it that they had not had sexual intercourse the night before, and so would not bring bad luck into the Poro. They must also swear that they brought no "witch" or poison. This big *mæ̃* was the face of a woman, perhaps a relic of the earth mother idea, just as the Poro was "the earth itself."

Each zo carried his small personal *mæ̃* in his pocket. He prayed to it every day if he did not forget. He *must not* forget to wash it and pray to it every new moon. The water must contain some of the bark of the tree called *gei*, beaten off the tree with a stone. A boy *zo* who dreamed of a *gɛ*, or the Poro could rid himself of threatening trouble by so washing his *mæ̃*. A big *zo* who was angry might cool off completely by so doing. He would talk to it and ask it for good luck and help. It was a nuisance, this *mæ̃*, always demanding attention. But a *zo* must at least spit in its face and rub it against his forehead, then rub it between his hands and wish for luck. This was an acceptable substitute for washing it, except at new moon.

Just as no one was allowed to mourn the accidental or sacrificial death of anyone in the Poro, so no one was supposed to mourn a *zo*. The public was not even allowed to know he was dead if it was possible to keep it secret. They would finally say: "He has gone back into the water from which he came." No one ever saw the grave of a *zo*. The voice of the *gɛ* was heard, and all women went inside the houses. Then the *gɛ* and his companions took the body to the secret place in the forest, or disposed of it inside the sacred house in the *zo*'s quarters of the town. A big *zo* would be taken to the sacred grove far away where all really big men rest. There he would be placed in a sitting position between the prop roots of a cotton tree, itself called *gɛ* and greatly feared in its own right. There he would be covered with leaves, and closed in with a little fence of poles. No woman ever went near this grove. Few men even knew of its existence except the great men of the tribe.

This lore of the *zo*'s was handed down to the boy *zo* when he was old enough to accept the responsibilities, but he must pay a fee to his uncle if he was not a *zo* by direct line. This fee was: a person for sacrifice in the Poro, and a cat with horns, and a ewe sheep with horns, and a sacred agrey bead, and a chimpanzee's tooth. Since a cat with horns was impossible, and a "woman" sheep with horns almost as rare, he had to make up the deficit with money or the equivalent in whatever he could get. The sacred bead might cost him another person, for the price of such a bead was a slave. A chimpanzee's tooth might also cause considerable trouble, as these animals were taboo and could not be killed. It was a real adventure to be a *zo* in the old days!

Wai was a woman, a *zo*, and ritually a man. She was not the only such woman in the Poro chapter. There were one or two others in training to succeed her if necessary. *Wai* should not be thought of as the wife of *nangma*, though she was that in a ritual way while in the Poro. They lived together in the same house in the sacred grove, but sexual relations were taboo. In fact she was ritually sexless, even though she had a perfectly good husband and children on the outside. Her husband was always a *zo*. Moreover, a "man-*zo*-woman" would be denied entrance to the Poro if she was pregnant, or if the girls' school was in session. It probably never happened that *wai* herself was pregnant since she was usually old enough to be practically sexless before she attained full ritual status as "*wai*."

She was not only consort to the big *zo*, but the cult mother in her own right. She had under her the quartermaster and cook, but hers was the duty of cooking the last ritual feast of graduation which will be described later. Hers was the hand that condemned a man to death for breaking the laws of secrecy and chastity. Hers was the hand that flogged the wayward boy lying prone before *dunuma*. If a Poro criminal tried to escape by running away, she simply "put his name in her *mæ̃*, and sent a messenger with the *mæ̃* to catch him. When he saw the *mæ̃* he knew there was no further chance of escape, and came back without protest. Brought before the assembled Poro he was confronted by *wai* wearing her mask. She struck him on the forehead with a small iron rod shaped like a hook at the end, but with an edge like a small axe. At this signal, the executioner cut his throat. (Because of this power a man-*zo*-woman is called *bɔ̃ zɛ zo*, (pl. I, c) "killer of the bush.") His family were forced to furnish salt, pepper, palm oil, greens and all the fixings for a feast—except meat—he was the meat. All the Poro ate. The family dared not mourn or refer in any way to his death. In fact his name was never mentioned again.

Wai could have *dunuma* fetishes which gave her further powers of a big *zo*. She had her substitute for the other fetishes of *Nangma*. Finally hers was the custody of the great *mæ̃* on which all men swear at the entrance of the sacred grove.

A caricature mask which was a grotesque face of a chimpanzee, (pl. X, c) had also an important place in the education of youth. A strong man wearing it played the part of a clown, sometimes in town, sometimes in the Poro. There was a lot of slap-stick comedy and throwing around of heavy objects. If an onlooker got hurt or even killed, there was no protest. In the Poro this *gɛ* taught the boys good manners by always doing the wrong thing, and doing everything exactly backward in an unforgettable barrage of clowning. Thereafter a favorite way of cursing a man was to call him a monkey. The word for monkey in ordinary language is "*wai*," which heightens the humor of the performance.

SOME DETAILS OF OPERATION OF THE PORO IN THE MANO TRIBE

It should now be possible to understand some of the inner workings of the Poro from notes more or less as they were taken down. They are not complete, nor are they as accurate as observations of an eye witness. They describe procedures no longer to be seen even by an initiate. They are subject to the inaccuracies of any outsider writing about a secret society.

When the year came for the opening of the bush school, the big *zo* called *wai* and said: "This is the year when we should make Poro." She answered: "Where is the chicken?" They got a white chicken and killed it. *Zo* said to the chicken: "This Poro is a custom of our ancestors. This year we will make Poro. Let us have good luck." *Zo* kept the left wing, *wai* the right, as mementos of the occasion. The chicken was cooked and eaten with boiled rice. It was taboo for either of them to touch the vessel with their fingers while eating. As they ate with their fingers this required no small amount of skill. Every grain of rice had to be eaten without touching the bowl. Penalty, another white chicken, and do it all over again. Incidentally the accident of touching the bowl meant that some rival *zo* would be making trouble for them. The chicken was killed by breaking its neck with the back of a blacksmith's hammer handle. No knife could be used. It was dismembered with the fingers. *Zo* and *wai* then discussed and fixed details of time and place.

All roads through the sacred forest were stopped, and signs of taboo set up. The entrance was curtained with long streamers of fresh raffia bud leaves hung on a fence of plantain stalks and cotton tree poles between two great cotton trees (*Bombax*). The outside of this fence was like a curtain of water falling over a dam, or a low waterfall. It was impossible to see through it. It was symbolical of falling rain, and the Poro itself was the earth—the "good old mother earth." In the center of the curtain it was possible to enter by stooping low and parting the curtain. This was the entrance of the Poro. No one entered by any other way.

Inside, the men built a house for *zo* and *wai*, huts for the other officials, and dividing fences for the three grades of initiates: commoners, chiefs, and those destined to be *zo*'s and *gɛ*'s. In some cases the boys built their own quarters after they entered.

When all was ready, a man wearing the mask *Zi kū gɛ* walked on the road crying out: "The *gɛ* will catch men today." The wearer of the mask impersonated the character of his mask, and felt that he was for the time being possessed with the spirit which dwells in the mask.[4] The name *gɛ* means spirit, but refers to the mask unless it is definitely stated that the man is not wearing his mask.

Tea blɪ si (pl. III, b) stopped traffic on all roads leading to the Poro, and flogged people caught on the road after warning had been given. He had an assistant and interpreter with him. No *gɛ* talked the common language, but that of another tribe. This overlapping of languages may give a hint of the path of spread of the Poro.

Very early on the first morning *dɛ bu gɛ* (pl. III, d) went first into the Poro grove, carrying the sacred razor and a fetish to ward off harm. The fetish, called *bua*, was a cow's horn filled with a brown mass with a chimpanzee's tooth stuck in the middle. Following him went the officials who were to do the work, carrying their property. This occurred long before daylight.

When the boys were ready, the chief's son went in first. He was called *bua* after the fetish carried in first. He was to be the leader of his age group in the Poro and afterward. He was given the horn *bua*, for his badge of office, and was responsible for his group, making complaints to the proper official if anyone misbehaved.

At the entrance the boys went through a ceremonial "death." In the old days they were apparently run through with a spear and tossed over the curtain. Onlookers heard a thud as he was supposed to hit the ground inside, dead. Actually, the boy was protected by a chunk of plantain stalk tied on under his clothes. Into this the spear was thrust. A bladder of chicken's blood at the right spot was punctured and spilled to make it all very realistic to other boys and women who could not resist the desire to see their sons, perhaps for the last time. Inside the fence *sa yi gɛ* (pl. III, e) and

---

[4] Hereafter, I shall use the name of the mask to indicate a man wearing it since that will convey better the fundamental Poro idea that it is the mask, not the man, which is doing the work.

two assistants, all masked, caught the boys in mid-air, and dropped a heavy dummy to complete the delusion. The boys were actually unharmed, and were quickly carried away into the deep forest which is the Poro grove.

T'to gɛ had medicine on which boys must swear secrecy. *T'to blı gɛ* (pl. III, a) administered the oath not to tell a woman anything, not to see a woman, not to run away. The penalty was death. They were shown the *Kafu*, a tray containing toes and fingers of boys who had paid the penalty.

The making of the fire and fireplace was very important. The fire was kindled from a sacred fire kept eternally burning, and originally from the first of all Poro groves more than a hundred miles away. The hearth stones were gotten by *gɛlɛ wi gɛ* (pl. III, f) who went to town and said: "I have come to get three stones to carry to the bush." Then with the blacksmith's big sacred two-handled sledge hammer he broke off three chunks from the anvil stone, or from any big stone near town. All people watched him. Then he showed the stones to the people and carried them off to the bush. There the big *zo* placed them with suitable ritual, putting "medicine" under each. They were to hold the cooking pot over the sacred fire.

On this hearth food was to be cooked, much of it sacrificial. In fact, a human sacrifice was necessary before any fire could be put there. A slave boy was brought.

Bɔ̃ kɛ tutu had medicine which he gave to the slave to make him blind and insensible to pain, for there must be no crying in the Poro. Then *bɔ̃ zɛ gɛ* (pl. IV, b) took his sacred razor and cut out the liver of the living victim. Then *sie kū gɛ* (pl. III, c) kindled a fire which did not smoke, using specially prepared (magical) firewood, lit with sacred fire. *Bɔ̃ bulu kpa gɛ* was the cook who cooked the liver for all the big people of the Poro to eat. He must stir the pot with a stick of calamus vine. To have used any other stick for stirring human meat would have meant that he himself had to bring a human for another sacrifice.

Meanwhile the rest of the slave was being prepared for cooking to be eaten by the assembly. First bits of skin from the middle of the forehead, the abdomen, the palms of the hands and soles of the feet were taken by *bɔ kbo si* and incorporated in the fetish medicine of the big *zo nangma*. He also took the left second toe and the right thumb and little finger to add to the tray of *Kafu* medicine on which all boys were again sworn on pain of death never to tell about the things they had just seen. The blood of the sacrifice was sprinkled over the tray of medicine. Each boy ate one cola nut and one raw cassava root to seal the oath.

In the southern part of the tribal area *gea gɛ* went to town and sat all day and night until the people caught for him a small red-billed blue bird that makes a noise something like that of the *gɛ*'s shrill, rolling voice. This he carried to the big *zo* who cut its head off with the razor and cooked it with medicine. Another *gɛ* stirred the pot. All ate together.

White clay—the symbol of the spirit world—was mixed with the first food eaten by the boys to make them strong and less afraid. If a boy had to go a short way in the bush, he rubbed white clay all over his skin, and called out a warning to all who were not supposed to see him. This use of white clay was explained to him by *bɛlɛ kpɔ gɛ*, the white clay spirit. If any woman should happen to see him through no fault of her own, she would be told that she had seen a spirit, but she had better not say anything about it. She should have run away when she heard the warning.

If she deliberately refused to run away, she was caught and tied. Her relatives were notified and asked to bring a quantity of salt, four loads of rice, pepper, palm oil, beni seed, and a cow. Then the woman was killed anyhow, and all eaten in a great feast in the Poro. If the woman's people were wealthy or influential they could possibly save the woman's life by paying three more cows, but the woman could never speak again as long as she lived. She was given some kind of "medicine" which paralyzed the organs of speech, or more scientifically speaking, she was probably hypnotized. At any rate she never talked even one word to anyone. If she did she would have been killed, and she knew it. She could not even talk in her sleep!

She was made to eat some medicine out of a small iron mortar, which was then put upside down near the fire. Around it was put an iron ring. On top of this, each person present piled a stone. For one week this pile of stones stayed there. During this time the woman was in the Poro seeing everything, but was not initiated as a member. They showed her plenty. At the end of the week she went back to town, literally "dumb with fright."

The bull-roarer, *vu ni*, was used during the first part of the Poro merely to terrify the women. It was one of the voices of the spirits used especially at night when the high men of the Poro walked about without their masks. The men were quite frank to admit that it was merely a bit of frightfulness to keep the women under control.

Another voice of the spirit, gɛ na, was made with a set of whistles of pottery, three or four, each blown by a man (pl. XIV, f). The effect was amazingly sweet in the middle of the night when everything was quiet. A Poro official called out in a falsetto voice: "The spirit, the spirit is talking." This happened during the first part of the Poro when the boys were circumcised.

This circumcision was a minor rite among the Mano people. The cutting was done by a zo of special standing. The boy sat on a pole supported by two forked sticks, with his feet on a lower cross piece. The juice of an herb was rubbed on to deaden the pain, the foreskin pulled as far forward as possible and cut off with the razor while another man held the boy from behind. The wound was rubbed with strong, country lye soap. A boy was still an outsider even after being circumcised until the spirit had "eaten him," that is until he had been scarified with the special marks of the Poro.

The foreskins were saved, dried and turned over to the woman zo who was head of the girl's Sande school to be cooked at the proper time and eaten by all the girls to help heal their wounds. The clitoridi and labia minora cut out in the Sande school were likewise saved and dried and given to the property man of the big zo of the Poro. When the boys were circumcised he had these parts ready. After a few days when the healing had begun these parts were cooked up in a fine soup called tɛni, and eaten by the boys to hasten their healing. This was one of the reasons that the Poro and Sande were never held at the same time, but alternately.

The operating zo had medicine prepared for him by bɔ kbosi from the soles of feet and the palms of hands of sacrifice victims mixed with herbs and charred. This medicine was supposed to prevent undue hemorrhage. The juice of a vine was also squeezed on the wound, and another leaf wilted in the fire was wrapped around it. This stayed on four days, then was removed and the boys allowed to go and sit in the water of a stream. As soon as the wounds were healed the business of training began.

Bɔ̃ kū gɛ or gɛ na, went to town to catch boys who had not voluntarily entered the Poro, provided the consent of the parents had been given. This consent was seldom withheld unless there was some reason for waiting until the next session of the Poro some years later. The gɛ of course knew beforehand where the boy was hiding. He pretended to find him with the aid of a pointer made of the penis of the first sacrifice, which pointed to the house where the boy was hiding, and the door flew open!

Another official, who was really the quartermaster of the Poro, had power to catch any stranger on the road and force him to enter the organization.

Gblɔ zɛ gɛ (pl. II, d) had the task of killing any boy who tried to peep into the mysteries from the outside. The culprit was caught, tied, made insensible by putting poison into his nose and eyes, and seated on the fire that would not smoke, specially prepared for the occasion. The toe, thumb, and little finger were added to the tray of Kafu medicine. After he was properly roasted, he was consumed by all the zo's of the countryside called together for the occasion.

A similar fate awaited any boy who had previously ridiculed the Poro as nonsense, something he would "never join whatever happened," especially if he had cursed it or one of its officials. Another offence leading to death was to try to imitate the voices of the spirits.

The real initiation ceremony was that of scarring with the marks of the Poro, supposed by some to be the marks of the great crocodile spirit who had swallowed the boys and in whose belly they stayed during their sojourn in the bush as spirits. These marks were in two rows around the neck, down the chest where they branch into several double rows going around the sides of the chest to join in the back and go up to the neck again. The process of scarification has already been described as a duty of gɛ nangma, the big zo. When the scars had healed they said the spirit had eaten the boys. They were initiated, but not yet graduated, or as they say, the great spirit had eaten them, but they were to remain in his belly until his time came when he would give them rebirth as men.

This process of scarification was not a simple matter. It was dangerous and sometimes fatal from hemorrhage or infection. To guard against hemorrhage, tɔ kū gɛ was sent to town to collect a white chicken from each mother and promise to take good care of her boy. In the Poro they killed and ate all but a selected one which was fed a bit of the feast and consecrated with the prayer:

"Let the blood go into the chicken, not fall on the ground." Excessive bleeding, supposed to be caused by witchcraft, would be prevented by the chicken. This fowl was watched with much concern so that no harm came to it. It was eaten with a ceremony of thanksgiving when all was safely over.

Yumbo so gɛ caught any blood that ran down from the wounds in a basin. It must not fall on the ground, which would be a sign to the spirits that another spirit was about to join them. This caught blood was cooked by *di a blı gɛ* and eaten by all men in the Poro, not by the boys.

If the boy was not reassured by all this and became unduly alarmed or hysterical, a few leaves of *fla lɛ* were squeezed into a moist ball and used to stop the bleeding. The boy was then forced to swallow the bloody mass of leaves. "His blood went into his belly." This caused much gas in his stomach, and he was naturally uncomfortable. It gave him something else to think about. He was the nervous type, and was said to have "big mouth in the presence of big people." The others made fun of him: "*zai bo lu* has given him belly," (he is pregnant) but no one said he had swallowed his own blood. When the boy's father thought he had had enough discipline, he asked the *zo* people to stop it all. Then they took the bud shoots of *zu fılı kɔ*, rubbed them between the hands, squeezed the juice into a gourd, added one egg and gave it to the boy. He drank that and his belly cooled off. All this was horse play; the bleeding was not enough to worry about.

If the bleeding was serious, that was another matter. They took a big pollard shoot of *lolo* and let the red sap drip on the wound. This mingled with the blood and hastened coagulation.

Kala kala gombo was the official who dressed the wounds until they were healed, using loops of bark to clean them and a brush of owl's feathers to apply palm-kernel oil. The boy was told to lie on first one side and then the other, then on his face, then on his back, so that the wounds would not make big sores.

Dā ya bɔ̃a (pl. III, g) washed the wounds twice daily, at sunrise and sunset with hot water the first two days, then with cold. At noon he applied medicine called *ki a kpo*. In troublesome cases the *nyɛ gɛ* was called to squeeze other juices onto the wounds. He was the teacher of medicine as we know it—herbs, roots and poisons used as drugs.

If a boy was badly infected and got blood poisoning from it, *mi glı gɛ* (pl. IV, d) called the boy to him, asked him if he was sick, sent him for firewood, and burned him alive. This sacrifice was not eaten, but the charred remains were powdered to make magic medicine to prevent any other boy from getting the same infection. It was a drastic but remarkably efficient control of an infection that might easily have become epidemic while each boy was going around with a hundred tiny wounds on his body.

When the wounds were first healed the scars were white. To hasten pigmentation the skin was rubbed with calcined *lolo* fruits powdered and mixed with palm-kernel oil.

But it was not all blood and terror in the Poro. *Dā ya bɔ̃a* was the guardian of the boys. He treated their minor ills and regulated their daily habits. He received and himself tasted all food brought in from the outside. He could detect poison in the food and had the power to kill anyone bringing in poisoned food. He was especially watchful toward visiting *zo*'s who might want to spoil the reputation of the big *zo* in charge of the chapter.

The camp doctor *nyɛ gɛ*, was also a good fellow, and was highly respected. He taught herbal remedies to those wanting to follow the medical profession. He was never seen outside the grove. His was the responsibility of the health of all concerned. He even had an assistant to give the boys enemas. This was frequently necessary toward the end of the session when all the boys had successfully passed their period of discipline, and were being deliberately fattened for the re-birth "graduation" entry into the town from which they had been absent for two or three years.

During this time the boys learned to build houses, to make their own farm and follow the trades of their choice. Just as in any other school food was a big problem. They got some from their farm in the bush. Their mothers sent them as much as they could spare. This would have been enough for them, but their fathers and other men would drop in to visit and enjoy the bounty that was considered legitimate at the expense of whomever could pay. Various officials existed for no other purpose than to raid, beg, steal or commandeer food for the continuous feasting.

Five days after the opening *gɔ gɛ* the "leopard gɛ" went to town, caught all the dogs he could see, took them back to the big *zo* who killed them with his own hand. They were cooked and eaten by all. Next to human meat, dog meat was most sacred.

The "snake gɛ" was very quick tempered, and talked to no one outside the Poro. He gave all the big men of the town a mixture of herbs to attract snakes and told them to bring two snakes apiece the next day. All the people hunted and killed snakes. They were taken to the Poro, cooked and eaten.

The "bush hog gɛ" called a great hunt. After the kill had been taken to the town he appeared masked, and claimed all the credit. He took the liver and brisket for himself. At sunset he went back into the bush. The meat all went with him. He was the town's chief hunter in disguise.

The "greedy gba dɛ gɛ" (pl. III, h) went about everywhere collecting and begging food for the boys in the Poro. "The shamer" went to the farms when they were cutting rice and called them names for being so selfish as not to give him any for his boys. He and his assistants went back loaded down. The "hawk gɛ" went into town and caught all the chickens he could see, aided by his "interpreter." Another gɛ was privileged to catch ducks. When anyone killed a great hornbill the gɛ of that bird came and demanded his share, or more likely imposed a fine of ten shillings for not calling him to the feast. Some were pure extortioners with little or no excuse for making people pay fines of one kind or another. The fruit-eating elephant came and demanded fruit of /5. The people gathered it, and he ate what he wanted then carried a supply to the bush. A gɛ disguised as an old woman went about begging food. Long ago the Mandingoes were especially disliked by the hierarchy of devils in the Poro. One of them called himself gbā gɛ "the dog" (pl. IV, f) and went out to catch Mandingoes to be cooked and eaten in frank cannibalism.

Inside the Poro there was a well-organized community. The boys learned by doing the things they would do in after life. One of the officials who had a tortoise shell for his medicine, containing fetish, was the police judge or magistrate. He was a sort of fact-finder who heard the evidence before presenting the summary to *wai*. She pronounced the sentence or imposed the fine. For instance, for fighting both must pay regardless of guilt or "who hit first": one sheep, two cloths, one load of rice, palm oil and salt. They were warned that the next time the fine would be heavy. Then all cooked and ate happily together, the cloths going to *wai* as "costs."

If a boy cursed another he was likely to be turned over to the official punisher who made him kneel on a pile of cracked nut hulls. He must stay there until sunset unless his people would ransom him for four anklets. Another gɛ was sent as messenger boy to tell the parents that their son was being so punished. They rushed the ransom back so that the boy could get up.

The warrior gɛ taught them war songs, and dances, and all the tactics of primitive combat. The age group preserved this lore when they got back to normal life in the organization known as *gɛ yumbo*, or the blood spirit to be described later.

When a boy died a natural death in the Poro, he was cooked and eaten, all except his heart which was saved to be eaten at the feast of purification at the end of the session. The skin from the forehead and abdomen was incorporated in the big *zo*'s medicine.

At the end all the boys were washed or baptised by the big *zo* in a stream, or in medicated water with sacred leaves which he picked himself. Each one was given a new name, by which he was called for the rest of his life. They were then rubbed all over with white clay and went to the raffia curtain fence near the town. They could not yet see their folks, but all the townspeople came near the outside of the curtain and danced. They brought cooked rice and animals which were cooked by *wai* in person inside the fence. On this occasion *wai* did not wear her mask, but if she had *dunuma* she rubbed some of it on each hip. This soup was made in many pots, sheep, goat, chicken and duck, so that all could eat and no one break his taboo. It was a day of great rejoicing. The boys went back and slept once more in the bush.

On or before this day all the parents were obliged to pay the *zo*'s their fees of two cloths each. A bit of magic was supposed to guarantee payment. When the boys were scarified, a bit of blood on four blades of grass was saved by the big *zo*, and covered with cotton string. When the fee was paid he gave the packet to the father, who threw it into the water, and the boy got well. If not paid, the big *zo* hung the packet over the fire and the boy wasted away until he died. The *zo* gave the fathers who had paid, some magic medicine to protect him against "witch." This was appreciated because every man with a bit of property lived in constant fear of being poisoned for his wealth, and not without reason.

Finally, the boys came to town, smeared with white clay, and pretending to be new born by the gɛ, not knowing their own mothers or anyone else among their old associates. For one day they were given "the keys of the town." Those who had died in the Poro were not mourned. No one mentioned them, but on that day each bereaved mother found a broken pot at the door of her hut. Until then she did not know. She could not say anything about it, just carry on.

There were quite a number of gɛ's not definitely connected with the Poro school proper but with the fundamental idea of spirits returned from the other world by way of the sacred grove where the Poro was held. The Mano people speak of the spirit world as "up," but they never direct their prayers in that direction, rather to the remains in the grave, or to the spirit hovering near. It might seem on first thought that the lack of a logical arrangement of their spirits and gods in a heaven of some sort was due to its degradation by their spirit impersonation, so that the men's whole concern was to keep the women and children terrified and to use the higher knowledge of the inner circle of priests for selfish ends. This idea is not without foundation, but there is another explanation. It is simply that they had the corpse as their only tangible evidence of the deceased ancestor, whether in the grave, embalmed in the loft of a sacred house, or propped up between the buttress roots of a giant cotton tree in the forest. It was usually in the last named place that the remains of great men and their spirits could be approached. So it follows that the important gɛ's were thought of as coming from the forest. The sacred house in the town was a kind of holy of holies. Here sacrifices were made as when the celt *lai* passed from father to son with the sacrifice of the grandson. Here a great ancestor priest might be kept embalmed. Here the masks were guarded by men in direct line of descent from the priest for whom they had been originally made. It was in this house that the priests were supposed to be buried, though in the case of a big man, his peers would take him away secretly into the forest at night and put him to rest at the foot of a great cotton tree, even if they had to tunnel through the floor of the house to the next house in order to escape the vigilance of fond relatives not supposed to know even that he was dead. He was supposed to be transferred without death to the realm of the spirits. Later on when it became necessary to tell where the man was, they would announce his death, allow mourning by the relatives, and show them a recently disturbed area on the floor, saying that he had been buried there by his peers. Men of less importance were sometimes buried inside the house where death occurred. A big man seldom stayed in his own house if he was seriously sick, for fear that someone would take advantage of his illness to give him poison. He went to stay with some doctor, or in the sacred house where no one could see him but his peers. His actual death could therefore be kept secret for some time.

The story of one sacred house came to me in a peculiar way. Seven old masks and four smaller replicas were brought to me one night for sale. They had come from a sacred town at the far edge of the Mano country. Once a large town, it had only two huts left. Most of the people had died and the rest ran away from the curse that had settled on the town because the keepers of the masks had broken some sacred law. The blacksmith shop had caught fire which was a sure sign of the wrath of the spirits. No one would live in the town except one old man who was the custodian of the masks, and his young son and daughter in the adjacent hut. The old man was too feeble to walk or see. The young man wanted to be free of his accursed masks. No other town would let the masks be transferred to its sacred house, lest they bring with them the curse of the broken laws. No woman would marry the young man because he was destined to care for the masks when his father died. No one dared get rid of the masks. Finally, after three days dickering with the one who was to bring them to me, the boy decided to overrule his old father's objections and sell them to me, curse and all. Then he called the people who had fled from the town to show them that the masks had all "run away."

They were all very old, and had not been used for many years. The oldest and most powerful was called gɔ gɛ, (pl. IV, c) god-spirit. It had been the first mask in that part of the country, brought with the original settlers from the east. It was spoken of as "He who has the town in his hand;" that is, the very earth on which the town was built. Another was the *mi gli gɛ* mentioned above as the one who burned the boy whose wounds had become infected. The four smaller ones were replicas of old ones that had been ruined by boring beetles and cockroaches, lest the spirit residing in the old mask have no place to rest. The other five were Poro officials whose function had been "forgotten" by the feeble old man, who had once worn one of them.

No one outside the family of keepers could go inside this house. The masks had been kept in the loft. When the house was first built all the gɛ's danced and "talked." Four humans had been sacrificed to solemnize the occasion. The town had been exempt from obligations to the tribe in time of war. Even when the tribe was brought under the rule of the government, the town had conveniently been exempt from taxes. It was the mother town of the Poro in that area.

One of the old *gɛ*'s was the man spirit, *gɛ gɔ̃*, who came to town perhaps once in two or three years. He called all the people together and blessed them. They gave him plenty of presents, or a piece of red cloth. When the people fought among themselves in town, he would come and stop them, telling them they had broken the law and must pay a sheep, a load of rice, and some money. The sheep and rice were cooked and eaten the same day by the town fathers. *Gɛ gɔ̃* might speak from inside the sacred house, or walk in town with a red cloth over his head.

Lu bo bie (pl. IV, e) the *gɛ* that breaks big trees, was the elephant *gɛ*. This mask was kept in the sacred house and used when any person was spoiling the town laws, or refused to pay his debts. The matter had to be settled at once or the "elephant" would break down his house.

Gbana gɛ, the spirit of thunder, could even stop wars between two clans. The *gɛ* was immune to bullets or other weapons, When he walked between the fighters, they stopped. When he told them they were fighting foolishly, to go home, they did.

Some of these masked "spirits" now appear purely as entertainers. Whether they are old *gɛ*'s whose original function is lost, or new creations purely for entertainment, it is impossible to say. One of these, *dia mi a ga* (pl. IV, a) is so fine a dancer and singer that no one will pass through a town while he is singing. A traveler will sit down to watch, and at the end of the day will say: "Oh, I started to go to that other town today."

Such a dancer will have an attendant with a broom to sweep down the raffia skirt. On the tip of the peaked headdress is a bit of magic medicine which is supposed to make the rain pass by when the clouds see this *gɛ* dancing. It will not rain that day.

Another dancer can make himself tall or short at will by some mechanism hidden under his skirt. But the most popular of all dancers is the one on stilts. He is "the dry leaf eater" so light and airy is his dancing. He is not really one of the Mano dancers, but from the Gio.

Fania is another *gɛ* not to be seen outside the Poro, but is said to be a dancer. *Gɛ fwɪ fwɪ* is a very clever little fellow, and his name is a byword for nimble fingers. *Yɔ gɛ* is a small-boy play devil, which is nothing more than a boy covered all over with dry plantain leaves tied on. He dances around for fun, collecting a small present occasionally from some benevolent father, in imitation of the real dancers.

THE PORO AMONG THE GɛH PEOPLE

The Gɛh people live next to the Mano, and have a modified form of Poro. They do not consider scarification necessary, nor do they take any of the ritual quite so seriously as do the Manos. On the other hand they have a larger number of masks, and consequently more contact between the Poro and the outsiders. The Mano say of them that they have too many masks, so many in fact that it would be almost impossible to keep the women from discovering that they were really worn by men and not pure spirits. The Gɛh people have put the Poro more where it belongs. It comes closer to being what a fraternity is in America, but has in addition the tribal initiation and circumcision firmly fixed as the basis of its ritual.

When a boy is to go to the bush, the patriarch of the family calls all living members together and says: "Your son is to go to the bush. You must come so we can cook food for the gods." Then they take plenty of cooked rice and chicken to the grave of the family ancestor. The old father says: "Oh, my dead father, you must call all the people there (spirits) to come and eat here with you. Your son is to go to the bush. You must come and be god for us. You must help him so it can be easy for him. You must bring him good luck." The liver and the heart of the chicken with a bit of the rice is put on the grave for the spirits, then all the living family sit down and eat the rest. When they finish eating each takes some cold water, dashes some onto his face and on his foot, while invoking the spirits' aid for the boy. "God, you must help this boy," says one. Another: "This my son has never done anything bad against me. We have no palaver. You must help him to be a good boy and take the initiation easy."

The night before the opening each family observes this custom. Then bits of the rice from all the pots are put together and set out on the road leading into the town. One old man will carry it there for all the people, and put it down saying: "All you gods coming along this road, you must eat this rice so that all our boys can have good luck in the bush tomorrow." All the aunts and sisters who have died can come and eat of this common pot of rice on the road. If such an offering were not made one of these female spirits might appear to the boy that night in his sleep and deceive him by giving him some magic thing to do which would only cause his death when he was circumcised. Much or all of the night is spent by the entire village in dancing and revelry. The next morning the boys are taken to the bush before daybreak. They are not seen again until initiation is complete.

Another preliminary event might be the finding of a mask called *yi loa glü*,[5] (pl. VII, f) cold water spirit, on the doorstep before dawn on the day preceding the entrance. The finder is supposed to have dreamed about this mask. No one is supposed to know how it got there. The man dresses up and puts on the mask. All the people throw cold water in his face, offer him a fowl and cola nuts, pray to him for success. Cold water is everywhere a token of good faith. A man may owe another a debt, and be unable to pay. He can avoid trouble by giving him some small thing, saying: "I cannot pay you today, but here is your cold water. I will pay you the full amount."

Tie blı sia is placed on the road close to the entrance of the bush where he can catch and flog anyone walking there, and spoil his goods. He is called the fire eater.

On the day of opening when the old men who escorted the boys into the bush have returned to town, *yɔ pu glü* (pl. V, a) follows them to town. They put a bucket of whitewash (clay) in front of him. Each woman in town must come to salute him. Before they speak to him each must dip into the whitewash and smear it around her eyes. At the end of the Poro he is paid one white chicken and one length of white cloth, collected from the women by the young girls.

There was formerly a sacrifice for the sacred fire. The *zo va* (pl. VIII, h) (big *zo*) put poison in the victim's mouth to make him insensible, then cut out his liver and larynx.

There is a story about a small *mæ̃* (pl. II, e) made to commemorate an event that happened many years ago. There were two women *zo*'s trying to spy on the Poro, wearing two finger rings made of squirrel's teeth which were supposed to make them invisible. They were caught,

killed and eaten by all men in the Poro. I have the small *mæ̃* with squirrel's teeth imbedded in it which was carried by the *zo va* who caught the women, as a memento of his prowess over the magic of the women. I have also the mask of the *zo va*, himself, so there is a possibility that the incident actually happened.

Si blı glü was guard of the *ka sɔ*, medicine in the Poro on which all members swear. It is a pot full of trinkets of those dead by false oath, with two emblems of lightning. The oath was: "May the lightning strike me dead if I tell anything that I have seen."

Dra ya bɔa was a jester and entertainer in the Poro.

Diā (pl. VIII, e) was "a good devil." He said to the boys: "You must not make witch. You come here for a long stay. Behave yourselves so you can get well quickly and go back to your people." He also went to town at night accompanied by a boy already initiated to collect food. He was paid at the end of the Poro: a sheep, brass anklets, chickens, cloth. He was a kind of godfather to the boys.

Mi glı glü not only burned the ones who broke the unforgivable laws, but also punished the boys who needed it by making them kneel down (with elbows also down) on a pile of cracked nut hulls.

For cursing in the Poro, *so ze glü* imposed a fine of five anklets, two white chickens, ten white colas.

To kpɔ glü was the tattler who reported anyone misbehaving. This was because no one would ordinarily report another for fear of retaliation. A man wearing a mask whose duty it was could do so without fear of this. It would probably be an event all knew about, but no one would report.

There were two truant officers who would watch any boy who went aside, to be sure he was not trying to slip away for a few minutes to meet someone in the forest. These also questioned any father coming to visit his son to make sure he had not had sexual intercourse the night before.

Dai da glü (pl. V, d) was the father of medicine. He made all treatments for the boys. He knew much. He treated gonorrhoea by blowing water with plant juices into the urethra with a long reed. He was paid at the end of the session—a cock and five bundles of firewood from each family who had a boy in the bush. If there were many boys his pile of wood was almost as big as his house, and the neighbors probably helped him burn it.

Si si glü came to town only when nobody had

---

[5] *Glü* is the Gio word meaning *gɛ*.

died in the first group initiated. He was called the "good news devil." He came at night followed by all the men, absolutely naked, to recruit more boys for the next class of initiates.

Shortly before the end of the Poro, *dra ya bɔ̃a* went to town calling the names of the boys who were in the Poro. The people told him they were in the Poro, then he began to cry: "All my boys are gone." The people laughed at him. Then he became serious and called the names of those who had died, saying: "These will stay with me in the bush. They will not come to town again." Then the mothers of those boys knew, but could not mourn.

A few days before the graduation procession, *bo glü* went to town and told the people to clean it up. He watched at night and if he caught anyone soiling any part of the town, he fined him four chickens and one striped cloth. This same *gɛ* would come to town at the time of new rice when everyone was likely to have a touch of diarrhoea. If he caught anyone, he would say: "Don't soil this place. Don't waste it here. Go away. Don't dirty the place just because you had plenty to eat."

The boys always came to town wearing new clothes, and all the family finery. A day or two before the day of the procession, *bɔ kū glü* came, seized all the rings from everybody and carried them to the Poro. The boys had rings for every finger. *Nyung kū nɔ ngɔ*, also came to town and caught all the beads from the women so the boys could wear them on the grand day. *Tu kū glü* caught all the horns to be blown in the triumphal march.

For this occasion the boys should be fat and happy because it was a time of great rejoicing and the boys were to come out as men ready to catch their brides. For weeks in advance they were fattened with all that the land afforded. Various officials had been collecting food and raiding stores on all sorts of pretexts.

Gɔ glü, the leopard, came near town at night growling and demanding rice already cooked with soup on it. The women would cook rice and put gravy on it and set it down at a respectable distance. Then the boys would come and get it. If any woman came too close to him, she was fined one cow. He did not wear a mask.

Gɔ gbi glü was a mask made in memory of Giu who was the father of cola eaters. Its wearer collected cola for the Poro.

Mini aɔ̃ glü (pl. VI, g) went to town in the daytime when women were beating out rice. He would take the mortar stick out of a woman's hands and beat a little, then go the next until he had beaten a bit in each mortar. Each woman visited had to give him a load of rice. He would say: "Where is the rice I have beaten?" Nothing would satisfy him short of a full load.

Gbla blü went to town and said nothing for three days. The fourth day he demanded a sheep. The women were glad to get rid of him so cheaply.

Zɔ glü (pl. V, i) the stutterer could say nothing right. He so amused everyone by his foolish attempts that when his companion (pl. V, e) helped him out he said quite glibly: "Yes, that is just what I was trying to say." He always got what he asked for, and carried all kinds of dainties back to the boys.

Kpa blı glü was the grasshopper eater. He cried out at night that all people must catch grasshoppers for him. The following morning everyone grabbed these insects off the bushes very early before they got warmed up by the sun, and were still easily caught. Then they cooked them with a little rice. The *gɛ* came and asked for them. They fed him enormous quantities, but he was never satisfied, because he had a bag hidden behind his mask to catch all he "ate." He carried them to the boys.

Gba blü (pl. VII, d) was the lightening *gɛ*. When a thunder storm was coming up they would dress him quickly and set him on the road in front of the entrance to the Poro to protect it from lightning. He did not go to town. He sat there and told the lightning to stop or go on and strike some other place.

Da glü, the diviner, sat sometimes at the entrance to catch any one with witch. Any visitor had to swear on this man's medicine horn that he had no witch. If he intended to do any harm in the Poro this man would somehow find it out and turn him back.

During Poro *nīa sɛ* would go to town to greet any stranger visiting for the night. He would politely ask questions and make the fellow feel rather important, then collect an anklet and a chicken from the host of the stranger, and carry them into the Poro.

No one could curse when *n'na glü*, (pl. V, b) was around. If he heard any cursing he would sit down in front of the house until the fine was paid. It might be as much as a cow. It went into the Poro bush like all the rest.

Without warning a voice would call out in the middle of the night: "Zɔ or no zo, you all make fire." Then everyone would have to get up and blow up the fire. If anyone did not do so he paid heavily. All the gɛ's from the Poro came and sat down in front of his house which meant that each must be sent away with an acceptable present.

Yau wɔ gbi (pl. V, c) and his wife were two masked beggars who begged large quantities before they would dance and go away satisfied.

Wana glü was something of an extortioner. He would go to town in broad daylight and walk around. It was taboo for anyone to look him in the face. Everyone went about with faces to the ground. Anyone looking into his face had to pay two cutlasses.

Ma ya wa ya went about wearing many hairpins. No one else could wear one in his presence. He seized all he saw. They could be redeemed for twenty colas each.

After the wounds had healed the boys had a special feast of palm cabbage. It was ordinarily taboo to cut a palm tree for its cabbage, or tender bud. *Glu si glü* superintended the cutting, and called out warnings so that no one would come near to see what was going on.

Tɔ zɛ glü was the chicken killer. No one needed to feed him because he was licensed to catch any chicken in sight. He had several attendants to do the catching.

Zā (pl. VII, e) was the crested hawk. If anyone killed this taboo bird and tried to eat it in secret, this gɛ was almost sure to find it out and come with all the town people at his heels singing: "*Zā wing gbi zā.*" He collected five loads of seed rice from the offender to be divided amongst all the women who had boys in the Poro.

A shrivelled up little mask was worn by the crawfish catcher (pl. VI, c) who went with his attendants and dug crawfish out of the banks of streams, took them to town and showed them to the people saying: "Here is some food for your boys in the bush." Then he took them to the Poro. He was paid for his trouble: five mats, twenty cola, two chickens.

There was also a fish trapper who could raid all the fish traps on any one day and take the contents into the bush.

Drɔ kū glü was the frog catcher. Toward the end of the session he would go and tell the people: "Only three days are left. Catch me frogs." That was an easy one. They caught plenty, so that the boys feasted for three days on frogs.

On the eve of graduation *kwi tɔ̄ glü* went to town. He could seize as many as ten ducks. People saw him coming and hid their ducks if possible. The Poro had a final feast of duck.

The boys came out of the Poro in new clothes. They gave all their old ones to the owl, *klun glü*, who spent many nights hooting in the town just to keep the women frightened. The owl was supposed to be a witch, capable of most anything.

When the boys "came out" they could do or have anything they wanted for one day.

Entertainers and Special Spirits

From this Gɛh section I learned about seven gɛ's that seemed to be nothing more than dancers and entertainers. One of these may be thought of as the spirit of the dance. The mask represents a woman's face, but was worn by a man. He danced in town on moonlight nights. His name was: "Small boy can't see where the moon goes down" (pl. V, g). He danced until two by two the revelers went inside, then he disappeared. Others dancing in the daytime for presents of food or money were: *wi gbɛa glü, tie glü, ko kɛ glü, tā kɛ glü, gbie ka, gɛ lɔ kɛ lɔ*.

Another *dū glü*, (pl. VIII, f) came representing an old man with a cough. He acted like someone who had seen better days, and did not know that his skill had gone. Those who were initiated laughed at his acting which was really good, but non-initiates who laughed were fined for lack of respect.

When a man's daughter gave birth to a man child, *bea glü* visited the new grandfather. His women must give him the crusts of scorched rice left in the pot from the feast made to celebrate the event. The women made all manner of fun of him, even cursing him with impunity. He only laughed.

At any time of rejoicing the small boys not initiated were allowed to wear a mask called *pɛ glü*, but the entire body had to be covered with plantain leaves.

Nya wɔ̄ was a very popular young woman. When she was about to die she begged that they make a mask for her so her friends would not forget her. This was done before she died. She saw it and was satisfied. Her parents were still living in 1936, but were very old. This was said to be a common custom.

Ma die (pl. V, h) was a woman of so generous a reputation that she was immortalized by a mask. The wearer danced at the time of farm cutting while the women cooked for the men cutting farm. The wearer sang of the fame of *ma die*, who cooked a pot of rice that never got empty. This was to please the spirit of *ma die* so all would have plenty to eat, and the farm would be fruitful.

Sie glü (pl. VII, a) was the name of a mask made in honor of a man who was both greedy and generous. He collected huge supplies for the Poro. When he died the people made this mask. They prayed to it when they went to plant rice asking for fertility and plenty.

Dī zi sie, (pl. VII, c) crooked mouth, was a caricature of a woman with facial paralysis. It could be ridiculed, but it must be fed soft food as eggs, rice, plantains. It was prayed to by those who had this affliction.

Kupa ya glü was made in memory of a very flirtatious woman, *kupa ya*. The wearer was a man, who sat pouting and said: "My fashion is bad. My husband beats me. I can't stay in any place long. Palmwine vexes me. Rice makes me mad." People drove him from town laughing.

M'liu di was the rice mother. When the first farm was cut, each man brought a white cola and presented it with his cutlass saying: "This farm we are about to cut, let us have plenty of rice in it, and plenty of cassava." They broke an egg and rubbed it on the mask: "Let no one steal our cassava and rice out of the field."

Dɛi glı glü was the farm burning *gɛ*. The wearer gave sacred fire for burning the farms. The mask must be sprinkled with blood of a chicken sacrificed to the fire.

At rice-cutting time they made a play with two masks, one representing the rice birds, the other representing a spirit protecting the sleeping bird and driving the flies away, though they say the protector was himself asleep. This happened during the time that everyone was busy keeping the rice birds from destroying the crop.

Ka glu (pl. V, f) seems to have been a sort of household god. It was kept covered with a white cloth when not worn. A white chicken was killed for it every new moon, cooked with rice and eaten by all in the house. The head man threw a bit in the face of the mask, praying to it: "We must stay well. We must not be sick. We must have children. We must have good luck."

When contemplating a long journey, *Yi lo glü* was addressed by spewing water out of the mouth, or chewing cola and spitting part of it into the mouth of the mask, asking for protection from harm on the journey. On returning, thanks were expressed by sacrificing a black chicken and sprinkling the blood on the face.

Tie glü (pl. VI, e) was fed before going on a hunt. Four white colas and a white chicken were "given to it," but actually eaten by the hunters, except for a small portion thrown on the mask.

Yo glü (pl. VI, b) was prayed to when preparing rubbing-chalk for rheumatism.

Blɔ̄ glü (pl. VIII, i) had medicine for tumor of the jaw. This mask was a caricature of a man who died of this disease. It was worn by a man who tried to cure this condition by cutting a small hole in the tumor and putting medicine in it. He also gave the patient something to drink and isolated him inside a small fence.

Si bo glü was a "bad devil." He liked to curse people. Women's hairpins were taboo to him. A crier went ahead of him telling all women to hide their hairpins. It is difficult to see his place in the scheme of things.

Gbala ko pie (pl. VI, a) danced boisterously, throwing gravel into the faces of bystanders. To stop him the chief had to bring a black cat, a strip of white cloth and some cotton; then tell him to go and sit down in his house. If the black cat was not available, black cloth would do.

Another one dressed in the bush, went to town, danced and raised rough-house, beating people with a double-pronged iron hook.

Du gbı glü (pl. VI, f) was the cow eater. He was seen only on state occasions, as when a cow was killed. He was given money saying: "Here are the bones of the cow you ate." For each cow eaten a calabar bean was added to the beard. When the old men dreamed at night of the cow eater, they must kill a cow the next day, the share of the wearer being the liver. Whenever a cow was killed to the ancestors this *gɛ* must be called.

I yɛ glü (pl. VIII, g) dreamed of war and prophesied certain things to come, advising how to meet the enemy.

Zai bo lu (pl. VI, d) would sit on the side of the road whenever there was a petty war in town, catching and fining anyone passing with a spear or knife or any kind of iron. No one could make palaver while he was in town. He could stop a fight by simply walking in and fining both parties regardless of the nature of the quarrel. Both parties brought a sheep and a roll of cloth. The whole town cooked and ate the sheep and divided the cloth among the big men.

Dinga (pl. VII, b) used to catch a man and his

wife if they quarrelled at night. He demanded the cloths both were wearing. They must also bring him a duck and cook it for him to eat. He pretended to be very hungry, and could not wait. Old men who knew the "devil business" ate with him. It seems probable that they helped him spot the quarrelsome couples. The mask was also fed with some of the food.

A fine of one cow was put upon any woman who cursed a man to injure his sexual powers. It was imposed by a man wearing a special mask.

Several masks in this area were small replicas of old masks that had broken or become motheaten, (pl. VIII, a–d). Then the spirit of the old mask went into a sort of retirement in the small new one, but had to be remembered by a sacrifice to the group of small ones spread out on a white cloth once a month. Occasionally in the Poro all ate a sacrificial meal to all these small masks spread out in a circle.

THE PORO OF THE GIO TRIBE

The Gio, like the Gɛh, circumcised but did not scarify the initiates. They put even less of terror into the ritual, and held the women less harshly under the dominance of the supposed spirits. Yet they had many zo's and gɛ's like the Gɛh people, and were the artists who carve the big masks for the Mano people. They also made a few masks of cast brass, using the lost wax process, which they also used to make figurines of an endless variety.

The masks described below do not tell the whole story of the Poro in the Gio country, but they do show the variations in the officials, and the continuity of the main idea of the Poro. The general organization was the same as that of the Gɛh tribe. The language was almost the same.

Sɔ pu blü, the white cloth gɛ, dressed in white cloth danced all day the day the Poro opened. His pay was two white cloths paid by parents of the boys to be initiated. They collected cola nuts, pooled the lot and bought the white cloths with it.

Zi mia glü sat at the entrance of the Poro to escort strangers, especially women, past the entrance and prevent peeping.

Zua kpa glü (pl. X, d) taught respect of elders and proper conduct. He showed the boys the wisdom of tribal laws.

Nya kɛ bõa was in the Poro with the boys constantly instructing them in manners and conduct, in the smallest details, such as precedence in eating, etc.

Bla glü (pl. IX, e), the sheep gɛ, danced in public, carried the boys to the bush, taught them medicine and took care of their wounds, and finally escorted them back to town as men.

Yi si glü had a small boy assistant to carry water to the house of every mother who had a boy in the bush. He put medicine in this water that was supposed to reveal any poison. This water must be used to cook food to be sent into the Poro for the boys.

Nya kɛ ya ba (pl. IX, a) watched the cooked rice. He could be seen by all, men and women. When women cooked food for the boys, this gɛ sat and guarded the pots of rice as they brought them. Then he sent all the women away while he called the boys to come and carry it into the bush. Some of the women gave him cola; some chewed it and spit it into his face, which was not considered impolite, but quite the thing to do to a spirit.

Kuɛ glü called for food to be brought him. He came near the town, but stayed inside a raffia fence built for him so no one could see him.

Zie gbing glü, the spirit on the road at night, went from town to town at night demanding food for the Poro. He did not tarry, was in a terrible hurry, and covered a lot of territory. Perhaps there were two or three of "him." He was said to fly from town to town at great speed.

Bei ta glü planted cassava. He went from farm to farm at planting time, planted four or five sticks, in each farm, and said: "You see? I have planted my farm." When the Poro opened he went to the farms and took all he wanted for the Poro.

Nyu glü came to town and collected palm oil from all the women to carry to the boys. He was paid two cloths.

So glü was the fish trap expert. He followed people to their traps and took toll from each, or might even rob a trap for the Poro.

Biu da glü collected dried peppers for the boys.

Kpa blı glü collected grasshoppers. He said: "Where are my grasshoppers?" The women went in the houses and got dried grasshoppers and gave them to some man standing near saying: "Go give him his grasshoppers. We are afraid of him. He is a bad devil."

Gbu gbu glü, the cassava snake, came to town bringing some cooked food in a pot. He set it down in front of him saying: "I am a cassava snake. You may do anything you like to me but don't touch my food." Children came and started to eat. Their parents paid, two buckets of rice each, for the food of the boys in the bush.

When a boy died in the Poro the *gɛ bɔ a ga* went to town at break of day and said: "The spirit has carried away your boy (calling his name) in the bush. You will not see him again, he is dead." Then he returned to the Poro. This was his sole duty.

Bɔ zu glü washed the boys ceremonially at the end of the Poro. The rest of the Poro was essentially like that of the Gɛh tribe.

Outside the Poro there were various *gɛ*'s who came and went from the spirit world to town. One came to thank a man who had been to a far country and brought back a wife. He talked a lot of flattery and got a present.

Gbēin glü prowled about at night. Anyone seen by him was likely to be challenged: "Who is that?" The proper answer was: "I don't belong to anyone. I belong to you." Whoever did not answer correctly was fined a black chicken and whatever eggs he could get.

Tŭ'piɛ glü carried a fan, fanned a victim vigorously, commenting on the heat, and asked for a gift for his fanning. He collected from everyone according to his ability to pay. He was a great beggar.

Kba glü had a big mouth always open. In fact it could not shut. He went in town and said: "Let no man speak when my mouth is open." He then demanded a sheep which was cooked for all the people to eat. No one could say anything until he had eaten with them and gone. If anyone spoke, they had to bring another sheep.

Nya va glü (pl. IX, c) was a mask with big eyes. He extorted a fine from every man he thought was making eyes at him, or who had big eyes. The fine, however, was only a cola nut.

Nya ti glü, the blind mask, was worn only at night. He groped about town feeling his way. He was not to be seen by any small boy. Fines were collected from boys who peeped.

Kpa lu lü did not wear a wooden mask but a thick net veil of black cord twisted from palm leaf fibers. He walked on high stilts and was purely an entertainer. He was like the *dɛ kpa glü* of the Gɛh tribe.

B'lı, the porcupine, represented by two masks, has a story that shows the origin of a clan taboo. The first mask (pl. IX, g) was made at the death of a hunter who had killed many porcupines. He had been warned, but kept on, and died of gangosa which made his nose shrink until it was like a porcupine's nose. The people made a mask of him when he died, and one man wore it at his funeral. The wearer warned all men in the name of the porcupines, that they should stop exterminating these animals. The son kept on in spite of the warning. He also died of gangosa. The people made a mask of the son before he died. This mask, (pl. IX, f) worn as a *gɛ*, decreed that porcupines were thenceforth taboo for the clan. No one should ever kill one again. The porcupine is still taboo in the Boya clan of Srɔ section in Gio.

Gea glü (pl. X, a), the lesser hornbill, was a "sassy devil." When any petty palaver was on, this *gɛ* was likely to come into town to settle it. Men were prone to settle quickly when they saw him coming, because he would likely render a hard decision. If they did not all agree to his decision he would go into a rage and seize anything in sight and make off with it.

Di va glü (pl. X, b), the big mouth, was given to great exaggeration. The mask was made of a man who carried a stock of tall tales, and made much of nothing. As a *gɛ* this character runs into town to act as judge in a fight. His exaggerations are so ludicrous that the cause of the fight is forgotten. His fee is two mats and the weapons used in the fight.

Dɛ kpa blı was called the dry leaf eater. He could make himself tall or short at will. He was merely an entertainer.

Bɔ was a god of fertility. When men were ready to plant rice they brought all the hoes before this mask. Four men washed it in cold water in which was a live puff adder (*Bitis gabonica*), and prayed to it for good crops. Then they drank the water and went to work, eating nothing. They must finish the planting before they ate, but could drink palm wine, while working. When all was planted they had a grand feast cooked by all the women of the town, symbolizing hunger followed by the plenty of harvest time. This mask had been in one family for many generations.

Zing glü was a mask to the tiny migratory birds appearing about harvest time. They often made nests in the thatch. At harvest time the wearer of this mask collected a bucket of new rice from each quarter of the town. He was the first to eat new rice. No one else could eat any until he had his part.

Mini zɔ glü sang while women beat out new rice. All could see him. He had a drummer, and all beat rice to his rhythm.

Gɔ glü (pl. IX, d) was the leopard spirit. When he came to town they killed a cow for him. He was worshipped: "Take care of the Poro for us."

He included a leopard skin in his costume, or the skin of a chimpanzee, the symbol of *wai*. He could not put his hands on his knees to rise from a sitting position lest he spring up like a leopard and reveal the identity of the one wearing the mask. No one could spill cold water on him lest he growl like a leopard. Leopards dislike water very much. He was one of the biggest in the Poro.

Mɛ mā glü (pl. IX, b) was so called because he could beat other men. He was the artist who carved all the other masks. This mask is the portrait of a boy, beautifully done. He was the boy who showed such talent in carving masks that he was the teacher of the art. When he died his portrait, made by his successor, was worn as a mask by his successor who went about flogging everyone, even other *gɛ*'s and big men. He used the stick that had been used to stir the human sacrifice pot. No woman could see him.

At Tapi town in Gio it was taboo to kill chimpanzees. They were spoken of as brothers. In other parts of Gio they might kill one, but they must call *klua glü* (pl. X, c), and give him the head and liver to carry to the *ki la* men, or gathering of the peers in the Poro grove. Failure to do so involved a penalty of ten chickens to be eaten in the grove by the *ki la* men.

THE PORO IN OTHER TRIBES

From the Krā tribe located to the east of Gio I had only two masks. One was a *gɛ* who danced at any important feast, as when a big man won a famous palaver. The other was the *gɛ* who presided at the building of a suspension bridge (pl. XI, a). These bridges are all over the interior among the hill tribes who do not like the rivers, make no canoes, do not know how to swim, and do not fish in the rivers. These bridges are built in secret by the Poro men with all roads leading to the spot closed. No outsider is allowed to come near. Women still think that these bridges are woven by the *gɛ* flying through the air and spinning them as he goes back and forth. They are actually true suspension bridges essentially similar in design to our great steel structures, and woven entirely of vines. Even repairs on these bridges are made in secret.

I have seen carved wooden bowls, ceremonial spoons with carved heads on the handles, and a mask of a woman used in the Sande, all done by Krā artists with a skill that outranks that of any other tribe in Liberia.

From the Konor tribe in the northern part of the Ivory Coast I have seen three masks of rather fine workmanship. Their functions were similar to those from the Gɛh and Mano tribes. One of these called *ti* (pl. XI, c) was said to be a "good devil," for luck and popularity. He came to town when a cow was killed at a big man's funeral. He imposed fines on peeping boys who were not supposed to come near him. He would walk around calling out: "Take time, don't hurry and spoil your work. Remember *ti* and be careful." This mask was washed with cold water, the water rubbed on the face of the worshipper with a prayer for good dreams. There was a small pot with it to hold palm wine which was drunk with a prayer for good luck and inspiration in dreams.

The other two were different interpretations of the sheep *gɛ*, which in Mano was the deity of medicine while in the Konor tribe it was the god of war. No woman ever saw him. He came to town on the eve of war, or to celebrate victory. He demanded a human sacrifice on the spot. Failing a human, he would accept three cows, but an agrey bead must accompany the cows, otherwise a human would be demanded in addition. The price of one of these beads was a slave, or more recently, a cow. No one could come very near him, only so far, then retreat backward still facing the *gɛ*. He carried in his hand a cow's tail. His attendant carried two war bells matched in tone, which he rang constantly during the ritual.

The fat of the sacrificial victim was saved to be rubbed on the mask to feed the spirit residing within. The same fat was used to anoint those about to go into war to make them immune to spears, bullets, etc. But they must stand erect, never cringe. To stoop would have spoiled the charm and invited casualty. Before putting this mask on the wearer would spit in it and wave it around his head. This was repeated three times.

This mask (pl. XI, b) had a beard to which was tied the beads he had acquired. The eyes were surrounded by a zone of red woolen cloth. On the forehead were two sheeps' horns, carved with the mask from one piece of wood. There was an elaborate headdress with it of red cloth and leopard skin.

The other interpretation of this war *gɛ* had also sheep's horns but was an entirely different face. It had an elaborate wig instead of a headdress, but it had an even more elaborate cape (pl. XIII, b) and back piece made of red cloth, leopard skin, and sheep's mane. It was decorated with twelve epaulets around the neck piece, each with a symbolic design embroidered with thin strips of leather. The back piece was similarly decorated with six plaques. These symbols were in part: sun, moon, star, fire, rain, leopard, lizard, crocodile, snake, spider, turtle, suspension bridge, and arrow. To him was killed also a human, but in addition a duck, because the African duck does not "talk," only hisses. "So may the enemy be dumb and their war cries like a hiss and impotent," bringing out the idea that the war cry breaks down the morale of the enemy, and so is part of the battle as much as other weapons.

The mother cult of Buzi and Gbandɛ differed considerably in its outward appearances from that of Mano, but the fundamental principles were much the same. I know only that the masks were much heavier and not in the nature of portraits. They were more like demons. The chief of these was called *Dandai* (fig. 2).[6] It was a mask about three feet long, carved out of a large log of very light wood. It appeared in public three times:

(1) To call the boys to join the bush.
(2) To announce their coming out of the bush.
(3) To bring them back to town.

He talked with a voice modified as though his mouth were full of water, or in a throaty rumble. The language was secret, or at least foreign so that he needed an interpreter.[7] He spoke very fast and in short sentences, sometimes giving out a rumbling sound.

Men brought him things to eat, usually cola and money which he snapped up with his great crocodile mouth. A bag hidden behind the jaws caught everything. Occasionally he pretended to eat a person, hiding him under his voluminous skirt, and dribbling red juices from his mouth, which was stained red with the juice of cola nuts.

He did not dance. His mask was too heavy. He usually walked slowly, with occasional spurts of running. He could see only through his mouth, as the mask was too large for the eyes to fit. He was usually surrounded by attendants who guided him around by secret signals. Occasionally he sat down to rest, the man (underneath) kneeling and resting the chin of the mask on the ground.

He was seen by all, but the women stayed inside the houses until he called them. The head of the Sande must come and give him a chicken as a sacrifice, but she dared not approach near enough to deliver it to him herself. He was superior to any other demon. He held a whip in the free right hand, the left being necessary to work the lower jaw.

He impersonated the founder of the bush, in which respect he was like the Mano gɛ. He was supposed to swallow the boys and give them rebirth at the end of the Poro. The scarifications were marks of his teeth. He came to town once during Poro accompanied by the boys. This differed remarkably from the Mano Poro, which has made much of the idea of their being spirits and invisible. It is doubtful, however, that women saw him at this time. Sacrifices of chickens and cola were brought to him by a man crawling on hands and knees. Even the head of the Sande must hand her sacrifice to a man who took it to him.

The founder of the Poro in Buzi country was a very old man when he died. His death was kept secret as long as possible, then his work was carried on by a successor wearing a mask, probably much smaller than this one, and imitating his voice which was tongue-tied, and unnatural. The story of the mummy kept in the loft of the hut probably refers to this founder. The Buzi did mummify certain people. When a boy died in the Poro they mummified the body by smoking it, and kept it until the end, when it was turned over to the family for burial.

THE SANDE SOCIETY FOR GIRLS

Concerning the Sande I know little in detail. It was an organization for the education of the girls. They were taken to the bush like the boys to live for a variable number of months in the camp prepared for them beforehand by the men of the tribe. While there, they were seen by no one except the big *zo* woman and her assistants. This head woman conferred with the big *zo* of the man's bush, for he was overlord of the Sande as well as the Poro. It was death to any other man who was so foolish as to trespass on their territory. Sexual intercourse was taboo, and if a Sande girl became involved with a man, he was killed in the old days. Later on he was merely required to pay to the Sande the equivalent of the bride price.

The girls were circumcised by cutting out the clitorides and the labia minora. They were taught all matters pertaining to sex, as well as the art of pleasing a husband. They learned to cook, take care of the household, sing and dance, the

---

[6] He is the great red-mouthed crocodile supposed to swallow the boys and leave the marks of his teeth on their bodies.

[7] The Kpelle gɛ speaks Buzi. The Gbandɛ, Mano and Gio gɛ's speak Kpelle.

FIG. 2. DANDAI.

art of poisoning, and especially how to make simple herbal remedies for sickness. They were divided into three classes: the commoners, the chief's daughters, and the *zo*'s. The *zo*'s were especially trained in the use of herbal remedies and poisons. For this training the old women and *zo* women doing the work were paid at the end of the Sande. If a girl had been betrothed before entering, her future husband paid these fees. Her relatives could bring food, but had to leave it at a designated spot where it was picked up by the *zo* women. For misbehavior the girls were flogged.

The idea of death and rebirth does not seem to have been so clearly established in the Sande. But the girls were brought out of the bush by a masked official who was greatly feared. They were smeared with white clay as symbolic of the spirit world just as were the boys. They were taboo for a month after they came out. Then they were taken by their husbands who gave a feast in honor of the occasion.

The special symbol of the woman *Zo* was a Janus staff with two horns. The Janus spoon with double bowl (pl. XIII, a) is from the Krā tribe, where it was used by the head of the Sande in a special ceremony at planting time, at the time the girls entered the Sande, and at the final burial feast for a paramount chief. A similar spoon was used by the Mano in a secret fertility ritual held every three or four years.

A Janus mask from the northern part of Liberia which was sold in Monrovia to a tourist is shown in pl. XII, b. Although it had never been used it was supposed to be a replica of a mask used in the Sande. Two other Sande masks should be mentioned in this connection, since they were made for tourist trade, yet represent a very high type of native art. Pl. X, f, is a mask made by a Bassa artist who probably expected it to be put to legitimate use. Pl. XII, a, is a mask made by a Krā artist in a serious attempt to reproduce an antique for a collector who refused to buy new carvings.

The mask shown in pl. XI, f, is of very poor workmanship and is included in this collection mainly because of the Berber symbols carved on the cheeks. It came from French West Africa, just north of Liberia, with the story that it had been worn by a man whose duty it was to scarify a double row of marks around the waist of girls to indicate their eligibility for marriage. Where such a practice would fit in with the Sande organization cannot be said at present. The Berber symbols may indicate a custom from a far country.

Except during "graduation" ceremonies, the Sande masks are seldom seen in public, and are very few in number when compared with the Poro masks. From the Gio country comes an interesting mask which was worn by a medicine man, who was a sort of specialist in obstetrics. The face, however, is that of a woman, as was the rest of his costume. Being a man he was not allowed to attend a woman in child-birth, but he was called to help by a midwife who had a difficult case of labor. He sat in front of the house in consultation with the midwife inside, gave her advice and medicine to help her in her difficulty and was well paid for his trouble (pl. XI, e).

Another mask from the Gio country was held in high esteem by the midwives, but was not worn. It was the object of prayer offered by the midwife and the pregnant woman, who slept with it under the blanket at the foot of the bed. From time to time the woman would wash the mask with water, then rub the water over her body, praying for a fine baby and an easy delivery. When her time came this mask was set up by the midwife and held a prominent place in the ritual of childbirth. After the baby was born a sacrifice of thanksgiving was made to this mask. It is interesting to note the two human breasts carved on the forehead of this mask (pl. XI, d).

During the time neither Poro nor Sande was in session, masked dancers appeared in public. Some of these were pure entertainers, who appeared on gala occasions to heighten the festivities, but they served also the function of keeping the population constantly aware of the ever-watchful spirit world. They were supposed to be spirits from the jungle. They were of three main types. One performed on stilts (pl. XIV, c and d) and wore a heavy net veil instead of a mask, probably because he needed to see better than was possible when looking through the tiny slits serving as eye-holes in the wooden masks. The second type of entertainer wore a rather beautiful mask with conventionalized features (pl. XIII, c). All of these danced in full costume, frequently with a tall headdress decorated with bells and surmounted with a tuft of feathers. Some of these also sang rather well and were accompanied by drums, rattles and other musical instruments. The third type was the masked clown who frequently wore the burlesque chimpanzee mask, called *Wai* (pl. X, e). Another type of masked dancer from near Monrovia is shown in pl. XIV, a.

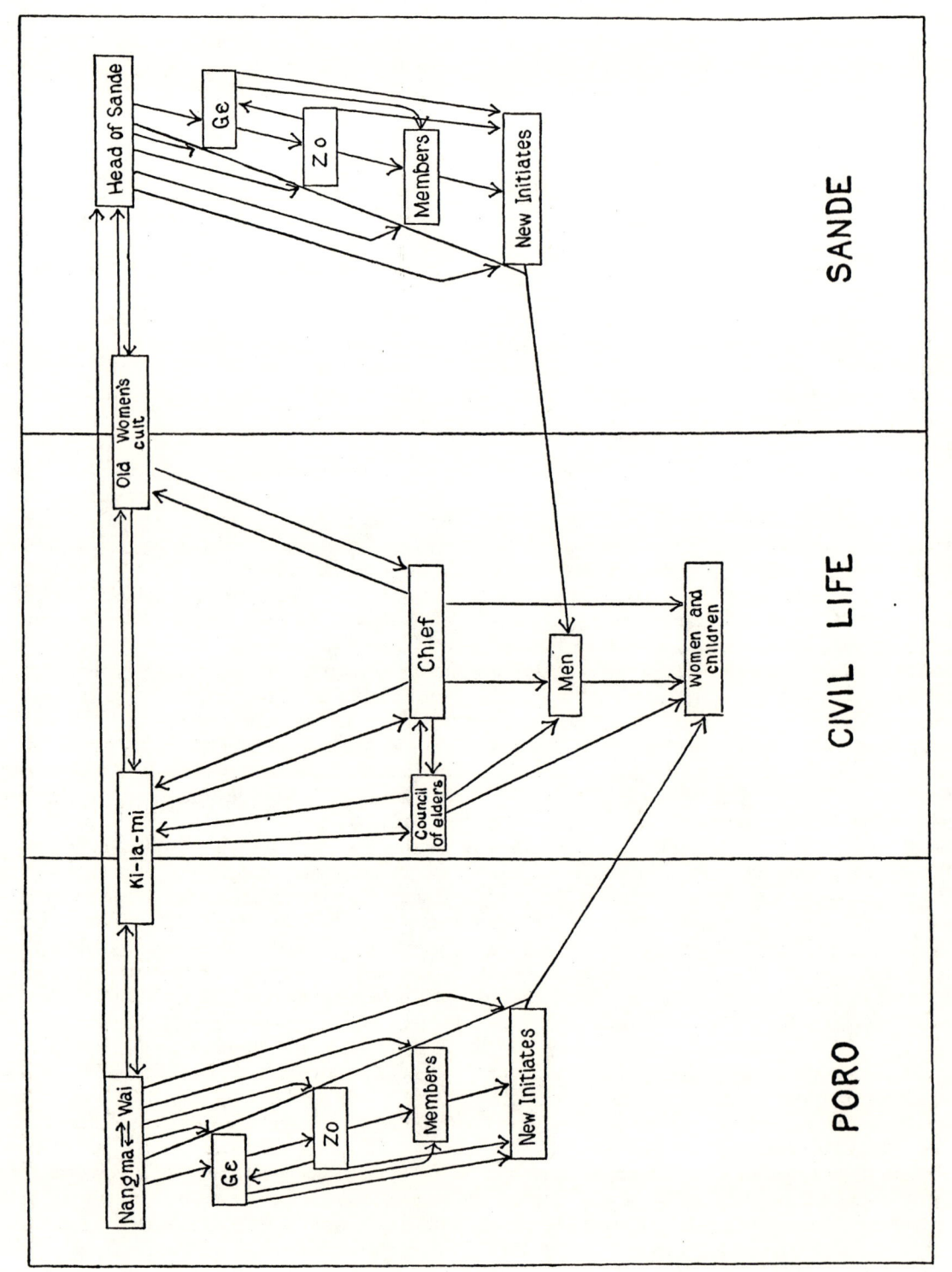

Fig. 3. Chart of social authority trends showing dominance of the Poro over all of society.

Still others appeared in public to participate in public functions or execute justice as Poro officials. These have already been mentioned in the description of the Poro masks of the three main tribes represented by this collection.

THE POWERFUL INNER CIRCLE OF THE PORO

The Poro *gɛ*'s were used in all important events: to stop village quarrels, or control fighting warriors; to catch, try, condemn, punish or even execute social criminals; to intensify the holiday spirit of great occasions; to promote fertility of the fields and bountiful harvests; to cultivate public sentiment, regulate hygiene, build bridges and sacred houses; and to conduct and administer the Poro school which was all things to all men. In the old days, among the Mano people at least, control of tribal affairs rested in the hands of a few privileged old men of high degree in the Poro who worked in secret and ruled by frightfulness. These old men were frequently the *gɛ*'s themselves, wearing the masks and carrying out the decrees of custom. Although it is a question as to whether they wore the masks or the masks wore them—whether they acted the parts of the characters or whether the characters inspired movement for arm, leg, and tongue—the fact remains that these old men perpetuated the system, and profited by it. Only a very wealthy man of advanced years could pay the fees and hope to pass initiation into these higher degrees reserved for nobility.

These old men formed an inner society of patriarchs. They were the peers. They were called *ki la mɪ* because each carried with him always a skin on which to sit, preferably a striped or spotted skin. On any big question they went into the sacred grove to deliberate. Their decision was final. They had an organization among themselves and were sworn to obey their leader. They were men of peace, and settled all palavers by arbitration. They could not fight or be fought, nor could they be arrested or tried in the tribal court, but one could be tried by his equals. They were sacred even before death so that the transition from earthly to heavenly beings was an easy one—so easy that their death was kept secret. When one of them died no one knew until a death mask had been made. Even then, his family could not mourn until a death fee of one pound sterling had been paid to the members. Sometimes they kept the death a secret and continued to collect cows from the family "to make soup for the sick man." This abuse of power was manifested in other things, and in many ways. All of the *ki la mɪ* were *zo*'s and had secret burial attended to *zo*'s only.

There was within this group another circle, the *ki gbuo la mɪ*, the big skin men who were the real royalty of the tribe. One of these men had a dignified poise about everything he did. Everyday affairs were executed with an air of being in a definitely circumscribed area of action with polite rules of conduct approaching ritual. The standing of such a man would be recognized in other tribes and other Poro systems, though the details of the Poro in a distant area might vary so much that the ordinary initiate would not be allowed even to see the least bit of the ritual. This higher brotherhood was very strong and closely knit.

In explanation of fig. 3, it should be pointed out that the chief was the nominal center of civil life, but that the real power lay in the hands of the *ki la mɪ* who could act through the council of elders or even depose a chief. Ordinarily the chief consulted the elders or the old women. Many of the more important elders were actually *ki la mɪ*. The position of the *ki la mɪ* was half civil, half Poro. This body was the court of final appeal when the Poro was not in session. Moreover, certain cases could not even be tried by the chief, but had to be taken before the *ki la mɪ* assembled secretly, preferably in the Poro grove. A chief could not declare war without consent of both the *ki la mɪ* and the old women's cult. Ordinary women and children had nothing to say about public affairs.

When the Poro was in session, the men were entirely under Poro laws and influence. The entire organization exerted an influence of taboo and frightfulness upon the women and children. The power of the *Nangma* and *wai* was exerted either by relay down the line of officials or directly upon each group. The lesser officials as masked "devils" exerted the chief pressure upon the women and children, and constituted the only visible evidence of the workings of the Poro on the world outside. It is chiefly with this phase of the Poro that this paper deals. Much of the internal working of the Poro is still a mystery. In fact the organization shown in the diagram is partly conjectural. It is entirely possible that the Poro, like the organization of the Druids, had two doctrines, one for the initiated, one for the vulgar outsiders. In this paper it has been impossible to say much about the inner secrets, except as revealed by bits of information collected here and there during ten years of residence. The picture drawn here is a true one of the Poro's contact with the outside world and the means used to guarantee secrecy. The inner circles have scarcely been penetrated.

It is certain, however, that during the boy's stay in the sacred grove he learned tribal lore and the rules of polite conduct, as well as his trade or profession. He was equipped for life, but there were still many things he could not learn until he reached middle age and was admitted into a higher degree. The old men reached still higher levels, paying stiff fees with each step upward. The higher degrees were limited to certain families. In general, wisdom and science were reserved as a monopoly of the chosen few, and that monopoly was almost entirely hereditary.

I have said little about the initiations into higher degrees for the simple reason that I know little about them. There was, however, a system of post-graduate work in various fields. There were schools in "leaves," or the practice of medicine; "lightning," or prediction and control of rain, thunder, and lightning for personal ends; "rivers," or the demons of the waters and fertility; and finally "frightfulness," or the art of the innermost circles of the Poro itself.

The total effect of all this was ultra conservative. Private wealth was opposed by rival poisoning. Any individual inclined to be too progressive for the community as a whole, especially if his family standing did not allow it, was doomed eventually to destruction by some jealous rival, or even by common consent of the other men. From what I have seen of its workings in its more recent emasculated forms, I am willing to advance the hypothesis that the lack of progress of these West African tribes and similar people has been due in no small measure to their socialistic totality, pulling down and destroying the progressive individual, or sacrificing him deliberately to their conservative ideals. Inventive genius was not only suppressed, it was taboo in such a system. Even the abuse of privilege and power by the high and mighty ones was kept in check by the systematic use of poison by both men and women. To fight poison there was only a subtler poison; and frightfulness was overcome by a frightfulness more terrible still, until the all-highest could simply sit and say, "I am what I am."

BIBLIOGRAPHY

BIBLIOGRAPHY

The Poro and Sande in Sierra Leone, Liberia and Adjacent Countries

ALLDRIDGE, T. J.
- 1901. The Sherbro and its hinterland. London.
- 1910. Sierra Leone, a transformed colony. London.

BROWN, G. W.
- 1937. The Poro in modern business: a preliminary report of field work. Man, vol. 37, no. 3. London.

BUTT-THOMPSON, F. W.
- 1926. Sierra Leone: its history and tradition. London.

CESTON, J. M.
- 1911. Le *Gree-Gree* bush (initiation de la jeunesse) chez les Négres-Golah, Liberia. Anthropos, vol. 6. St. Gabriel-Mödling, Vienna.

CHEVRIER, A.
- 1906. Note relative aux coutumes des adeptes de la societie des Scymos. L'Anthropologie, vol. 17. Paris.

COLE, I. A.
- 1886. A revelation of the secret orders of West Africa. Dayton.

DAPPER, O.
- 1668. Description de l'Afrique (trans. from Dutch, J. B. Labat). Paris, 1732.

DICTIONAIRE D'ETHNOGRAPHIQUE MODERNE.
- 1853. Paris.

FRAZER, J. G.
- 1913. Balder the beautiful, the fire-festivals of Europe and the doctrine of the eternal soul. Vols. 1 and 2. London.

FROBENIUS, L.
- 1898. Die Masken und Geheimbunde Afrikas. Halle.

HAMBLY, W. D.
- 1937. Source book for African anthropology, part II. Field Museum of Natural History, Anthropological Series, vol. 26. Chicago.

HENRY, J. M.
- 1908. Le culte des esprits chez les Bambara. Anthropos, vol. 3. St. Gabriel-Mödling, Vienna.

KOELLE, S. W.
- 1853. Outlines of a grammar of the Vei language together with a Vei-English vocabulary. London.

LAING, A. G.
- 1825. Travels in West Africa. London.

LANGLEY, E. R.
- 1932. The Kono people of Sierra Leone: their clans and names. Africa, vol. 5. London.

LOEB, E. M.
- 1929. Tribal initiations and secret societies. University of California Publications in American Archaeology and Ethnology, vol. 25. Berkeley.

MARRIOTT, H. P. F.
- 1899. The secret tribal societies of West Africa. Ars. Quatuor Coronatorum.
- 1899–1900. The secret societies of West Africa. Royal Anthropological Institute of Great Britain and Ireland, Journal, vol. 2. London.

MIGEOD, F. W. H.
- 1913. Correspondence regarding unlawful societies. British Parliamentary Paper (Command paper no. 6961). London.
- 1916. The building of the Poro house and making of the image. Man, vol. 16. London.

NEEL, H.
- 1913. Note sur deux peuplades de la frontière libérienne, les Kissi et les Toma. L'Anthropologie, vol. 24. Paris.

NEWLAND, H. O.
- 1916. Sierra Leone, its peoples, products and secret societies. London.
- 1922. West Africa, a handbook of practical information. London.

PAROISSE, G.
- 1896. Notes sur les peuplades autochtones de la Guinee Francaise. L'Anthropologie, vol. 7. Paris.

PENICK, C. C.
- 1896. The devil bush of West Africa. Fetter's Southern Magazine, April, 1893, quoted in the Journal of American Folklore Scrapbook, vol. 9. New York.

SIBLEY, J. L. AND WESTERMANN, D.
- 1929. Liberia, old and new. London.

SMITH, L. F.
   1905. West African Bundoo. Journal of the Royal Army Medical Corps, vol. 4. London.

THOMAS, N. W.
   1916. Anthropological report on Sierra Leone. Part I. Law and customs of the Timne and other tribes. London.

THURNWALD, R. 1929. Social systems of Africa. Africa, vol. 2. London.

VOLZ, W.
   1911. Reise in das Hinterland von Liberia. Berne.

WALLIS, C. B.
   1905. The Poro of the Mendi. African Society, Journal. London.

WEBSTER, H.
   1908. Primitive secret societies. New York.

WESTERMANN, D.
   1921. Die Kpelle, ein Negerstamm in Liberia. Gottingen.

WINTERBOTTOM, T.
   1803. An account of native Africans in the neighbourhood of Sierra Leone. London.

ZELLER, R.
   1912. Die Goldgewichte von Asante. Baessler-Archiv, vol. 3. Berlin.

SIMILAR SOCIETIES IN OTHER PLACES

BASDEN, G. T.
   1921. Among the Ibos of Nigeria. London.

CUREAU, A. L.
   1915. Savage man in Central Africa. London.

DALE, G.
   1895. An account of the principal customs and habits of the natives inhabiting the Bondei country. Royal Anthropological Institute of Great Britain and Ireland, Journal, vol. 25. London.

DELAFOSSE, M.
   1931. The Negroes of Africa (trans. F. Fligelman). Washington.

DENNETT, R. E.
   1910. Nigerian studies. London.

FARROW, S. S.
   1912. Faith, fancies and fetich. London.

GRAY, W. M.
   1825. Travels in western Africa, 1818–1821. London.

HAMBLY, W. D.
   1935. Tribal initiation of boys in Angola. American Anthropologist, n. s., vol. vol. 37. Menasha.

MEAD, M.
   1934. Tamberans and Tumbuans in New Guinea. Natural History, vol. 34. New York.

ORTIZ, F.
   1906. Hampa Afro-Cubana. Los Negros Brujos. Madrid.

SELIGMAN, C. G.
   1913. Some aspects of the Hamitic problem in the Anglo-Egyptian Sudan. Royal Anthropological Institute of Great Britain and Ireland, Journal, vol. 42. London.

TALBOT, P. A.
   1923. Life in southern Nigeria. London.
   1926. The peoples of southern Nigeria. Oxford.

WILLOUGHBY, W. C.
   1909. Notes on the initiation ceremonies of the Bechwana. Royal Anthropological Institute of Great Britain and Ireland, Journal, vol. 39. London.

PLATES

PEABODY MUSEUM CATALOGUE NUMBERS FOR SPECIMENS ILLUSTRATED IN PLATES

PLATE I. Scale ¼
 a. 37-77-50/2563
 b. 37-77-50/2564
 c. 37-77-50/3005
 d. 37-77-50/3013

PLATE II. Scale ½
 a. (Dr. Harley's property)
 b. 37-77-50/2615
 b. 37-77-50/2615
 c. 37-77-50/2963
 d. 37-77-50/2993
 e. 37-77-50/3004
 f. 37-77-50/2882
 g. 37-77-50/2883

PLATE III. Scale ¼
 a. 37-77-50/3000
 b. 37-77-50/2653
 c. 37-77-50/2820
 d. 37-77-50/2657
 e. 37-77-50/3008
 f. 37-77-50/2876
 g. 37-77-50/2788
 h. 37-77-50/2881

PLATE IV. Scale ¼
 a. 37-77-50/2672
 b. 37-77-50/2798
 c. 37-77-50/2967
 d. 37-77-50/2966
 e. 37-77-50/2744
 f. 37-77-50/2819

PLATE V. Scale ¼
 a. 37-77-50/2802

 b. 37-77-50/3041
 c. 37-77-50/2785
 d. 37-77-50/2804
 e. 37-77-50/2708
 f. 37-77-50/2654
 g. 36-77-50/2755
 h. 37-77-50/2784
 i. 37-77-50/2707

PLATE VI. Scale ¼
 a. 37-77-50/2972
 b. 37-77-50/2799
 c. 37-77-50/2762
 d. 37-77-50/2859
 e. 37-77-50/2988
 f. 37-77-50/2824
 g. 37-77-50/2685

PLATE VII. Scale ¼
 a. 37-77-50/2818
 b. 37-77-50/2989
 c. 37-77-50/2699
 d. 37-77-50/2880
 e. 37-77-50/2983
 f. 37-77-50/2992

PLATE VIII. Scale ¼
 a. 37-77-50/2743
 b. 37-77-50/2964
 c. 37-77-50/2962
 d. 37-77-50/2733
 e. 37-77-50/2763
 f. 37-77-50/2760
 g. 37-77-50/2647
 h. 37-77-50/2719
 i. 37-77-50/2991

PLATE IX. Scale ¼
 a. 37-77-50/2717
 b. 37-77-50/3019
 c. 37-77-50/2688
 d. 37-77-50/3017
 e. 37-77-50/2873
 f. 37-77-50/2649
 g. 37-77-50/2650

PLATE X. Scale ¼
 a. 37-77-50/2875
 b. 37-77-50/2648
 c. 37-77-50/2969
 d. 37-77-50/2874
 e. 37-77-50/2765
 f. (Dr. Harley's property)

PLATE XI. Scale ¼
 a. 37-77-50/2691
 b. 37-77-50/3024
 c. 37-77-50/3022
 d. 37-77-50/2870
 e. 37-77-50/2791
 f. 37-77-50/2565

PLATE XII
 a. (Dr. Harley's property)
 b. 33-55-50/114

PLATE XIII
 a. 37-77-50/2690
 b. 37-77-50/3034
 c. 37-77-50/2851

PLATE XIV
 e. 34-34-50/271
 f. 34-34-50/265
 g. 34-34-50/269

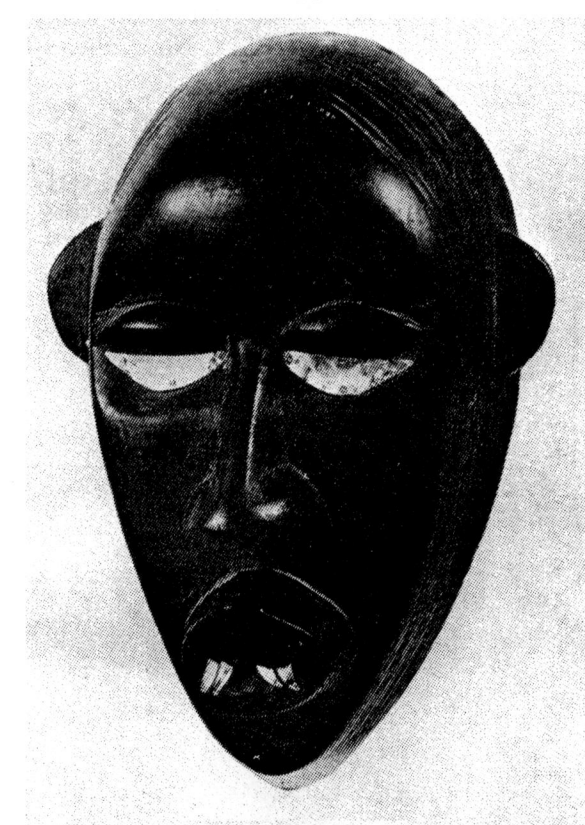

a. Mandingo tribe.

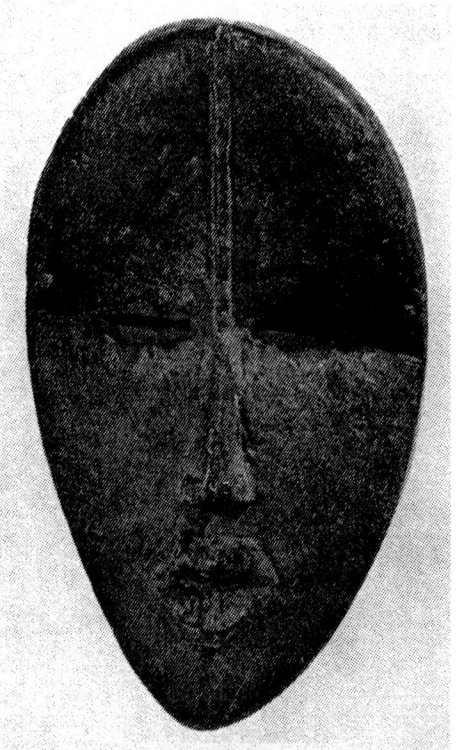

b. Da glu. Mandingo tribe.

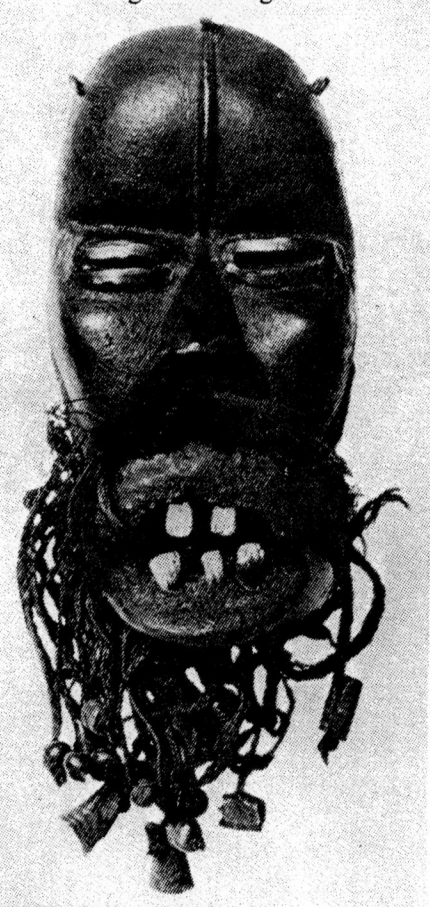

c. Bɔ zɛ zo. Gio tribe.

d. Zo zɛ Gɛ. Mano-Konor tribe.

1. MASKS FROM VARIOUS TRIBES.

PEABODY MUSEUM PAPERS　　　　　　　　　　　　　　　VOL. XIX, No. 2, PLATE II

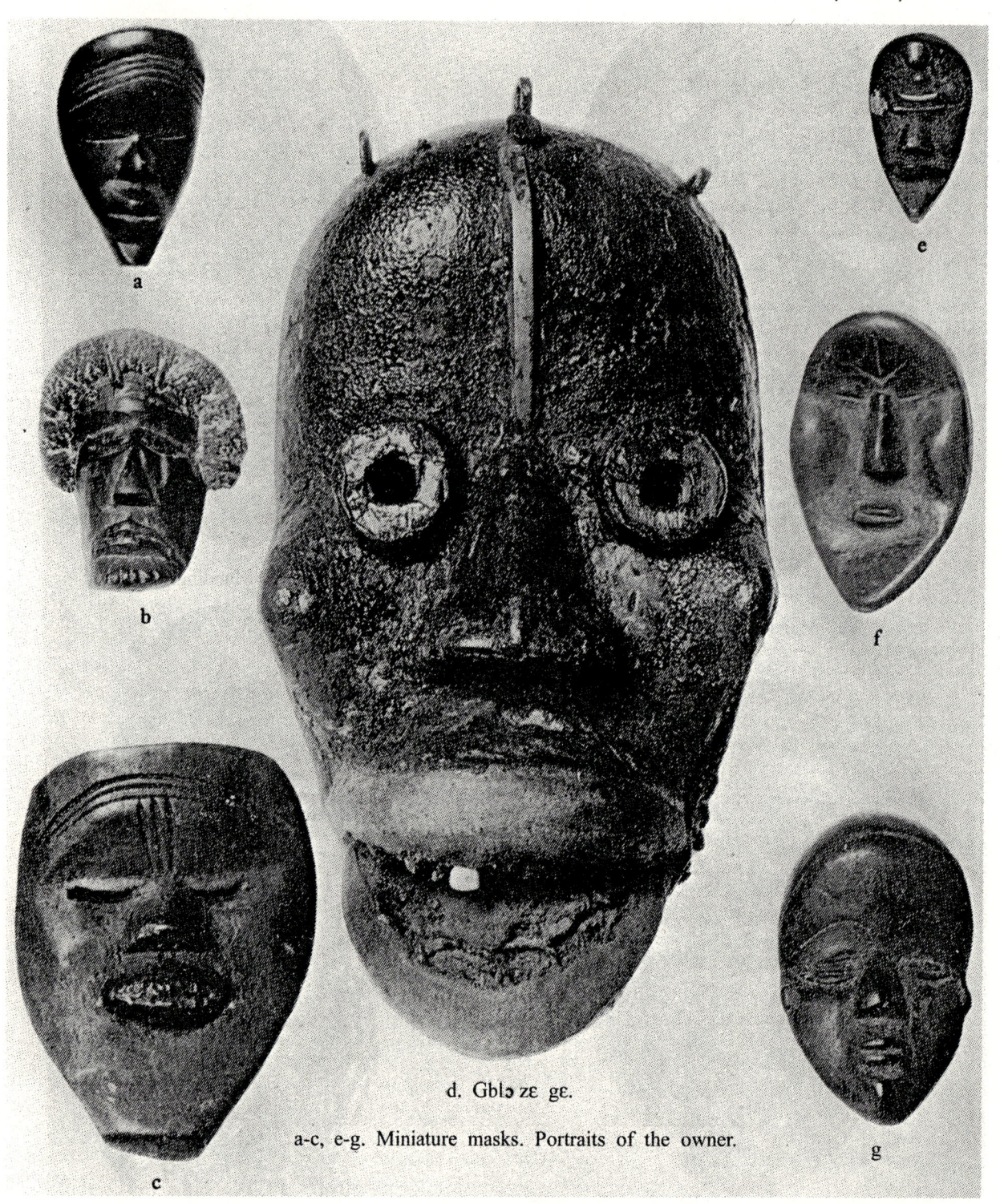

d. Gblɔ zɛ gɛ.
a-c, e-g. Miniature masks. Portraits of the owner.

II. MANO TRIBE.

PEABODY MUSEUM PAPERS VOL. XIX, No. 2, PLATE III

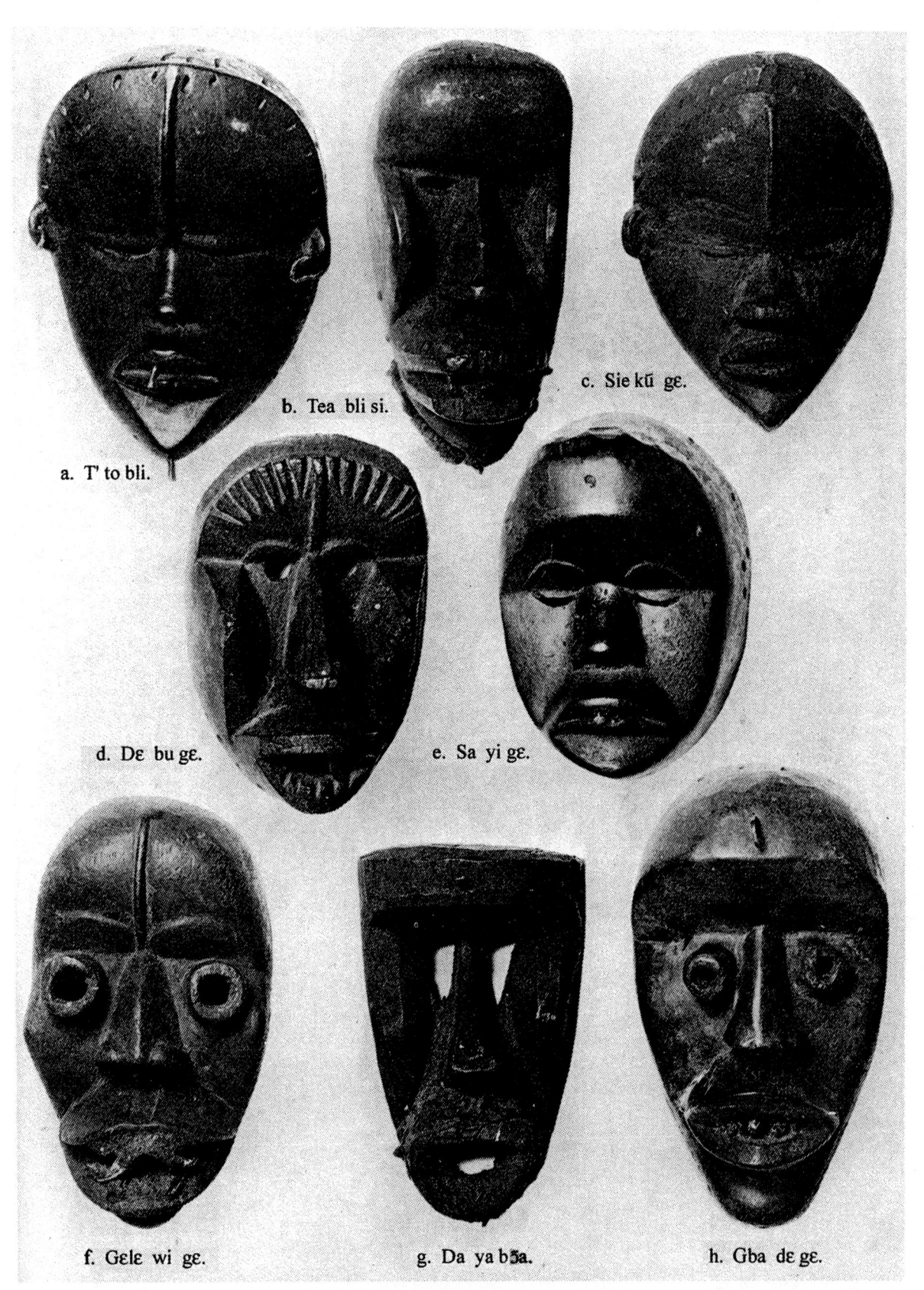

a. T' to bli.   b. Tea bli si.   c. Sie kū gɛ.

d. Dɛ bu gɛ.   e. Sa yi gɛ.

f. Gelɛ wi gɛ.   g. Da ya bɔa.   h. Gba dɛ gɛ.

III. MANO TRIBE.

a. Dia mi a ga.

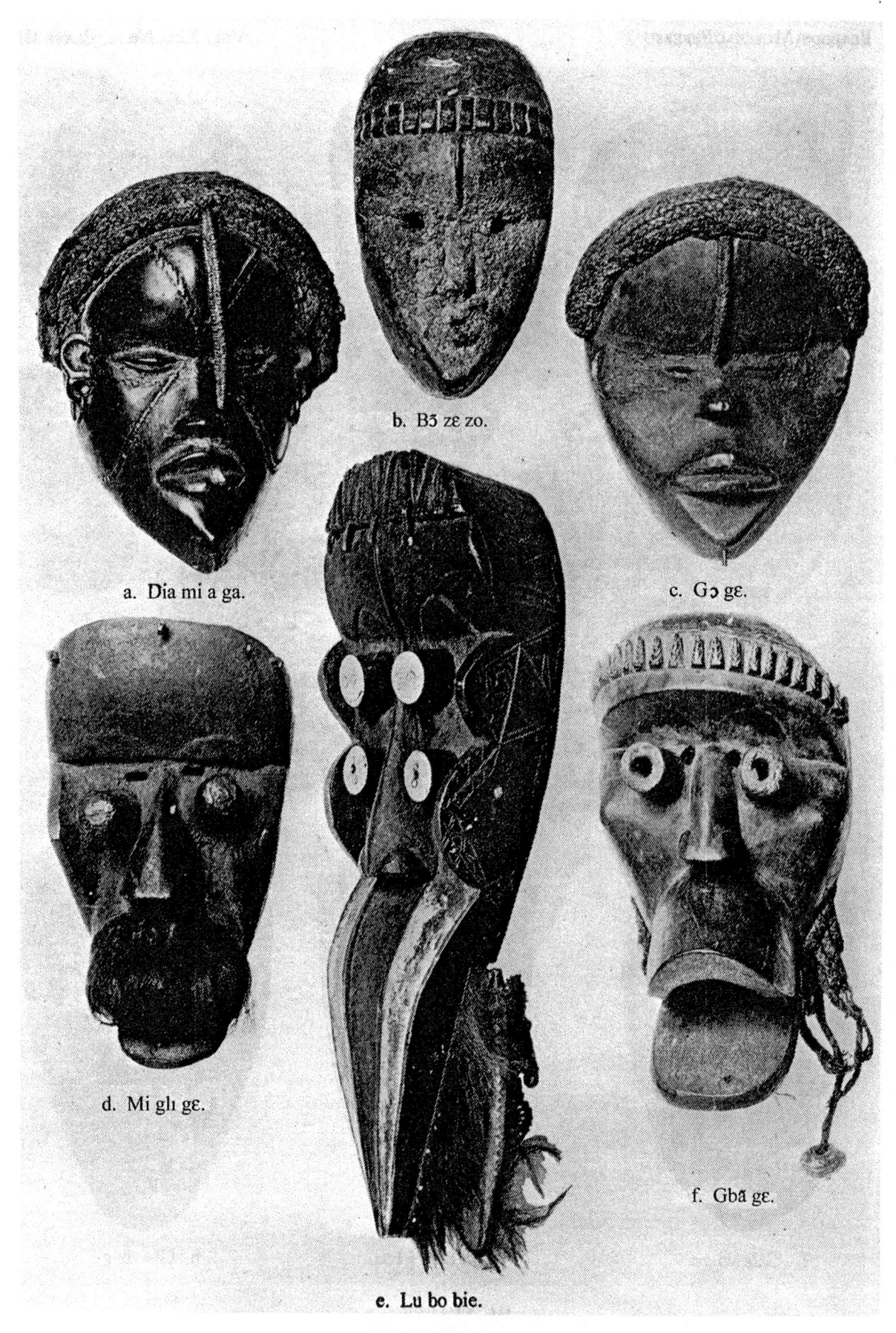

b. Bɔ zɛ zo.

c. Gɔ gɛ.

d. Mi glı gɛ.

e. Lu bo bie.

f. Gbā gɛ.

IV. Mano tribe.

a. Yo pu glü.
b. N'na glü.
c. Yau wɔgbi.
d. Dai da glü.
e. Companion of zɔ glü.
f. Ka glü.
g. God of the dance.
h. Ma die.
i. Zɔ glü.

V. GEH TRIBE.

a. Gbala ko pie.
b. Yo glü.
c. Crawfish catcher.
d. Zai bo lu.
e. Tie glü.
f. Du gli glü.
g. Mini aō glü.

VI. GEH TRIBE.

PEABODY MUSEUM PAPERS VOL. XIX, No. 2, PLATE VII

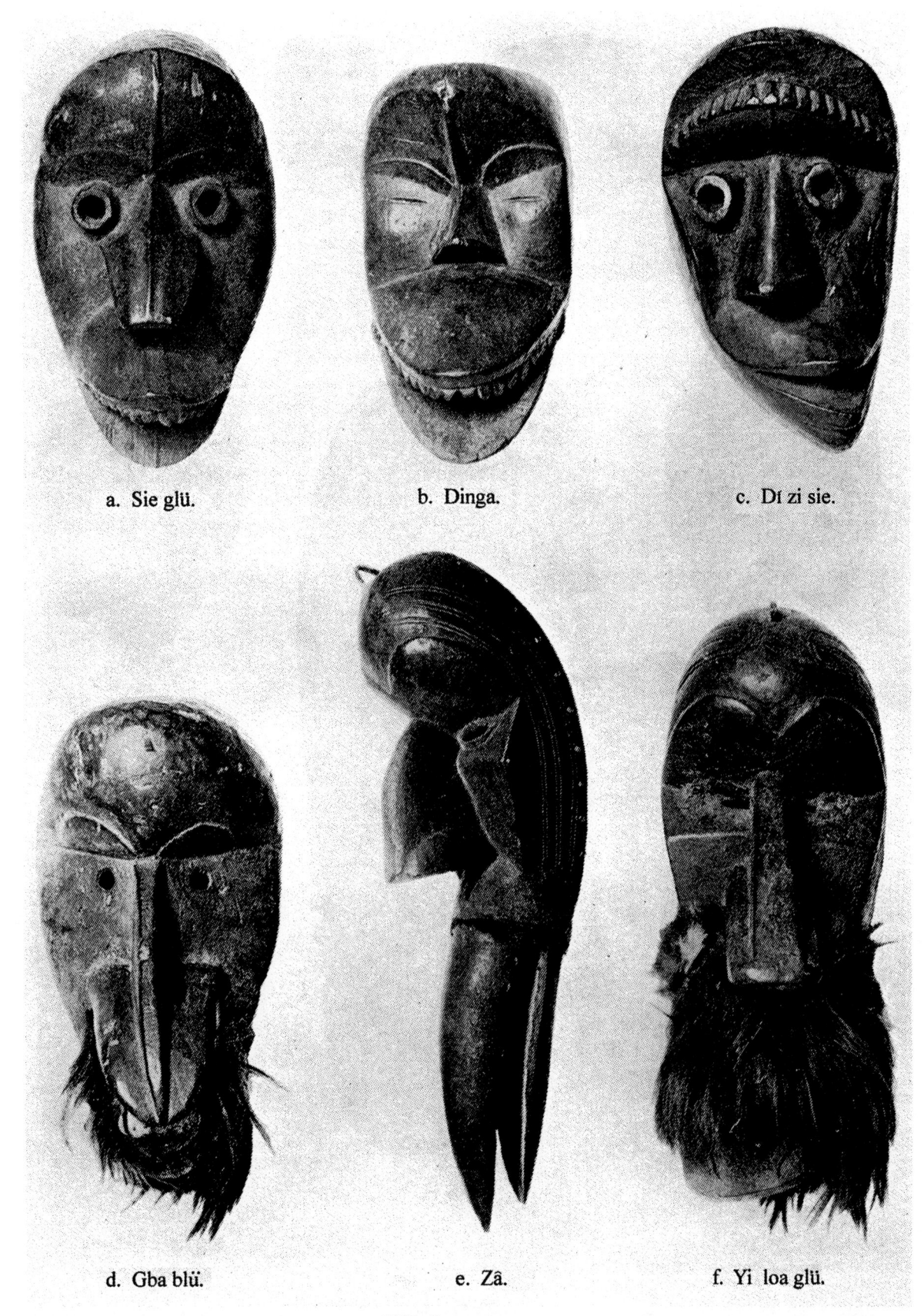

a. Sie glü.   b. Dinga.   c. Dĭ zi sie.

d. Gba blü.   e. Zâ.   f. Yi loa glü.

VII. GEH TRIBE.

a-d. Small replicas of old masks.

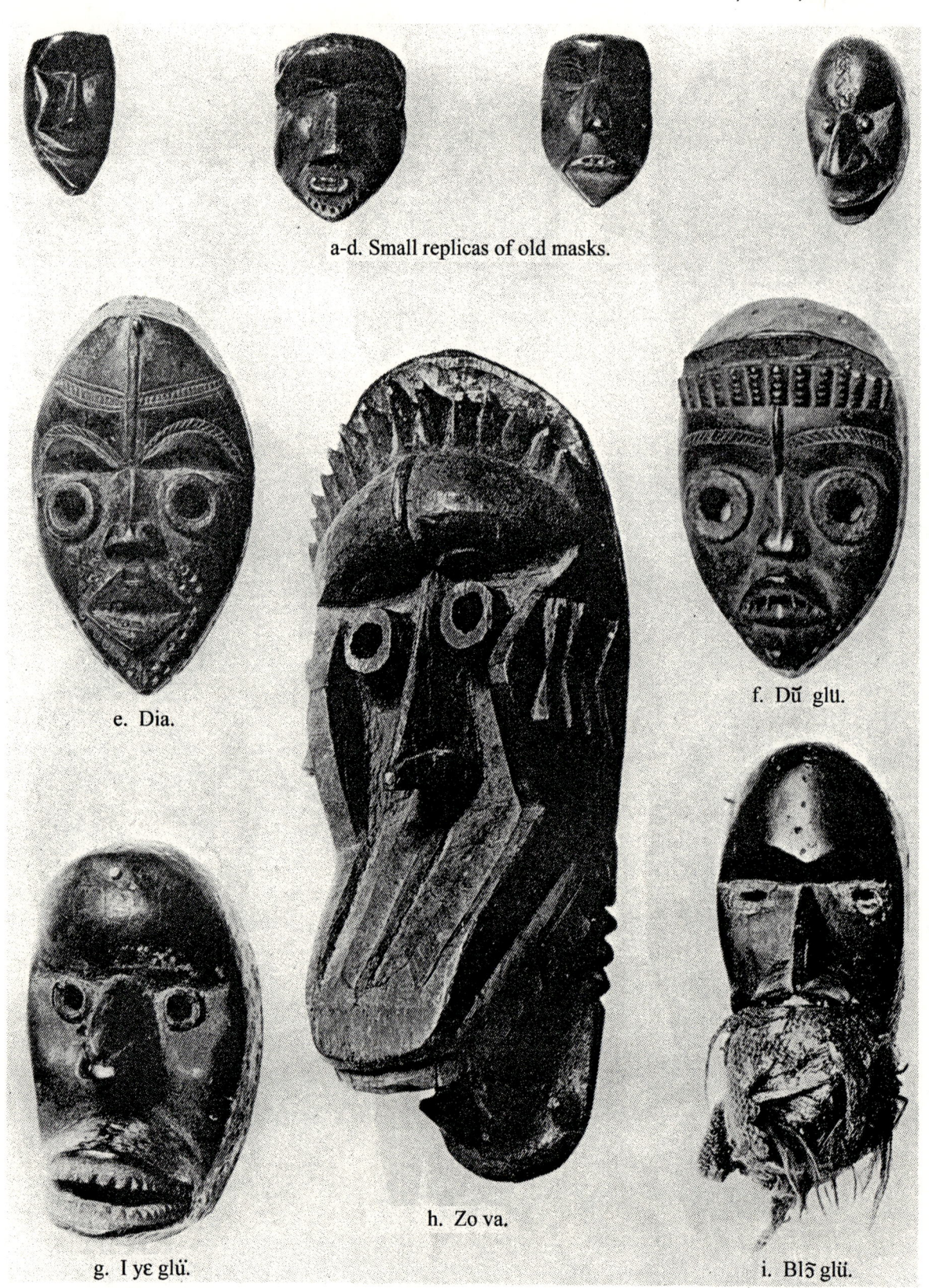

e. Dia.

f. Dŭ glü.

g. I yɛ glü.

h. Zo va.

i. Blɔ̃ glü.

VIII. Geh tribe.

PEABODY MUSEUM PAPERS　　　　　　　　　　　　　　　　　　　　VOL. XIX, NO. 2, PLATE IX

a. Nya kɛ ya ba.　　b. Mɛ mã glü.　　c. Nya va glü.　　d. Gɔ glü.　　e. Gio bla glü.　　f. B'li.　　g. B'li.

IX. GIO TRIBE.

a. Gea glü.

b. Di va glü.

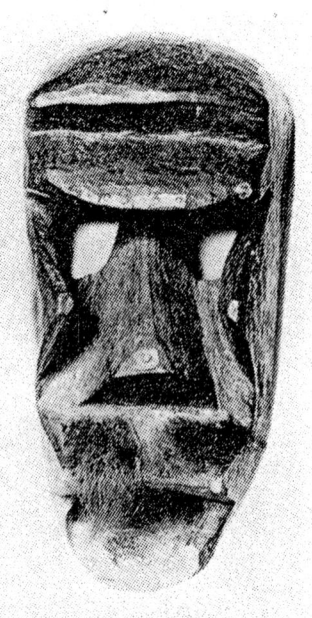

c. Klua glü.

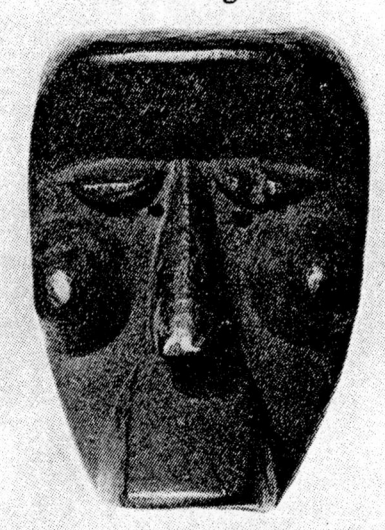

d. Zua kpa glü.

e. Wai.

f. Sande mask.

a. Krā tribe.

b. Konor tribe.

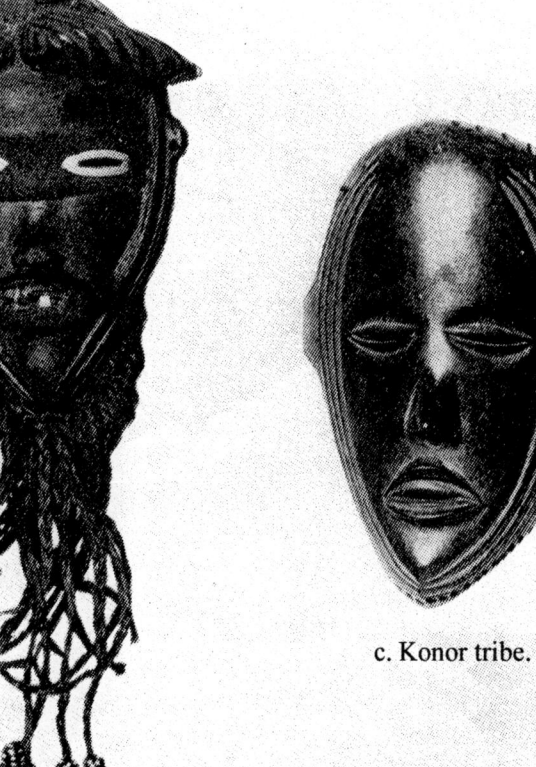

c. Konor tribe.

d. Gio tribe.

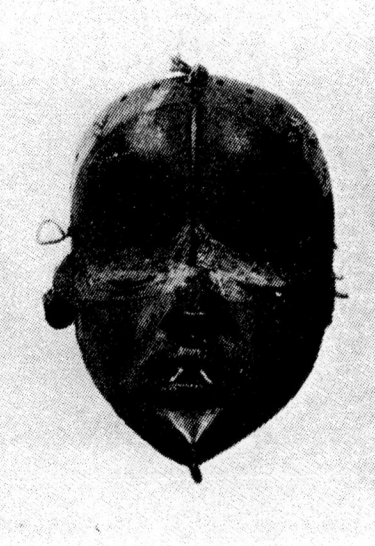

e. Gio tribe.

f. Mask showing Berber influence.

XI. Masks from various tribes.

a. Sande mask made by a Krā artist.

b. Janus mask, replica of one in the Sande Society.

XIII.

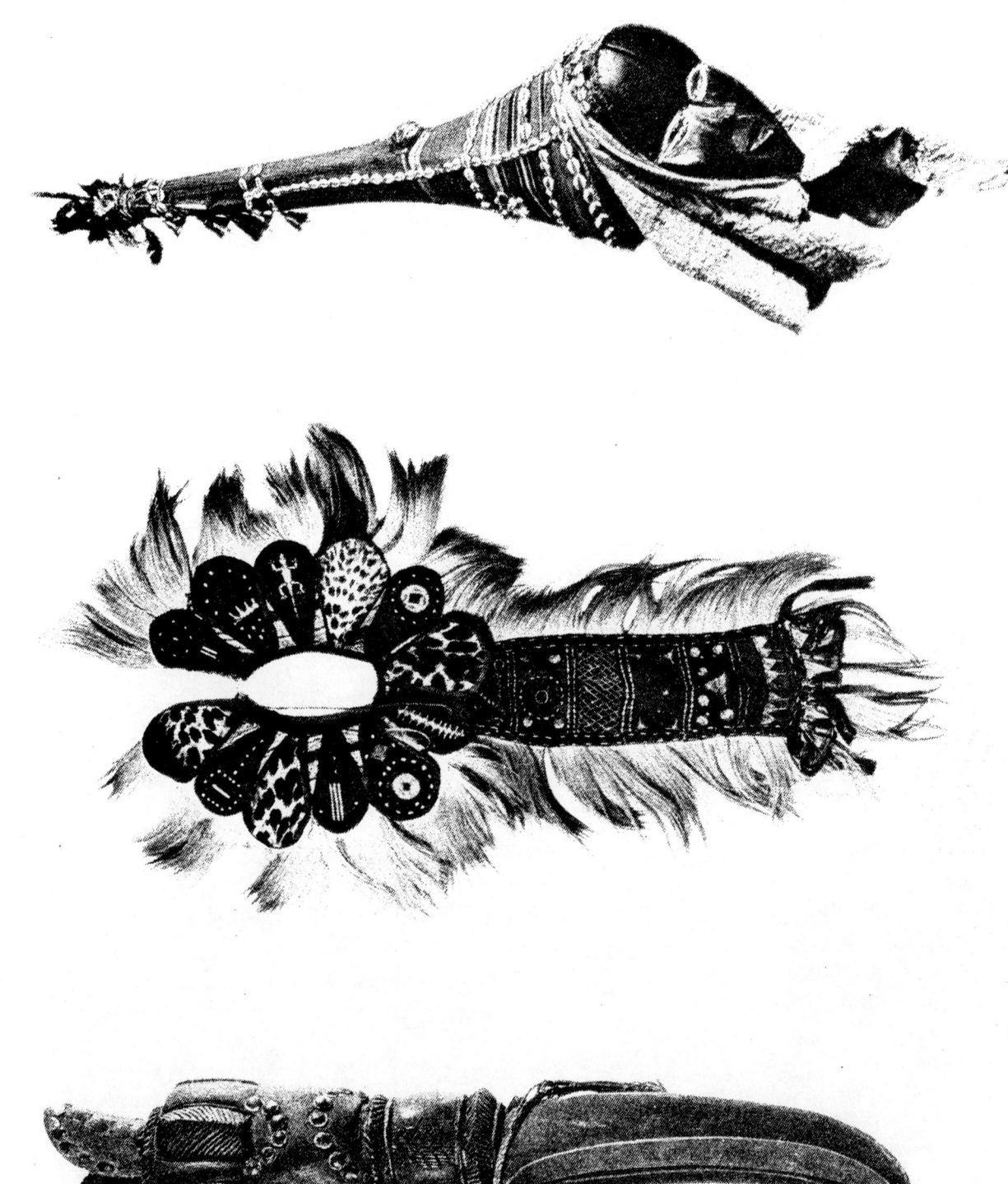

a. Janus spoon. Krā tribe.　　b. Headdress worn by god of war. Konor tribe.　　c. Mask worn by dancers and entertainers.

a. Masked dancer from Monrovia.

b. Entrance to Poro.

c, d. Dancers representing spirits from the jungle.

e. Scarifying knife.

f. Whistle used in making "voice of the spirit".

g. Scarifying razor.

MASKS AS AGENTS OF SOCIAL CONTROL
IN NORTHEAST LIBERIA

Frontispiece, Small personal mask, *mã*, of an important man, *zo*.

PAPERS
OF THE
PEABODY MUSEUM OF AMERICAN ARCHAEOLOGY
AND ETHNOLOGY, HARVARD UNIVERSITY
VOL. XXXII — NO. 2

MASKS AS AGENTS OF SOCIAL CONTROL IN NORTHEAST LIBERIA

BY

GEORGE W. HARLEY

CAMBRIDGE, MASSACHUSETTS, U.S.A.
PUBLISHED BY THE MUSEUM
1950

This Facsimile
of the
Original 1950 Edition
Published by the
Peabody Museum of American Archaeology
Is Strictly Limited to
200 Copies
of Which This Is

Number 105

ISBN 1-57898-266-9

Martino Publishing
P.O. Box 373
Mansfield Centre, CT

Ethnographic Arts Publications
1040 Erica Road
Mill Valley. CA

Ethnos Inc.
Las Vegas, NV

FOREWORD

IF THE people now living in northeast Liberia were suddenly to disappear, most of the material culture left behind would be destroyed rapidly by termites and decay. They would leave behind them no ruins of temples or dwellings. Their paths would scarcely be distinguishable from the trails of the animals through the forest.

A century or two later their town sites might be marked chiefly by hearthstones in groups of three, associated with burned earth, charcoal, and pottery fragments. There would remain a few wrought-iron implements of good workmanship, some from native-smelted ores. There would be found a moderate amount of rather crude, heavy, brass jewelry — more rarely, brass figurines of coarse heavy texture and rough finish — and some rather well formed but poorly burned pottery. The beads associated with such a cache would consist chiefly of recognizable trade beads, but would include a few belonging to the local culture — of brass or iron, or the perforated canine teeth of chimpanzees or leopards. Cowrie shells would establish the contact of these people with other West African tribes.

If some accident were to preserve more perishable materials, there would be found coarse homespun cotton cloths and garments, wooden hairpins and combs, and fragments of woven raffia stuff. Simple basketry of various fibers might be found to give a general idea of the little things cherished by women. A carved wooden stool, an occasional clay pipe of a shape reminiscent of the stone pipes of American Indians, a fish hook, a razor, bows, arrows, spears, and knives with leather-covered scabbards might give a picture of the pastimes of the men.

If the physical remains of this culture could be recovered in sufficient detail, the investigator would undoubtedly be impressed by the frequent occurrence of wooden masks, found singly or in groups. Where a group of masks together indicated the location of a storage place for cult objects, there might be associated with them a few large ceremonial spoons, and rarely a human figure carved in wood. Near by might be discovered various articles of costume and ritual, such as headdresses decorated with cowrie shells, red cloth, and feathers.

Without following further this imaginary picture of a culture left behind by a vanished people we might place a student in a similar position, by letting him go through a museum where were displayed articles collected from northeast Liberia, and try to deduce from them what sort of culture these tribes possessed. Given a very complete collection, and perhaps photographs of the people in their various activities, such a study still could not give a student a complete picture. There would still remain unknown to him the large realm which we designate as the social organization.

Going one step further and giving the student accounts and descriptions written by travelers through this country we could convey to him bit by bit some idea of the social structure. After comparing this with descriptions of people in similar and better-known environments the student might consider himself fairly well informed. It might even be that an anthropologist had passed that way, had spent considerable time photographing and measuring the people, and had described the things they did and how they did them. He might have stayed around long enough to have recorded part of the language and collected a large number of folk tales and an occasional joke.

If the anthropologist had been a careful investigator, he would undoubtedly have made note of the fact that many things he wanted to know were hidden from him, and that the most important things in the lives of these people were not discussed with outsiders. He might even have had an occasional frank informant who would tell him that these things were known only by the old men. If the men had talked at all, it would have been merely to say that such things were sacred and fully understood by only a handful of men in high positions in the secret societies.

If the investigator had been of such a mind he might, by paying suitable fees, have been allowed to join some of these secret societies, but unless he were of African descent he would not have been allowed membership in the inner circles, or more than a superficial contact with the more sacred properties of the priesthood. Even if he had secured some of these objects, he would have found it very difficult to obtain any detailed information as to their use. In any event, if he had joined a secret society, he would have had to swear on pain of death never to reveal any of the things he had learned, so that the advantage of membership to him as an anthropologist would have been completely neutralized by this oath of secrecy.

It is with a feeling of high privilege, therefore, that I find myself, after twenty-three years of residence in the midst of these people, the possessor of an accumulated knowledge of their most sacred objects which begins to fit together into a more or less comprehensive picture of the socio-religious forces which underlie their reactions to the more important crises of life.

The recently published report by George Schwab [1] was more than ten years in the form of a manuscript which gradually evolved into its present form. Schwab had to be content with only an occasional glimpse of the Poro and other secret societies. What little material he has from the northeastern tribes on these societies was compiled almost entirely from notes I placed at his disposal a good many years ago. In 1941 I published a study, *Native African Medicine*,[2] which succeeded in penetrating a little deeper into the fundamental conceptions designated, for want of a better term, as religious. About the same time I made a study of one hundred and sixteen masks which had been collected over a period of ten years.[3] By the simple process of inquiring about the function of each mask as it was secretly brought to me, I accumulated enough information to make this preliminary study of the great secret society known as the Poro.

This collection of masks representing Poro officials was made during the period when the Poro had been completely suppressed in this area by the Liberian Government, and the people had practically given up hope that it would ever function again. It has since been revived, but in a very modified and emasculated form, so that it is no longer the great educational institution it once was.

In the old days a group of boys would be taken into the sacred Bush (forest) whenever a chief's son arrived at the proper age, so that he could become the leader of the group. The boys remained isolated in their own small community in the forest for several years. During this time they were under very strict discipline. It was not unusual for the boys to see one of their comrades suffer the death penalty for some unforgivable offense. They received instruction in tribal history and tradition, the rules of polite conduct, formal and ritual dancing, and, as a matter of course, specific training for the parts they were to play in life as members of the tribe. They were divided into groups: one for the rulers, one for professional men, and a third for commoners. In these schools each boy learned his trade. The importance of what was going on was impressed upon the boys by high ritual administered by officials wearing masks, as did all Poro officials. Some of these rituals included a human sacrifice.

A boy graduated from this school thoroughly inculcated with a sense of loyalty to the traditions of his tribe. There were certain things that were simply not done. To reveal any of the secrets learned in the school was punishable by death.

My *Notes on the Poro in Liberia* published in 1941 presented the information available at that time concerning the Poro masks. They were supposed to represent spirits from the Bush. Their general effect when they appeared in public was to keep the women and children in ignorance and fear.

During the past eight years one hundred and fifty more masks have been collected. The information which came with them gradually changed in character because of two circumstances. One was an attempt on the part of the government officials to destroy the cult

---

[1] Schwab, 1947.
[2] Harley, 1941a.
[3] Harley, 1941b.

houses and completely suppress the forlorn hope of the elders that the old customs would some day function again. This had the effect of placing on the market masks which were not strictly Poro, but had to do rather with priestly control of public conduct. The other circumstance was that the old "owners of the land" began to die off with no successors who knew how to take care of the sacred masks — since the function of controlling the people had now been taken over by the central government. As several of these patriarchs had been my personal friends, it was only natural that their sons should bring their sacred relics to me. Everyone knew that I collected masks and that I had never betrayed the confidence of anyone giving me information about their use. Nor had I ever shown an unsympathetic or disrespectful attitude toward their sacred objects and beliefs.

The present study resulted from the realization that the information regarding these masks and their functions opened up a broader and higher category of relationships than that of the Poro alone — which I had previously considered as all things to all men. At that earlier stage of information the Poro organization seemed all powerful, yet I gave a tentative description of an inner circle and a pyramiding of power until one high mogul sat and said: "I am what I am." It is not now certain that this pyramid was *within* the Poro. It was within the cult of the *masks*, of which the Poro was the most highly developed form for manifesting the power of the ancestors toward the people. Above this, the operations of the high priest and his council were secret even from the Poro initiate until he had reached the higher levels of the cult. A level might finally be reached at which a man's prestige extended across tribes that had no true Poro.

There was undoubtedly a wide network binding all the priests together under a supreme council. This was presided over by high officials selected by a kind of divine right from two or three families of supreme hereditary standing in the whole of Liberia. That this was true, I have had a definite clue from a member of one of these families, though I have no detailed or supporting documentation.

In the light of this new information it seems that the Poro should be considered as the logical development of ideas inherent in this larger conception of the functions of masks and their wearers. The present conception is that the masks are visible manifestations of a type of ancestor worship,[4] debased, perhaps, by the necessity of using the masks as practical implements to guarantee the smooth working of a system of government founded on strict adherence to custom. This discussion of their use in a system of social control is based upon information obtained bit by bit from various informants. It applies particularly to the Mano and Gio tribes in northeast Liberia.

These tribesmen are agricultural people, living in villages in the forest country. They build round huts of sticks, mud, and thatch. They clear the forest and burn over the ground to plant rice and cassavas. In these farms they interplant small amounts of corn and vegetables and sometimes grow a little cotton. Their artisans include weavers, who use a very simple loom to produce narrow strips of homespun which are sewed together into garments. The blacksmith is an important craftsman in the community, fashioning hoes, knives, cutlasses, and formerly spears and arrowheads. Clay pots are made by the women. Mats, baskets, and such simple articles are woven by men or women from raffia, reeds, bark, and other materials.

---

[4] That the essential religion of these people should be considered as a type of ancestor worship is further indicated by their frank prayer and sacrifice to ancestors at the grave; or at some great tree symbolic of the noble dead who were not buried but "went back into the forest"; or at the crossroads to contact those ancestral spirits who still walk the paths of their old haunts.

It is also worth noting that a mask is the same word used to designate the human spirit and the spirit of the ancestors. That this spirit idea is the very basis of the cult of masks is shown by the fact that where this cult has branched out and developed in its most all-pervading form, including the Poro, the term gɛ is also used to designate the great spirit which is supposed to swallow the boys, keep them in his belly during their seclusion in the Poro, and finally give them rebirth as full-fledged, but new-born, men. The marks of his teeth left on their bodies are evidence that they have been admitted into full tribal membership.

A group of professional men in the tribe are called *zo's* or "doctors." This term is not confined to herbal doctors or medicine men in the more magical sense, nor to "professors" in the sense of learned men with authoritative opinions on any subject. The term includes all of these, as well as master craftsmen, heads of guilds, priests, and chiefs of hereditary standing. These categories are not always separate, but often overlap. One individual might at the same time be a leading blacksmith, a town chief, and a priest; and other such combinations could occur. A *zo* is always an individual who deserves the respect of the community on one or more counts.

Before the subjugation of these tribes around the turn of the century by the coastal government their social and religious organization had persisted unchanged for a long time. The old, indigenous government functioned on two levels, not mutually exclusive, but overlapping. The first, which might be termed the civil phase, was concerned with the everyday management of the town and its citizens, common laws governing conduct, etc. On the second level, which may be thought of as religious, were the mechanisms for handling the crises and emergencies of life. It was in this second level of government, calculated to deal with the powerful, hidden, spiritual forces, that the masks found their special place.

The first, or civil, mechanism of social control included the external organization of chiefs and minor officers and was perfectly evident to casual observers. It was known and understood by all members of the group, including women and children. It was based upon a patriarchal system that controlled the people in a more or less democratic manner.

The head of the family ruled his immediate household. It was an easy step from this domestic rule to the authority of the "quarter chief" who heard complaints and settled petty palavers in a few families living side by side in the town and united by close ties of kinship. He would not hold formal court, but would talk matters over with interested people, sitting around almost anywhere. Everyone present had freedom of speech and of opinion. If there was a disagreement of a more serious nature, or if anyone objected to the quarter chief's decisions, a more formal hearing would be held by the town chief. From here appeals could be carried to the clan chief. In all this, women had little to say unless called in as witnesses.

Town chiefs and clan chiefs had the custom of calling in the elders to help decide matters of complicated or obscure nature. They might sit in the town council and express their opinions openly and informally, but as a matter increased in importance, the meetings of the elders became more and more secret until they reached the final high council. This met at night in a secret part of the sacred Bush, presided over by a high priest with a simple but highly effective ritual.

There was a definite tendency for a special matter to be handled by a secret organization. One of these which enjoyed considerable prestige and power was composed entirely of old women who on occasion would lead a solemn procession through the town, wearing masses of beads, little horns of medicine, chimpanzee teeth, and ragged old garments. Each walked with a long ornamented staff, and each of the more important ones wore a square pad of homespun cotton balanced on top of her head. The leader carried a kind of censer fashioned of a gourd or small pot, not smoking but nevertheless emanating a powerful, invisible *mana* (inherent power), for these old women were smelling out witches. This was one occasion on which the men took a back seat.

The corresponding organization among the men was a kind of peerage called the *Ki La mi*, "skin people," because they carried animal skins to sit on. There was a stiff initiation fee, and a limitation of membership to individuals of outstanding intelligence or high hereditary standing. They conducted all their official deliberations in great secrecy. *Ki La mi* were exempt from the call to war. In fact, their great taboo was against fighting or quarreling of any kind. Even to shove one of them aside by the shoulder was like an insult to royalty. The same elders who appeared informally in the chief's council could be called into secret session as members of this closely knit *Ki La mi* organization.

If one of the members died the fact was kept secret; to the common people he was merely sick. Even among the members he was spoken of as having "gone somewhere." Necessarily all funeral and burial ceremonies were arranged and conducted by his peers.

Within this group was a still higher group called *Ki Gbuo La mi*, against whom personal insults or violence was considered no less than treason. When one of these men died it sometimes happened that his death was not only kept secret but was, in fact, minimized by making a death mask before his burial. This was carved in wood, as a rude portrait or characterization, and in it his spirit was supposed to find an abode at least reminiscent of its former fleshly habitation — although that spirit was free to come and go between its former haunts and the town of the dead where God the Creator — *Abi* (Gio), *Gɔ* (Mano), *Zena* (Gɛ and Krã) — was chief.[5]

In this way a man of priestly or, indeed, of "royal" standing, who was highly respected and, as we shall see later, almost worshipped in life, passed by easy stages into the realm of ancestors. And since Abi was too far away to be reached by ordinary human beings such an individual became an object of worship as an ancestor. It is easy to understand how the death mask of such an individual would be revered, not only in the name of the man himself, but in the name of ancestors in general. He was more than an intercessor between men and God the Creator. Because he was not far removed in time and space he became very nearly a god himself. It is in this transition of ideas from God the Creator to "a god" who was a recent ancestor that we have the key to the essential religious force which held together and controlled the deepest trends of thought and action of these people.

When the town chief called in the *Ki La mi* they might sit for a while in open council; then, when the evidence was all in, retire inside the chief's house, or behind the fence where no one would hear, and "hang head" in secret deliberation, to decide, like a jury, what the verdict should be. Then they would return to the council and the chief would carry on, finally rendering the decision agreed upon.

In a higher court considering more weighty matters, the chief might postpone the case, saying that he was not ready to render a decision. The council of elders would subsequently meet at a secret place and decide the matter. The chief would later reopen the case, go through the motions of hearing further evidence, and, guiding the decision of the people to correspond with the secret agreement of the elders, or *Ki La mi*, render the decision.

In cases of offense against society, or against the Poro, or against the cult of the masks themselves, it would be impossible to conduct a public hearing, for the simple reason that to do so would be to reveal certain secrets that the common people must know nothing about. The trial, in such a case, would be conducted by the *Ki La mi* society secretly called to a secret session. The decision was reached and carried out by common consent of the elders without any obvious mechanism. If someone had committed an unforgivable sin, such as desecration or exposure to the public view of sacred relics, there would be no accusation or anything to point to the culprit. He would simply die through poison put in his food, perhaps by his own wife acting under instructions relayed to her through the powerful organization of old women. She would know that her husband was already dead as far as the social structure of the community was concerned. Without asking or caring about the "horrible details" she would simply do what she was told to do, because she knew that if she did not she would herself be eliminated in a similar manner. Indeed, she might know that she was destined to suffer the same fate as her husband anyhow. She was simply caught in a chain of events.

It was entirely possible that the death of her husband would be the subject of a public investigation in which she might be designated as the "witch" responsible for her husband's death. If the trial was by sasswood the same mechanism that established her guilt would automatically execute her. This would almost certainly happen if it were considered that the woman shared any knowledge or responsibility in her husband's guilty act.

This was not the only method of execution for a ritual sin, however. There were other ways of poisoning a man. He might be elimi-

---

[5] Schwab, 1947, p. 315.

nated quite openly after the lapse of a suitable period of time, by being found guilty of an entirely different charge, which might even be trumped up to fulfill the exigencies of the situation.

In matters of life and death there was a tendency to manipulate the mechanism of justice and its execution so that no one would appear publicly responsible either for the decision or its execution. The best example of this is the sasswood ordeal,[6] in which the poison cup, drunk by the accused, was supposed to make its own decision automatically. If the individual were guilty the sasswood executed him on the spot with the same infallible mechanism. There was no judge to be the object of resentment of those who dissented. No executioner whose bloody hands invited retribution by surviving relatives. To make the whole thing still further impersonal, the sasswood ordeal was presided over by an individual whose identity was hidden under a great mask, representing not an ancestor, but the great forest demon. The idea was inherent that it was on his authority this trial was conducted and that he had made this public appearance for that specific reason. There was also the idea that the sasswood tree whose bark had been used to make the poison potion was the real judge of guilt. A detail in the sasswood ritual[7] refers the whole responsibility to the tree itself.

In lesser matters, through trials by ordeal of various kinds, it is always the mechanism, not the diviner, that takes the blame. It is always "medicine" that does the work, not the operator or the doctor who prescribes the treatment. Of course there are exceptions. There are known cases of the operator coming to trial himself, accused of perjury. In such a case the defense would be that someone else was making stronger medicine. There was always an out, and it was sometimes a matter of who could get there first. But the essential idea remains unshaken, that it was the medicine, or mechanism, or mask, that did the work.

In the sasswood ordeal we have mask, medicine, and mechanism all sharing the blame. In lesser matters it might appear at first, in some of the examples shown below, that the mask was taking full responsibility. This is partly because we do not have full information about the mechanism used in each case. My use here of the term "medicine" perhaps needs modification. It is really the *mana*, or hidden power inherent in the drug, which does the work. The mechanism is merely to put that power into operation and protect it from contrary forces or powers that would tend to neutralize it; for it is well recognized that if the *mana* of any substance fails to work, it is either because their is present a more powerful opposing *mana*, or because the ritual mechanism has not been properly carried out.

In the case of a mask the inherent *mana* should be considered as the most powerful possible. It was an ancestral spirit, or the spirit of a totem animal, or the spirit of the forest, which might be thought of as the sum total of its animals, real and mythological. In fact, some of the greatest masks, embodying features part animal and part human, seem to represent an attempt to capture the *mana* of both the ancestral spirits and the animals of the forest, with its demons perhaps thrown in for good measure; for its features are half human, its voice and locomotion are human. Its general mien, however, is that of an animal and the animal features are undoubtedly emphasized. Finally, the masked figure is supposed to emerge from the forest and vanish again into its depths without leaving the slightest trace or having any visible habitation.

The system of government was, therefore, a socio-democratic government by chiefs whose authority was reinforced by a council of elders. That council sought to follow the customs and traditions of the clan. When a problem threatened to cause disagreement or a feeling of resentment on the part of the loser or his surviving friends and relatives, the elders sought to obtain a decree (and even the act of execution) from the spirit world itself, through the medium of the mask and the ordeal. This system had the effect of keeping the ancestors near by, and not only vitally in-

[6] Harley, 1941a, p. 153.

[7] Harley, 1941a, pp. 155–61.

terested in the affairs of men but able to do something about them! In the last analysis it was government by tradition, enforced by the fear of disapproval of the ancestors. Decisions were reached with the approval of the clan fathers both living and dead. The living merely used a technique, placing both the responsibility for these decisions and the blame for the administration of justice on the ancestral spirits.

CONTENTS

Foreword	v
Introduction	3
The mask as a fetish	6
Sacrifices	8
The Mā	9
Gɔ gɛ	11
Sei	13
Nya	14
Zawolo	16
Gbana	17
Other judges and lawgivers	17
Police	21
Messengers	22
Gɛ's presiding at public functions	23
War leaders	25
Instructors	26
Poro Gɛ's	27
Extortioners	33
Medicine and magic	34
Masks with animal features	35
Petty gods	36
Portrait masks	39
Dancers, minstrels, and clowns	40
Summary	41
Conclusion	43
References	44
Peabody Museum catalogue numbers for specimens illustrated in the plates	45

LIST OF PLATES

Frontispiece, Small personal mask, *mā*, of an important man, *zo*.

I.   *a*, Entertainer who may be seen by all, Gompa.
    b, *Mɛ fei gɛ*, ancestral mask with headdress.
    c, *Gɛ Na*, portrait mask.
    d, Boys' *gɛ*, wearing mask, Half-Grebo.
    e, Headdress, Gio.
    f, Mano dancer's mask and headdress.
    g, Headpiece with cowrie shells.
    h, Matching belt, part of *gɛ*'s costume.

II.   *a*, Conventionalized portrait mask, Bassa.
    b, Conventionalized portrait mask, Krā.
    c, Janus handpiece.
    d, Mace, carried by *Gɔ gɛ*.
    e, Handpiece belonging to *Wai*.
    f, h, k, Replicas of big masks.
    g, Twin *mā*.
    i, Collection of small *mā*'s.
    j, *Yongolo to*, carried from the Poro session by last boy.

III.   *a*, Headpad worn under a mask.
    b, Small stone adze, called *lai*, owned by *Gonola*.
    c, Ring belonging to Zawolo.
    d, Messenger-talisman of Zawolo.
    e, Brass chain of Zawolo.
    f, g, Scarifying hook and razor, belonging to Zawolo.
    h, Zawolo's ceremonial armlet.
    i, Knife, messenger-talisman of Nya.
    j–p, Flute and whistles used to create the voice of the *gɛ*.

IV.   *a*, *Gɔ gɛ*, mask of Gbana.
    b, *Zo zɛ gɛ*.
    c, *Blɔ zɛ gɛ*.
    d, *Gɔ gɛ*, mask of Nya.
    e, *Du gli*, "cow-eater."
    f, Mask of the *Gɔ gɛ* type.

V.   *a*, *Maa va*, red felt-covered face and headdress, "speaker" of *Nana gɛ*.
    b, *Zɔ gɛ*, who came to town to stop pestilence.
    c, *Nana gɛ*, a Konor mask with horns and headdress.
    d, *Gli dɔ gɛ*, judge of the sasswood ordeal.
    e, *Ma va (gɛ va)*, a mask with police functions.
    f, *Zuo wi nu*, broke pots in town for punishment.

VI.   *a*, *Lu gbo biɛ*, a judge between lesser *gɛ*'s.
    b, *Lu bo biɛ*.
    c, Crocodile mask.
    d, *Kma gɛ*, judge in major disputes.
    e, *Pia sɛ*, danced at planting time.
    f, *Dɛ gɛ*, diviner and judge.

VII.   *a*, *Ka da kɛ sɛ*, a powerful teacher and lawgiver.
    b, God of war.
    c, *Diɛ si*, messenger and "speaker" for *Gɔ gɛ*.
    d, *Gɔ gɛ*, "leopard."
    e, *Gbɛ gɛ*, judge in cases of adultery.
    f, *Ka gɛ*, "crab," messenger for *Lɔla gɛ*.

VIII.   Masks of various *Gɛ*'s of the Poro:
    a, *T'to bli gɛ*, swore boys to secrecy.
    b, *Gɛlɛ wi gɛ*, broke stones for Poro fire.

c, *Si kū gɛ*, "smoke catcher," made fire.
d, *Sa yi gɛ*, received boys into the Bush.
e, *Tɛa bli si*, closed off roads to the Poro.
f, *Dɛ bu gɛ*, carried sacred razor into the Bush.
g, *Bɔ ze gɛ*, cut out liver of the sacrifice.
h, *Mi gli gɛ*, Poro executioner.
i, *Dā ya bɔ̃a*, dressed the boys' wounds.
j, *Sie gɛ*, collected supplies for the Poro session.
k, *Tiɛ bli sai*, attacked and plundered passers-by.
l, *Gblɔ zɛ gɛ*, "executioner" of boys who broke the most sacred law of the Poro.

IX. Petty Gods and Patrons:
a, b, Masks commemorating man with facial paralysis.
c, Mask prayed to for cure of gangosa.
d, Patron of victims of jaw tumor.
e, *Dū gɛ*, "coughing spirit," entertainer and instructor.
f, *Yo gɛ*, patron of rubbing-chalk for rheumatism.
g, h, The stutterer and his "speaker."
i, *Dinga*, "duck," settled domestic quarrels.
j, *Klua gɛ*, patron of chimpanzees.
k, "The hungry one," collected food for the Poro.
l, *I yɛ gɛ*, diviner in war.

X. a, *Di gɛ*, judged palavers between sections.
b, *Kluɛ gɛ*, "chimp," ate of new rice.
c, *Nya gɛ*, "rice-bird," a collector of debts.
d, *Gbā gɛ*, danced at sacrifice to ancestral spirits.
e, *Ni bli bu gɛ*, "baby-eater," judicial consultant.
f, *Blɔ gɛ*, god of war, immune against gunshot.
g, *Siɛ dɔ wana gɛ*, "fire," attended killing of a cow.
h, *Ldoɛ gɛ*, a judge who stopped fights.
i, *Bā gɛ*, patron of blacksmiths and judge.

XI. a, *Gbea gɛ*, "crocodile," patron of fisherman.
b, *Mɔ gbɔ gɛ*, collected debts.
c, *Zi bo biɛ*, "road-making elephant."
d, *Kpo Gɔ̃*, Poro judge, much respected.
e, *Kpala*, "lesser hornbill," a judge.
f, A judge from the Konor tribe.
g, *Flɔ gɛ*, made medicine for boys in the Poro.
h, Function unknown.
i, *Tɔ̃ la gɛ*, executioner for offences against the Poro.

XII. a, *Pā kɛ la*.
b, No information available.
c, d, *Ka gɛ*, "crab," household god.
e, *Ma die*, patron of rice planting.
f, g, Portrait masks.
h, *Gbɔ gɛ*, could stop war.
i, *Dra ya bɔ̃a*, cared for boys in the Poro.
j, *Ga si gɛ*, helped clear farm.

XIII. a, *Zena*, prayed to by childless women.
b, *Nya wɔ̃*, portrait mask of a popular young woman.
c, *Ti:n gbi*, ancestral spirit.
d, *Gba gɛ*, danced for a new baby.
e, *Zei*, goddess of fertility.
f, *Longwa*, medicine dancer.
g, "Dancer," true function not known.
h, Figured for artistic interest, no information available.
i, *'Zi*, patron of babies.

XIV. a, No information available.
b, Goddess of the dance.
c, *Di kɛla*, goddess of victory.
d, e, No information available.
f, *Gbini gɛ*, ancestral spirit.
g, h, No information available.
i, *Tɔ bu gɛ*, patron of chickens, officiated at burials.

XV. a, Great clay head.
b, Small clay head.
c, Twinned pots.

MASKS AS AGENTS OF SOCIAL CONTROL
IN NORTHEAST LIBERIA

INTRODUCTION

THE thesis that God made man in His own image is reversed when man makes a human image and endows it with godlike attributes. We have seen how easily this came about when a death mask was made for a man of priestly standing. Similarly, a death mask might be made in memory of any famous or gifted individual and prayed to as though the spirit of that individual still resided in it, or at least could be contacted through it. Such a "living" mask was the object of sacrifice and prayer that it would continue to do the work it did as a human being. If this person had been a good provider, his mask might be the object of supplication for good crops and wealth, or success in any venture. The mask of a woman with a large family of healthy children became a goddess of fertility of farm and family. A man who had been a fearless and victorious warrior might be commemorated by a mask which became a sort of god of war.[1] In one instance a woman whose sons had been mighty in battle had her image venerated as a war goddess. For further examples of portrait masks, see pages 39–40.

The outstanding example of such immortalization was the great mask, the most reverenced object of the cult, which was the conventionalized face of a long dead and almost mythical man of great wisdom, the one who introduced the Poro to this area. This mask became the symbol, talisman, and oracle of the current living patriarch. By reason of being the hereditary keeper of this mask this patriarch was, through its power, the judge and leader of his clan, and as high priest of the mask he could obtain, through it as an oracle, the sanction of the ancestral spirits.

In addition to masks originating as portraits or characterizations of individuals there were masks of different origins — some of them not well remembered or understood by the people themselves. Their secret functions varied from those of clan oracle to personal fetish; their public impersonations from judges to festive dancers and clowns. Some of them clearly represented mythical, half-human beasts of the forest. A clearcut, simple analysis of their place in the lives of the people is difficult.

Perhaps the easiest approach to an understanding of the masks is to follow roughly the impressions and individual was likely to get through occasional contact with them as he grew up from early childhood to the point where he would be allowed to have full knowledge.

A boy's earliest memory was probably of a time when his mother grabbed him up and ran into the house, shutting the door and staying there kneeling and clapping her hands while weird, sweet music drew near and passed by, accompanied by sounds of many people walking. There might be some other sounds: of someone talking in a high rolling falsetto voice, of a clacking slit drum or a deep bellowing musical call, of a voice talking with a throaty gurgling growl resembling a leopard's roar, or of a varied commotion with hushed human voices — perhaps dying down to the sounds of men talking a palaver.

If he were old enough to understand and talk his mother would tell him that this was the *gɛ* and that he must not try to look out through a crack in the door, because women and children were forbidden to see the *gɛ*.

Perhaps on such an occasion he would steal a look, or accidentally get a glimpse of a masked figure. Very likely he would see nothing except ordinary men. One thing he *might* see would be a mass of men dancing backward on their heels, or at another time three men in costume leading a winding column in single file in and out among the huts.

There were *some* masked dancers which could be seen by women and children, either in the daytime or at night (pl. I, *a*). These were also called *gɛ's*, but they would be a

---

[1] Masks which were prayed to for success in war frequently were adorned by sheep's horns carved on the forehead. Perhaps this signalizes the prowess of the straight-haired African ram, which can break the horns of a goat. See pl. VII, *b*, and pl. XII, *b*.

boy's second memory, because the other one, from which his mother fled, would be much more impressive. Even as he became more familiar with the masked gɛ's who danced in public he would periodically be impressed by the generally potent fear of the gɛ which he could not see, and from which he and his mother continued to hide.

As he grew older he learned that a time would come when the gɛ would catch him, as he eventually caught all small boys — would catch him and eat him, or at least swallow him whole.

His father or uncle [2] might explain to him, as the time drew near, that he would not really be killed but that he would stay for a while in the belly of the gɛ, to be reborn, when the time came, as a real man. If the boy was destined to become a zo, or leader, either because his uncle was a zo or because he himself had been so designated by a diviner,[3] then much more was explained to him. The information was given in secret and gradually, as he became able to understand and to keep the information secret. He would eventually be told that the masked dancers were really men, not spirits from the forest. He would be allowed to see a tiny mask called mã, which his uncle prayed to, and he would actually have a small one made for his own personal use. He would be taught how to make sacrifice to it at the new moon and pray to it every morning. He would be told that it represented the "old people" who lived as spirits in "God's town," and that it also represented himself, because he would one day go as a spirit to live in God's town with the other spirits — unless he did some terrible thing which would make his spirit unacceptable and forever an exile, actually annihilated by being universally ignored. He gradually got the idea that spirits needed a little attention now and then to keep them alive, and that if he kept the rules and taboos he would some day have a really fine little mask made for him like his uncle's.

He would also be told about the voice of the gɛ that could not be seen by women. He would know that there was really nothing to see except men making the sound of the "voice." If his uncle were a big zo the boy would be shown the pottery whistles, the horn and clay-pot resonator, and other things used to create the voice.

He would learn that the gɛ did not swallow the boys, but that they were taken into the forest, where they lived in absolute seclusion and learned the duties and privileges of full tribal membership, as well as useful trades and occupations. There they would learn also all these things which he, as a zo, was already learning from his uncle. The others had to learn the hard way, under strict discipline of masked officials of the Poro or Bush school.

He was told all about the rituals of the Poro, and even instructed in the art of making the "marks of the gɛ's teeth," or scarification marks, denoting full membership in the Poro. Such a boy zo could go into the Poro at the end of the session, just in time to get the marks made on his own skin. Then he could help mark the other boys.

But even a privately instructed boy who was by heredity a big zo would not know about the high ritual masks of the clan fathers until he went into the Poro and had a fine little zo mask made for him.

A boy who was not a zo spent three or four years in the seclusion of the Poro Bush school.[4] During this time the high Poro officials were masked figures known to him as gɛ's. They were different, however, from the masked dancers called gɛ's he had seen in town. The masks of dancers were pretty female faces. Those of the Poro officials were mostly male faces, half human, half forest demon. Their eyes were prominent, even protuberant. Some of them had heavy beards and the mouths of animals with big teeth. Their voices resembled the leopard's growl, instead of the high rolling falsetto of the

---

[2] His cult "father." See Schwab, 1947, p. 283.

[3] A child might be designated as a zo if it showed any unusual symptoms thought to indicate an innate ability to contact the spirit world; such as epilepsy, petit mal, hysteria; or if it had an illness of an unusual nature, such as recurrent convulsions or prolonged unconsciousness. If a diviner decided such a sick child was an unrecognized zo, and prescribed "zo treatment," whereupon the sick child recovered, then there was no doubt about it and a mã was made for him.

[4] for more details of this institution, see Harley, 1941b.

dancers. They presided at high rituals, often including a human sacrifice. They administered strict and heavy discipline. These masks will be considered later.

At the very end of the session the boys saw *Gbini gɛ* as a man dancing with a mask on his face but no costume to cover the rest of his body. He had seen this mask before as a fully costumed "spirit" dancing in town and later presiding at the ritual of scarification in the Poro. Now he was permitted to see that the mask was worn by a man and was not a spirit from the forest. The boys may already have suspected this but no one dared talk about it. *Gbini gɛ* carried out his ritual dance as carefully as ever, and when it was over he made a sacrifice to his mask, thus demonstrating that it was the mask, not the wearer, that mattered.

No matter how old or powerful a man became he would never entirely lose his original respect and fear of the spirits symbolized by the masks and the voices. That respect and fear carried through to the masks themselves, rather than to the men who wore them.

THE MASK AS A FETISH

THE close relation between the masks and the ancestral spirits has been established. It is now necessary to consider their similarity or dissimiliarity to fetishes.

The native thinks of the unseen forces of life as spirit forces. He includes here much that scientific knowledge can explain by chemical and physical laws, but which to him has all the signs of the supernatural. This realm which is beyond his understanding is still close to him — too close for comfort. It affects his daily life. It is all pervading. Although he does not go around in a perpetual state of terror, yet where he feels the dangerous forces to be concentrated he seeks somehow to protect himself, or to institute measures designed to control these hidden "spirit" forces. These measures tend to become specific, portable, and packaged. Such a package we call a fetish.

West Africa is full of fetishes, but it is not enough to call the religion of these people "fetishism," and let it go at that. The use of the term, *fetish*, has been so abused that an explanation of its exact meaning should be presented here.

A fetish is usually prepared by a specific medicine man for a specific purpose, and often for a specific individual. The priest must be paid a fee or the fetish will be insulted and refuse to work, saying to itself, "So I am not worth paying for, eh!" In form, or in substance, or both, the fetish embodies the implication of hidden power. It is either shaped to represent some potent being, or it is composed of highly potent material. This physical unity of soul and substance is reinforced by giving it a name. At this point it acquires a living personality of its own — a spirit. It is a "thing" in its own right. This spirit must be respected. It must be "fed" to keep alive. It must be propitiated by prayer, which implies continued faith on the part of the person who is its keeper. The keeper must avoid offending the fetish, and to make this duty a definite one each fetish has its own taboos. If these taboos are observed then the keeper is *en rapport*. If not, the fetish may turn against him.

If the keeper observes the prescribed ritual in every detail, his request, or prayer, becomes little less than a demand — provided the favors he asks are within the definitely prescribed power of the fetish, and provided further that no one else is at the moment neutralizing the power of his fetish by directing against it a more powerful contrary force. It is assumed that a fetish which has been kept alive, and satisfied, and approached with suitable ritual, *must* respond with all its power in the specific matter for which it was created by the medicine man.

If the fetish fails to respond the keeper may conclude that he, or someone else, has inadvertently, carelessly, or deliberately broken the taboos of the fetish and offended it. If this failure has not already resulted in irretrievable calamity to the keeper, he will endeavor to carry out the proper ritual, "to pay the fine" to the fetish, or make suitable atonement, in the hope that the fetish will be appeased and will once more serve him.

Finally, fetishes can be killed. Most of them will die readily of simple neglect. A more potent one may not be so easily disposed of. Instead of dying when neglected it may turn against the negligent owner. A neglected fetish is, therefore, a dangerous thing. Even the simplest of them will be feared by a stranger who comes across one, for it may be "dead" or it may not. To get rid of a fetish no longer wanted it is necessary to carry it back to the man who made it. For a suitable fee he can reverse the process of manufacture and render the fragments inert and powerless.

A random collection of magical and sacred objects from West Africa would certainly include fetishes, but not even an expert could with any certainty sort them out by their appearance from lesser charms and magical objects. A bit of pith on a cord to be tied to the wrist may have been prescribed by a diviner to protect a child from measles, but that is not a fetish. An antelope horn may be filled with magical stuff to keep off witches, but this is only an amulet. A sheep's horn may contain a mixture of charred thorns and mild poisons, intended to be licked by the owner, and so to build up an immunity to poison. This is "medicine" and almost a fetish, but not quite. Yet the great fetish of *Dunuma* was a sheep's horn full of black stuff!

A fetish must have a name, an indwelling spirit, a "law" or taboo, and a ritual, as well as a specific purpose and power. The spirit of a typical fetish is the composite spirit of the several substances from which it is made, each with its own inherent power. A bit of stone for strength; some smooth bark from the invulnerable tree which is so slippery that even monkeys cannot climb it; a leaf caught floating in mid-air, for fleetness of foot; fruit known to contain a heart stimulant, for endurance — these might be incorporated in a *good* fetish to give a young warrior confidence and power. A list of ingredients for a *bad* fetish might sound like a recipe for witches' brew.[1] But a truly great fetish would contain substances from the human body, preferably from the heart, forehead, and larynx. It would have to be fed with human blood or fat.[2]

Outward form also contributed to the power of a fetish. A knotty vine, or a woody excrescence with a profile suggesting a human face, became almost a fetish in itself. If circumstances suggested a name for it, and trial and error pointed to an apparent taboo, it needed only that an occasional sacrifice be made to it to keep it alive and to establish it as a true fetish. Its proper function would have to be "discovered" by a diviner. This type of fetish, having presumptive power in its form rather than in its component substances, is comparatively rare.

Of fetishes which are representations of the human face, the more frequent were not found as natural formations but were carefully and deliberately carved from wood. This carving was either a portrait of an individual or the conventionalized face of a woman. The portrait mask was supposed to attract to itself immediately the spirit of the individual ancestor. The conventional form became inhabited by the great ancestral spirit — a sort of earth-mother ancestral goddess. The details of this ideology are not clear, but the conception is contained in the great *Mā* of the Poro, referred to as the "mother of all masks," and in the translation of the word Poro as "the earth."

To carve the likeness of an animal would likewise invite the spirit of such an animal to inhabit the wooden image — with unpredictable results. One did not indulge in such promiscuous creation of spirit abodes. There was too much risk involved. By common consent it was taboo for any layman to make any likeness of any thing in earth or sky or sea. Such carving could only be undertaken in great seriousness by one who knew the rules and was authorized to make a particular piece.

This prohibition, reminiscent of Mosaic law, reflects less a fear of the one true God than a fear of all the spirits; but it should be remembered that the greatest fear of all was directed towards the likeness of a human face — the ancestor mask.

By our definition, therefore, a mask may be considered a fetish, but it is something more. The spirit in a mask may be addressed by name. It is the object of sacrifice and prayer. It has taboos: no woman could see or know the mechanism of its wearing, and some masks had their own taboos as well. There is a feeling that the mask will not fail to perform its accustomed function. In all these respects it can be called a fetish.

But the mask was not considered likely to be neutralized by a counter force working against it. If a mask did not do its work it could only be because it had been neglected or because someone had broken its law. "Owners" of the clan masks might compete for prestige and for new territory, but there was no opposition of function between their respective masks.

A fetish might be made with a distinctly evil purpose. There were no masks that deliberately brought disease, calamity, or death as their fruits. Disease and death were firmly believed to be brought on by living people, perhaps with the aid of a "bad" fetish or "witch" substance or actual poison. A mask might be invoked to discover and remove such persons, who were considered public enemies.

---

[1] Harley, 1941a, pp. 143-49.

[2] See p. 8.

The final distinction that made a mask something more than a fetish was the belief that the mask could not be destroyed with impunity. It was impossible to have it destroyed by reversing the process of its manufacture. If a large mask were accidently destroyed by fire or decay a small replica had to be made, in which the spirit of the big mask might rest (pl. II, f, h, and k). If an individual lost his small personal mask he might have another made, but the lost mask constituted a terrible potential threat to his peace of mind and his very life. He would be like a spy who had let his confidential papers get out of his possession.

Upon the death of the owner the small personal mask might be buried with him or given to his son as an heirloom, or perhaps returned to the man who carved it. It might be inactivated by rubbing it with oil, but still it had to be cared for and put away where no woman would ever see it.

SACRIFICES

For an appreciation of the common practice of "feeding" a fetish or a mask it is essential to understand these people's conception of sacrifice, which, in turn, hinges on their conception of the life force. The Mano recognized three souls in a man, the first of these being identified with the intelligence. When a man lost consciousness or became insane they said: "He is not a person any more. The person himself has gone before." But there remained a second soul, the dream soul, for the person could still move, talk, even though irrationally; and a third, which departed with the breath. They watched these souls leave the body in succession. Sometimes the unconscious man "came back." The apparently dead sometimes revived. The body, therefore, was not to be disposed of too quickly. One or more of its souls might still be interested in it.

When the souls had finally gone, what was left was still the form and substance of a human being. Sometimes it used to be eaten as food without significance beyond the satisfying of bodily hunger. When it was used *ritually* as food, it satisfied more than bodily hunger. It then became a substance of potent soul-feeding power. (The more recently the person had died, the better.) For this purpose any part of the human body would serve, though certain parts were more powerful than others. The most powerful was the blood. It was usually the substance used to "feed" ritual objects.

We see here a link between food-substance and soul-substance which to the native was very real. Various substances could be "eaten," either literally or ritually, to reinforce hidden spiritual power. Of such substances, meat and bone of the human body were the most powerful, and could, indeed, augment man's own soul force. Also of high potency was the meat of the powerful man-eating animals like leopard and python. Eating these a man absorbed something of the spirit inherent in the animal. Such powerful meat was suited only to those who needed unusual power — the priests and the warriors.

When a sacrifice was killed it was "eaten" by the living priest, the ancestors *and the ritual object involved*. This was accomplished by offering some of the meat to the ancestors and smearing the ritual object with some of the blood. By the sacrifice all were equally bound in a covenant of continued cooperation. The inclusion of the ritual object in the covenant demonstrates that it, too, was conceived as having a soul of some sort.

It should be emphasized that no sacrificial procedure was complete without "prayer" that began with a statement of the reason or occasion for the procedure and ended with the covenant binding all parties. Included in the prayer, or implicit in it, was the assurance that the priest had faith in the power toward which the sacrifice was directed.

This conception of sacrifice explains the "feeding" of fetish and mask — usually at each new moon with more formal sacrifice once a year. As the object of sacrifice and prayer a mask becomes a fetish of a high order, embodying the spirit of a living man or of an ancestor or forest demon.

The most effective sacrifice was a man's own eldest son — not so much because he represented the greatest renunciation, but because it was assumed he would carry the message to the ancestors better, and would remember, after he got to their realm, that he could render his father a special service. He became at the same time son and "ancestor" and would continue to be interested in his father's affairs on earth longer and more vitally than would, for instance, a slave boy.

The spirits of those who have gone before are not terribly concerned with the affairs of human beings still alive, but they are not wholly unwilling to help if they are approached in the right way. They must be flattered, cajoled, and occasionally subjected to a bit of pressure to remind them that they are able to help their earthly connections a great deal if they will only take the trouble to do so.

Except for the highest of all sacrifices, a slave might be substituted. In recent times there is ample evidence that the slave was, in turn, replaced by a cow. For lesser sacrifices, the next official substitute was a sheep, then a white chicken, then white cola nut, chewed up and spewed on the sacred object. If no white cola were available, cold water could be used, not as a substitute sacrifice, but as a token, accompanied by the promise of suitable sacrifice "next time." This step-by-step degradation of sacrifice explains the significance of spewing water out of the mouth onto the ground by many African people when offering prayer to the ancestral spirits. Finally among the Mano people, at least, when offering daily prayer to the small *mã*, it was customary, merely to spit on it. This was considered sufficient provided the act were reinforced by sacrifice of chicken blood once a month. If this were inconvenient, water could be used.

White clay around the eyes of a mask was also a sort of a sacrifice, as well as a decoration. In several instances such application was made with instructions something like the following: "You are going far away, we want you to agree to go to America and do your work for the people over there." This was to assure the mask that its spiritual qualities were not being forgotten. In other cases it was apparently done to revitalize a mask which had been unused for some time.

Masks may be considered under four general types: (1) the small individual mask called *mã* and its Poro prototype which was called the mother of all masks; (2) the great oracle mask or "god spirit"; (3) the masks which functioned as public officials; and (4) those appearing as entertainers, dancers, or clowns. In the Gio country there was considerable overlapping of these types, but this classification will serve as a basis for studying the masks of the entire area of northeast Liberia and adjacent territories.

THE *Mã*

Each man of importance in the community had one of the small carved wooden masks called *mã*, just big enough to fit into the palm of his hand (frontispiece). No one but the owner was supposed to see it except when high ritual required him to show it. A woman must never be allowed to see it or hear its name. The *mã* needed a sacrifice of a chicken each new moon.[3] It was prayed to every morning by its owner, with a short petition for good luck and protection from "witchcraft," which was supposed to be the cause of accidents.[4]

Wai, the cult mother of the Poro, who was actually a woman but ritually a man, participating in the Poro sessions with men, also had her personal *mã* and was keeper of the great *Mã* of the Poro. Her special symbol was a little Janus handpiece (pl. II, *e*).

Boys who were to become *zo's*, either by inheritance or by special decree of the diviner, were given *mã's* while still young. If a diviner decreed that a girl child was a *zo*, entitled to become a *Wai*,[5] she also might be given a *mã*. The *mã* of a *zo* child was wound about with cotton string and kept by the child's mentor until the child was old enough to be taught how to care for it, pray to it, and help make the monthly sacrifice necessary to keep it active.

[3] Schwab, 1947, p. 278.
[4] Schwab, 1947, p. 381.

[5] Harley, 1941b, p. 12.

During the Poro session each boy of a "professional class" family got a *mã* of his own, which he was taught to revere and worship. An initiate who was a *zo* and already had a *mã* of his own was given a new one along with his new name.

Some of the big men who were *zo's* also got new masks to mark their acquisition of advanced "degrees," or their admission to the inner circle of elders known as *Ki La mi*, or the still higher circle of *Ki Gbuo La mi*, or peers.

A small *mã*, being a kind of portrait of its owner,[6] was by that fact a place where his own spirit was represented. It was also a place where he could contact the spirit world in general and the ancestral spirits in particular.[7]

The childhood *mã* was not very carefully made. It was merely necessary that it represent a human face. The *mã* made for a Poro initiate was supposed to be a sort of portrait, or at least have some character. A special one made for a medium who could go into a fit of hysteria or a trance and answer questions put to the ancestral spirits was very carefully made. It was of a conventional type with the oval face of a woman and resembled the big *Mã* of the Poro which was the mother of all masks. A special *mã* made for an old man on attaining distinction for any reason was definitely a portrait of the owner, and if for a big *zo* it had a coronet representing a row of antelope horns or a plaited headpiece.

The idea that the *mã* represented the soul of the owner was difficult to obtain and verify until one turned up belonging to a twin. It represented a dual personality (pl. II, *g*). To understand its significance it must be understood that twins of the same sex were thought to have one "ancestral" soul between them, and nobody could be sure which twin housed that soul at any given moment. Everyone was meticulously careful to treat them both exactly alike for fear of offending the soul should it happen temporarily to be in the neglected twin. They had to be fed the same food at the same time. Any gifts were in duplicate. To obviate this procedure, which was difficult to maintain throughout their life, the death of one twin was welcome, and was usually connived at, with the help of a diviner who supplied "medicine" to be given both twins to drink in the bath water. The weaker twin usually succumbed. Even then precautions were sometimes carried to the extreme of making a wooden image of the deceased twin and making further occasional identical presents, one to the surviving child and one to the image. Usually, however, the dead child was put into a termite hill, which was supposed to be a place no soul of any kind could survive. The soul was therefore firmly fixed in the surviving twin, and all was well. In the case of mixed twins it was even more complicated. The soul was a double soul. Usually both twins succumbed to the "twin medicine" in the bath water. The twin *mã* pictured in plate II, *g*, with two noses and two mouths, belonged to a survivor of mixed twins. It represents his double soul and confirms the idea that the *mã* is a portrait of its owner.

When a man died his *mã* either had to be turned over to someone who would care for it, or put on top of his grave. His son or nephew might keep it, or it could go back to the carver who made it. Such a man might collect several and in turn leave them to his son. One such collection of twelve finally was obtained from a grandson who no longer revered them and who needed some tax money.

During Poro sessions a larger *Mã*, plate II, *j*,[8] seven or eight inches long, was kept on a winnowing tray inside the inner portal of the sacred enclosure. A neophyte's first ritual act after fighting his way past the masked keepers at the outer portal was to swear to secrecy on this *Mã*. Initiates of all ranks swore on it that they had abstained from sexual activity the night before and that they brought no "witch" or evil intentions into the Poro. The Poro was a place of abstinence and peace. Within its sacred precincts all personal enmities were supposed to be forgotten. While the Poro or Sandɛ (the girls' school) was in session war was taboo.

The *Mã* of the Poro, called the mother of all masks, always had a woman's face. It was identified with "the earth itself," and with the

---

[6] See p. 4.
[7] See p. 4.

[8] See also footnote 41, p. 28.

ancestral spirits. The Poro was thought of as a place of the spirits. During their residence in the Poro the boys were supposed to be spirits "inside the belly of the *gɛ*" and invisible to outsiders.

This big *Mã* of the Poro could not be trifled with. Its keeper, *Wai*, was cult mother of the Poro. She and her consort, *Gonola* (see below), had power of life and death over the neophytes, and that power was exercised in the name of their masks. When a culprit escaped and fled for his life *Wai* could "put his name in her *Mã*," then send the mask as her messenger to the clan or tribe where he had hidden. The entire power of the Poro, which extended beyond tribal boundaries, could then be invoked to bring him back to justice.

Gɔ Gɛ [9]

As mentioned above, there were actually two systems for controlling or governing the people. One system functioned openly through town chiefs and elders with their palavers and councils which gave everyone a chance to participate in a more or less democratic manner. The other system was actually an extension of the men's cult which had its highest development in those tribes which had the Poro. This system functioned in secret through a high council of elders meeting at night in a sacred place, called together and presided over by the *gonola* or "owner" of the land. The *gonola* was also a high priest in that he was the keeper of the great mask referred to as *Gɔ gɛ*, "good spirit." When there was to be a meeting of the elders he carried this mask to the secret place, laid it on a mat on the ground, and covered it with a white cloth. Around it the elders sat and discussed the special palaver for which they had been called together by the *gonola*, who acted as chairman. When they had discussed the case fully the chairman guided their opinion into a judgment, which was tentative until approved by the mask, *Gɔ gɛ*.[10] In arriving at this decision the owner exercised the function of judge or chief justice.

The functions of *Gɔ gɛ* included that of lawmaker, since the session of elders hearing a case and rendering judgment would often decide that a decree was necessary to proscribe similar offenses. Such a decree, announced by the town crier, had the effect of law.[11]

This *Gɔ gɛ* mask is the great mask of the Poro referred to elsewhere as the *dunuma* mask.[12] It had some of the attributes of a living god when worn, and those of a sacred oracle and supreme judge at other times. It was the object of blood sacrifice and prayer. When it changed hands from father to son, or more properly from uncle to nephew, a high sacrament was eaten. In old days this was a human sacrifice to liberate a spirit to carry word to the town of the dead that the mask had a new keeper, a new high priest. It was appeased by the sacrifice of a chicken every new moon, and a sheep on occasions when a high palaver was to be talked.

Masks of this type are very rare in museum collections. Information including their names and functions is almost entirely lacking. Names given me were *Gɔ gɛ, Tɔ gɛ, Bu na gɛ, Zo zɛ gɛ, Gbɔ lɔ zɛ gɛ* (all Mano); *Wai wɔ* (Kpɛllɛ); *Gɔ glü* [13] (Gio); *Nana* (Konor); *Kma gɛ, Zena* (Krã).

They are characterized by protuberant eyes faced with perforated china or metal discs, red felt lips, a long beard hung with calabar beans, palm nuts, or heavy glass beads. As evidences of sacrifice they usually show black dried blood caked over the face and reddish

---

[9] *Gɔ gɛ* is the mask referred to by Schwab as the Big Devil, though he used this term in a very general sense to include the central idea of the *gɛ* who is neither a person nor a mask. It is better to use the term *Gɔ gɛ* in reference to this mask, though it went by different names, especially among those who did not know its real function. For some of these names, see below. The term "devil" or "country devil" is applied to the masks, and masked figures by English-speaking Christian Liberians.

[10] For details of the procedure, see p. 16.

[11] Sometimes other masks than *Gɔ gɛ* enjoyed the privilege of judging and making laws. See p. 17.

[12] In Harley, 1941b, p. 9, this term was used because I had no other name for the mask, though I had actually acquired one under the name *Gblɔ zɛ gɛ* with incomplete information as to its function. The term *dunuma* should correctly be used to refer to a fetish owned by *Gonola* or *Wai*, not a mask.

[13] The Gio word *glü* is equivalent to the Mano word *gɛ*.

remains of chewed cola nuts spewed into its mouth by the priest. Among the many masks collected by the author, this Mano Gɔ gɛ is the most interesting, and is also the one about which the most definite and the fullest information is available.

The owner of a Gɔ gɛ mask, here referred to for convenience, under the Mano name, *Gonola*, customarily received the high office and custodianship of the mask from his own father in a sacrament, accompanied by the sacrifice of his eldest son. *Gonola's* consort, *Wai*, also partook of this sacrifice. These priests ate the sacred parts, the forehead, heart, and larynx.[14]

Gonola also held command over all lesser *Gɛ's* in the clan. He could send them out as his messengers, policemen, or deputies. With the help of *Wai*, he controlled all activities of the Poro and the Sandɛ.[15]

He had power to stop war and fighting and could severely punish any breach of peace in the clan. His people could not make war without his consent. He and *Wai* together could plan war, or raiding parties so that they would not interfere with the sessions of Poro and Sandɛ.

He sanctioned and assisted in the creation or installation of a new *zo*.[16] As owner of *lai* (see p. 15), he called all the *zo's* of the Poro scarification ritual to sharpen their ceremonial razors on its edge.[17]

As a priest it was his duty to superintend the making of a new mask and its costumes.

When a mask was to be made the wood carver took his instructions from *Gonola*. A suitable tree was selected, and a sacrifice prepared for the propitiation of the tree. At the time of the sacrifice the tree was addressed and informed of the purpose for which it was proposed to use a portion of its wood, and a day was appointed for the felling. On that appointed day the tree was cut without further ceremony. Then it was allowed to lie for a few days just as it fell, "to get used to the idea." The idea in all this was that the stuff of the tree itself must be willing, otherwise the carving was likely to be spoiled before it was completed.

A few days later a chunk was cut off, and carried to an isolated hut in the forest, all roads being guarded or closed by taboo signs during the time the actual carving was being done. No woman was permitted to come near the place.

The kind of wood to be used for carving a mask was not fixed. For large masks a light wood was desirable. Cotton-tree wood (*Bombax buonopozense*) was usually preferred, though cork-wood (*Musanga Smithii*) was often chosen, and wild rubber (*Funtumia elastica*) was sometimes used because this wood was easily carved, and did not split readily.

If a high polish and fine permanent detail were important, a heavier wood was used. Close-grained varieties such as *Sarcocephalus Diderrichii* were preferred. *Chysophyllum perpulchrum* was a favorite with Mano artists. Durability, ease of carving, and resistance to cracking were requisites. Rarely an open-grained wood (*Chlorophora excelsa*) was used and the natural finish allowed to stand, but usually the character of the wood was concealed by the black coating of plant juices. In addition most masks acquired a patina composed of dust, smoke, and sweat rubbed into the surface by years of handling, and storing in the loft.

Tools used for the carving of the masks were the ordinary native axe, adz, and knife. Sometimes a knife was bent on the flat to scoop out hollows. The blacksmith's burning-iron was used for holes: eyes, tooth sockets, perforations for tying on the corona or "hair-do," beard, moustache, etc. These latter were sometimes nailed on with iron or brass nails, or pegged with hardwood pegs.

The smooth finish of the masks was achieved by shaving and scraping the wood down with a very sharp knife, then rubbing with leaves of the fig, *Ficus exasperata*, which are covered with microscopic hooked spines, more efficient in this work than sandpaper.

The black color and final polish was accomplished by repeated applications of a vegetable mixture, whose chief component is the leaves of the Calabar bean, *Physostigma venenosum*.

---

[14] Harley, 1941a, p. 132.
[15] Harley, 1941b, p. 31.
[16] Harley, 1941a, p. 132 and Harley, 1941b, p. 8.
[17] Harley, 1941a, p. 132.

This mixture was concentrated by boiling to the consistency of a thin paste which penetrated the wood to some extent, yet had enough body to fill tiny defects and pores in the wood. Its application and action was rather like old-fashioned liquid shoe polish. When it dried it could be rubbed to a high luster with the hand or a bit of rag. This concoction seems also to help protect the wood against decay and attack by insects.

The iron spikes sometimes driven into the chin and the crest of the forehead ridge were for extra lashings which served to secure to the mask the hood and the shoulder cape, or "shirt," which were "sewed" through the holes around the edge of the mask. Only one rule governed the arrangement of these accessories: no part of the wearer's anatomy could be exposed to view.[18]

The work of the carver was not referred to as a mask until it had been finished. Then it got its name, and was consecrated by a sacrifice to its newly acquired "spirit." If it was a portrait mask, the sacrifice was directed to the deceased person as his spirit was to come to inhabit the mask. (Details are not known concerning the procedure in those cases when a portrait mask was made while the person was still living.)

The position which the owner of the Gɔ gɛ mask held in the Mano community, and his secret ritual functions, can fortunately be illustrated by accounts of four actual known persons. The names given are, for obvious reasons, fictitious.

SEI

Sei was a man widely known for his power and independence. The fact that he was paramount chief up to the time of his death reflected his complete control over his people. He was *gonola*, also called *lɛkola*, hereditary "owner" of the land in the name of the clan. He was also owner of the forest, including the sacred grove [19] where the Poro and Sandɛ had their sessions. The Poro Bush was on one side of the town, the Sandɛ Bush on the other, each at a respectable distance but within sight.

Neither Poro nor Sandɛ could make preparation for a session without the mutual consent of Sei and *Wai*. He was *ex officio* commander of every secret organization of the clan. The masked *gɛ*'s of the area operated directly under his instructions. He possessed the great fetish known as *dunuma*, and the Gɔ gɛ mask that often went with it.[20] Into his keeping was given the personal medicine of any big man who died. This both indicated and strengthened his association with the realm of departed spirits, and so with the "old people" or ancestors.

In his function as owner of the land and the bush he could effectively bind the people to the home soil of their fathers. He could send a messenger to call a man back, wherever he might be, if that individual were involved in any matter of public interest. If the man refused to come, he became an exile, liable to be caught and sold into slavery by any aggressive individual unless the association of elders of whom Sei was the head gave some indication that the man was still under their protection.

Sei could also enforce exile as punishment for incurring his displeasure. Once when the son of a family in his town joined the Poro of a neighboring tribe instead of the local "chapter," Sei banished the family, which meant they had to leave his area and live forever after as foreigners in the other tribe.

There was a spot on the trail marked by three great trees and three sets of fire stones where Sei had met with the corresponding judge from the next clan to settle a boundary dispute. There had been cooked and eaten a great feast in which all the old men in the area took part in order to sanction and bind the agreement.

Wearing his sacred mask Sei could walk into a session of the Poro where a quarrel was brewing, say, "*Dunuma*," and stop the men in their tracks. At that word all present would prostrate themselves before him, none daring to rise until he was touched on the back with a bundle of small sticks that Sei held in his left hand. If anyone deserved punishment he might be left there all day. Anyone daring to get up would be killed.[21]

---

[18] Harley, 1941b, pp. 8, 10, and 11.
[19] Harley, 1941a, p. 129.

[20] Harley, 1941a, p. 171.
[21] Harley, 1941b, p. 9.

Wearing this mask he could stalk between two fighting bands and command them to stop.[22]

When Sei died government regulations denied him the traditional secret burial which was his due. But the night after he was buried publicly a score of men privileged to exercise the function of creating the effect known as the gɛ, gathered in the compound where he had died and all night long kept up the plaintive flutelike music of the pottery whistles, the throaty musical bellowing of a deep baritone voice chanting into a clay-pot resonator, the high rolling falsetto of a man talking through a blowing drum, and the gutteral bubbling gurgle that represented the forest demons. During this time no woman could leave the house in which she was hidden, except *Wai*, ritually a man, who was privileged to come and go as she pleased.

These makers of music and other manifestations of the voice of the gɛ wore no masks or any other emblem of ritual. In fact, it is barely possible that they were all stark naked. At least in the old days they would have been, for they were in the presence of a new ancestral spirit.

In recognition of this fact at Sei's public funeral his friends and relatives had addressed him by name as they stood by the open grave to throw in a cloth or some other tribute. They each made a prayer to him as a departing spirit.

"Let us have good crops."

"Let us not disagree about the division of our inheritance."

"Let us find money to pay all your debts."

"Let us prosper."

"Give us many children."

The master of ceremonies, who in this case was a civilized young man, had taken a palm nut and put it in Sei's hand, talking to him and asking him for good crops: "Let our seed rice germinate and multiply."

This palm nut was afterward taken and carefully hidden in the seed rice. Part of this was to be mixed with the seed rice of all the people.

NYA

Nya was another *gonola*, owner of the land and the forest, as well as keeper of the Gɔ gɛ mask (pl. IV, d) by virtue of which he was supreme judge of his clan. When exercising this function he actually wore his mask, with suitable costume completely covering him, even his hands and feet. He was dressed by the old men inside his own house and sat as judge in a near-by palaver kitchen inside the fence that enclosed his private quarters in town, guarded against all but the old men. Here would be brought to him important cases, such as the shedding of blood in a fight between two men.

Only the elders were present. The palaver was talked through an interpreter, since the mask spoke a secret language, with a few Mano and Kpɛlle words included. He spoke in a high rolling falsetto voice. If the culprit had shed blood with a knife he was fined one cow plus ten cloths. If he and his family could not pay on the spot that same day, his fine could be paid by someone else, in which case the culprit became the slave of the man who paid his fine. If no one spoke up the culprit was killed secretly in the bush.

If a cow was paid it was taken that night to a cleared area in the bush reserved for such purposes. It was killed, cooked, and eaten by old men assembled from all the towns within the clan. The feasting and talking continued all night. When they finished eating, the old men sat and talked, discussing any new laws and regulations appropriate to the occasion. These laws were recited to the young men by town criers at dawn the next morning. The Gbini gɛ, who was Gɔ gɛ's speaker (pl. XIV, f), danced in the chief town of the clan. In the old days, if the cow was not forthcoming, the culprit himself undoubtedly constituted the *pièce de résistance* for the feast which was held in the bush.

Nya's Gɔ gɛ mask did not dance. It did not walk about. It merely sat in judgment. When the trial was over the big men undressed the wearer and Nya himself attended the feast.

---

[22] The functioning of the keeper of the mask as high priest and judge will be brought out in detail with respect to other "owners." See especially pp. 14–17.

On other occasions Nya undoubtedly carried the mask with him to secret high councils, but at these times the mask was not worn. It was taken along to insure the presence and approval of the ancestral spirits. Furthermore, in its presence no man could tell a lie. No woman or small boy ever saw it.

This Gɔ gɛ mask had been made for Nya's father about the year 1870. When he sat in judgment wearing it he held a great iron knife in each hand (pl. III, i). When he went to the feast he ate with his left hand from a peculiar wooden bowl with a handle, carved from one solid piece. Only heads of the great families were permitted to dip their left hands into the bowl with him.

When the Government took control Nya was recognized as chief, and so he remained for two years. But he was a dignified and retiring individual and at the end of this time he was replaced by a more aggressive and younger man. When Nya became chief for the Government he put his mask away in a box and used it no more. After his death the mask, his knives, and wooden bowl came to me with this bit of information concerning their use. They came by consent of Nya's son, who knew nothing of their proper care and, being afraid of them, was actually grateful to have them find a sympathetic resting place in the museum.

As *gonola*, Nya was lord of the Poro and Sandɛ. Together with his consort *Wai* and his speaker *Gbini gɛ* he was responsible for the safe-keeping of the masks of all the other *gɛ's*. These, with other Poro property, were formerly kept in the loft of a sacred house or kitchen a short distance from town. This kitchen was inside the sacred Bush, near the place where the Poro sessions were held but some distance from the place of feasting. It was surrounded by a fence to keep out cows and other animals. No women or boys were supposed to go near. It was here that all the lesser *gɛ's* were dressed in their masks and costumes. In the kitchen itself a fire was kept burning every day. Here the old men were accustomed to gather and talk petty palavers. Poro initiates of lesser importance could also go there to sit and loaf and drink palm wine, but they could not go into the loft.

Besides the fetish *dunuma*, Nya had a *lai* ("sky stone," a small stone adz) on which the *zo's* of the Pʊro sharpened their ceremonial razors.[23] Because he had *dunuma*, he superintended the making of new masks, as when a big *zo* died and a mask was made in his memory. (No sacrifice was necessary to consecrate such a mask, because the spirit of the *zo* just dead was supposed to go into the mask.[24]) He supervised the making of new costumes for *gɛ's*. Any *gɛ* wanting to dance in his towns had to get his permission. This referred to *gɛ's* from other sections, for the *gɛ's* of that section were sent out by *Gonola* himself. They were his messengers, policemen, and henchmen.

As owner of the forest he was owner of its animals. The leopard, elephant, python, and crocodile were his. Any hunter killing one of these had to turn it over to him. In other sections the great barred eagle is also sacred to the owner of the forest.

The hunters would bring a leopard back to town on a litter, its head covered with a black cloth so no woman could see its face. Laying it down before Nya's house they would call him and say, "We killed this thing in the forest but we don't know what it is."

Then he would say, "That is a leopard."

They said, "Oh, is that a leopard?"

Not until he named it, could they refer to the animal as a leopard.

A python was brought in the same way except that its head was cut off so no woman could see it. Elephants were so scarce in that section I had no opportunity to find out what happened when one was killed. I think Nya would have gone into the bush where the elephant had been killed.

Nya's area included seven towns. He did not cut farms but received tribute from each of these towns.

He was the one who met Sei on the road to discuss the boundary palaver. In the other direction his territory joined that of another man in a similar position, whom I also knew personally. He is described here as Zawolo.

---

[23] See pl. III, *b*.

[24] See pp. 8–9.

ZAWOLO

Zawolo was also a *gonola*. His territory included some seven or eight towns. The mask which he cherished as his sacred connection with the ancestral fathers had been made for his great-grandfather Yini, who handed it down to Yembɛ, who was succeeded by Kɛlɛ, who was Zawolo's father. It was made about 1830, possibly earlier. Yini, in his time, fixed the place where he would meet a similar man from still a fourth section to talk high palavers. Because this man's mask was made after Yini's it was inferior in prestige, so that Yini's word was final in any difference of opinion.

When the elders were to be called for such a palaver the messenger would go to all the towns of the clan, warning all the women and children to go inside the houses. Another messenger, following soon after, carried in his hand the talisman of Zawolo himself (pl. III, d). He would tell the old men that they were called for a meeting. Only the *Ki La* men would be so summoned. At this time every man in all the towns would be warned not to get into any kind of palavers. This was done two or three days before the time set so everyone could be at peace with his neighbor and remember that weighty matters were to be discussed.

If the messenger carried Zawolo's razor in his hand instead of the usual tongs then the big men knew that a culprit was to be tried for his life. The inference was that someone had "spoiled" an unbreakable Poro law, and that the death sentence was likely to be passed regardless of how much he or his people could pay to get him off.

The place of meeting was called *Bu kpanala*. The old men assembled at night. A fire was built and all gathered around. When the matter involved both clans there were two groups, each with its high priestly judge who had brought his *Gɔ gɛ* mask with him, wrapped up in a black cloth inside a box or basket. When they were ready guards were placed on the roads to insure secrecy. The masks were taken out and each was placed on a mat in its prescribed place and covered with a white cloth. Four cowrie shells were placed in a row at each side.

Zawolo then sat behind his mask. On his left fourth finger he wore a big brass ring (pl. III, c); on his left arm, an iron armlet (pl. III, h); on the left wrist, a brass chain of intricate design (pl. III, e) which was an amulet of *dunuma*. These fetishes were supposed to give him power and wisdom. The mask in front of him was "to see how the other judge would cut the palaver." Apparently the keeper of the other mask, being secondary in importance, would hear the case, and Zawolo would be the one to have the final word.

After the old men had talked the case through and reached their decision Zawolo would uncover the mask, call it by name, and review the case, telling the mask:

"We have decided so and so. We want to know if you agree with our decision. If you agree let the cowrie shells fall up. If you disagree let them fall down."

Then he would take the shells and throw them like dice on the mat in front of the mask. The decision was supposed to be the decision of the ancestral spirits and it was final.

In ordinary life Zawolo was a physician, specializing in stomach troubles. It was he whom I once called in consultation and we agreed that the patient had an abscess of the liver. We drained it and the patient recovered. From this incident developed a friendship that lasted through the rest of his life. He taught me much of the native lore, and the use of herbs. In his last illness he came to me for treatment. When finally we both realized that he could not live long, he sent me his mask and other sacred relics and gave me the stories of how he had used them, then he went home and died.

I have never known a man more dignified and gentle, and I was a little surprised to learn that in the old days he had literally had the power of life and death over his people, for, as keeper of the great mask, he was a judge from whose decisions there was no appeal. The casting of lots before the mask was something of a formality. These old people were too sincere to decide everything by throw of dice upon pure chance. Old Zawolo knew how to throw them to get the answer he wanted. If he got an answer that did not suit him he could always invent an excuse for reopening the question and giving the cowries another throw.

GBANA

Gbana, the fourth "owner" of whom I have some information, was a grand old man with pure white hair when I last saw him. He always had a kindly smile. At the height of his influence he was judge for a total of nine towns.

When there was an important palaver to talk Gbana's messenger was sent to notify the old men. Anyone who failed to come was fined one cow. After they were assembled Gbana came down the path, preceded by a special messenger blowing a flute. When the flute was blown the assembled elders became very quiet. He brought his big mask (pl. IV, a) with him and put it on a mat as described above. This mask had been made for his grandfather about 1850.

Sometimes the council would be called to consider the making of laws or decrees considered necessary under the circumstances. Perhaps a town was not prosperous, or people were running away to other sections. Perhaps the young men were refusing to take responsibility in public affairs. Sometimes the chief was not receiving due respect, or the older men needed to be impressed with their responsibility toward the younger people.

Because of the isolated position of his towns, Gbana continued to use his mask and hold these councils for some time after the purely administrative responsibilities had been taken over by the central government of Liberia. These practices were not discontinued until 1938, some fifteen years after the area had been brought under control of the District Commissioner. In this case we have a man who was wise enough to adjust a native institution to the new conditons.

In the old days this mask and its keeper had discussed Poro and gɛ palavers. It had seen men tried and condemned to death. It had been smeared with the blood of any person executed because he had broken sacred laws. Almost one hundred years ago it had been made and consecrated by human sacrifice. During the first years of its existence it had been "kept alive" by similar sacrifice every year in the middle of the dry season. Later a sheep had been substituted for the human sacrifice. The number of victims who fell before its stern judgment is attested by the number of calabar beans and palm nuts tied into its beard.

It is hard to reconcile the gory history of this blood-stained mask with the benign clear-eyed patriarch under whose tutelage I myself once joined the blacksmith's guild. I can only do so by regarding him as a high priest, worshipping his ancestors in the manner which custom demanded.

OTHER JUDGES AND LAWGIVERS

The four Mano "owners" described above ruled their people with considerable power and prestige. Each was a big man in ordinary life, but a bigger man because of the secret power conferred on him through the ancestral mask of which he was the keeper. To help him in his work of judging and ruling his people, each had a number of associates who were of some importance in daily life; but they also were of more importance when they functioned as wearers of masks. Most of these masks had rather specific functions, examples of which will be given later.

In Gio, Krã, and Konor countries, to the north and east of the Mano, it seems evident that there was no exact counterpart of the Mano Gɔ gɛ. The Mano Gɔ gɛ did not walk about or appear in public, whereas his nearest equivalents in these other tribes could walk, dance, and even "hear palavers" (hold court) in public. The Mano were more inclined to have Gɔ gɛ settle things in secret session, while the Gio gɛ would accomplish the same result publicly in more dramatic fashion. He could, thus, fulfill functions which in Mano had to be carried on by some of the lesser gɛ's, in addition to functions corresponding to those of Gɔ gɛ as described.

On the whole these masks were used as badges of office by public officials of various types. It is convenient to give here a few examples of masks from the northern tribes whose functions resemble Gɔ gɛ's to some extent. First are notes obtained from five different sources concerning the functions of Gio masks actually called Gɔ gɛ. Others with different names follow to illustrate related functions.

Gɔ gɛ from the town of Tãwiɛ (French Gio country) used to walk about from town to town. When he came into a town the people had to kill a cow for him. His special taboo was that no water must be allowed to touch him at any time. He made laws for the townspeople.

Gɔ gɛ from Tāwiɛ (Butulu section, Gio) had a home in the bush and did not walk about, nor come to town. The zo people went into the bush to drink palm wine ceremonially with him. He made laws to govern the zo's. He also superintended such important events as the election of a new chief, palavers between clans, etc.

Gɔ gɛ (Gio) was sent for when a big chief died. He came and danced there four days, demanding chickens and other gifts. He would ask the people such questions as, "How many feet have four cows?" and would fine those who could not answer correctly as much as a sheep or four chickens. He would demand palm wine daily and all his followers would drink it. He would appoint one man to divide the wine so each man would have a full cup. If the last cup was not properly filled, the man would be told that he had spoiled everything and must pay a fine of one cow. When he was ready to proceed to the business of electing a chief he addressed the people telling them, "Your big chief has died. You called me here. Who do you want to succeed him?" They showed him the proposed successor to the office. He would ask the candidate, and other of the big men, seemingly foolish questions and put them to various tests (as above).

If the candidate did not demonstrate that he "knew how to talk," Gɔ gɛ disapproved of him and another candidate had to be brought forward. When the new chief had been agreed upon to the satisfaction of Gɔ gɛ and the elders he again danced all day. About noon he would demand of the people that they kill a cow "with two heads." They would retire outside the town and kill two cows, bringing the two heads and one body to Gɔ gɛ, who had them cook the meat for the zo's to eat. The gɛ continued to dance till dark and then left town that night. His special regulation was that no one must pass behind him. He never looked behind him. Only the big people could see him when he came to town. No one who spoke English — that is, had adopted any outside culture — would be allowed to see him.

Gɔ gɛ (Gio) sent a messenger before him, telling everyone, "Gɔ will come tomorrow. Shut up your sheep and goats and cows!" When he came he would catch and kill any cattle he found at large. When he came to town he used to make laws. He might say: "No one must fight here. The fine will be one cow. You all, do you hear?" Three times he would ask them and they would answer: "We hear."

Gɔ gɛ had a house in the bush, not very far from town. It was forbidden for any woman to go into that part of the bush. Gɔ gɛ sometimes came to town, demanded palm wine, and divided it among the zo people. The partakers of the wine received it kneeling, with the right hand extended, the right forearm supported by the left hand. When they were drinking they would not empty the small calabash, but would refill it three times. If anyone drained his cup Gɔ would ask him, "Why do you drink up all my wine?" and would force the man to sit beside him so he "could get sense." He would keep him there until his people paid the equivalent of one cow. Two white sheep would be accepted in place of the cow.

The one who dispensed the wine, likewise had to be careful not to pour out the last wine in the vessel until he had notified Gɔ that the wine was about to finish. Then Gɔ would graciously give him permission to empty the vessel. The dispenser had to kneel on his right knee while pouring out the wine for the company. This wine ritual was to teach the men a distinctive habit or conduct. It was used in certain areas only.

Gɔ gɛ had all the people in his power and care. He could make laws to govern them. They were obliged to kneel before him. No one was allowed to stand in his presence. He sat in the open door of his house, and the men gathered at a respectful distance in front of the house. No water could touch Gɔ gɛ.

An old white-haired man was the owner of this Gɔ gɛ, and kept the Gɔ house in the bush. When a leopard was killed, the hunters carried it to him. "Here is a thing that we killed — some kind of meat."

He would tell them, "Oh, that is a leopard!" After he had named it to them they could speak the name, "leopard." Then they would all dance and celebrate the kill. The old man would kill a cow for the hunters. On the way home the hunters could appropriate anything they wanted to eat, because they "had saved their country from war," they said. This was always the privilege of returning warriors. All leopards belonged to the old man who was the guardian of the Gɔ house. After the Government people came to the Gio country the house used to be built in town. Government messengers could not go there. The people could eat the leopard meat.

Tɔ kpɔ gɛ in the Gio country imposed restrictions and taboos. He could close certain streams to fishing for one year. An overfarmed section could be declared fallow for three or four years. If a man who wanted to raise cattle appealed to him he could decree that no one could buy the man's cow. She was to stay in town and have calves — perhaps for seven years. At the chief's recommendation a law could be passed against pulling up immature cassava when "hungry-time" threatened.

Ni bli bu gɛ (pl. X, *e*), also in Gio country, could be called to a town by its inhabitants. He would stay three or four days and make recommendations on any problem brought to him. He was evidently highly respected, for he demanded a small baby to be brought, killed, and cooked for him. He "ate" it all himself, actually stuffing it into a bag hidden below his chin.

Flɔ gɛ (Gio) could stop war. No one dared shoot at him. He would walk up and ask, "Did you tell me you were going to fight"? The answer was "No." He thereupon fined each party one cow. When the cows were brought he called representatives from each side to arbitrate. When the matter was settled both cows were killed and everyone joined in the feast.

Gba gɛ (Gio) came when a man had got into a fight, and sat down in front of the man's house to talk the palaver. The loser paid one hamper of rice, one white chicken, and four hundred white cola nuts. When the matter was settled the *gɛ* danced in town in honor of the winner, who was supposed to reward the *gɛ* with a cloth or at least a chicken.

Bã gɛ (pl. X, *i*), a large mask with cow horns, sometimes danced all night. Women could not see him. He sat in judgment in palavers between other *gɛ*'s. When a blacksmith's sacred hammer, *yini*, was broken this *gɛ* was called to preside while it was repaired. All the blacksmiths of the section came together while the best of them put the pieces in the fire with suitable ceremonies, welded them into a solid chunk, and forged a new *yini*.

Lu gbo biɛ (Gio) (pl. VI, *a*) settled palavers between lesser *gɛ*'s, sometimes talked palavers in his own town. He did not travel. He put restrictions on the fishing season in some streams. Sometimes he heard lawsuits for debt. He could carry difficult cases to Gɔ gɛ. He sometimes danced and then the people killed a sheep or a goat for him. The mask was kept in a bag in the cult house.

Za gɛ (Gio) was called to town by the clan head. He danced a little, after which he was told that the men would go to the bush tomorrow or the next day to drink palm wine. Next morning each big man took some palm wine with him to a secret place in the bush where the real business of the day was to be discussed: measures to be taken to stop too much buying on credit, or too much irregular sexual activity, or a warning to someone against boisterous conduct. Sometimes this *gɛ* would take a group of boys with him "to teach them good sense." One chicken or five cola nuts was collected from each boy.

Di gɛ (Gio) (pl. X, *a*) interposed when crops were poor in one section and the people of an adjoining section were accused of "making witch" to spoil them. He would call everybody together to talk it over. Apparently it was impossible to arrive at any real conclusion in such cases, but everything possible was done to settle the palaver. Then the *gɛ* said, "If any man does not fear famine let him go home but if any man prays to me he will have good crops." The people then brought him small gifts, whereupon he poured water on the ground, made a little mud, and rubbed some on the forehead of each person, promising that it would soon rain and the crops would get better.

Kma gɛ (Krã) (pl. VI, *d*) presided when the big people had a palaver to talk. Chiefs sometimes called him to settle disputes between clans or to catch a thief. When he settled a dispute the person judged in the wrong brought a cow, killed it, rubbed the blood on the mask, and carried the meat and guts to the place where the palaver had been talked, dividing the back, head, and one leg among the big *zo's* present. The rest was cooked and eaten by all those present. These palavers were held at night. No one might pass in front of this *gɛ*. When a thief was caught this *gɛ* would be called and the culprit brought to him. The man was forced to return whatever he had stolen and to pay the *gɛ* four cats and two gourds of palm wine. Such a palaver was held in town with all the women safely behind the doors of the huts. The *gɛ* took the cats home to catch rats. The palm wine was divided among the *zo's* present.

Gɔ gɛ (Krã) evidently presided at secret meetings of the elders to discuss important palavers before they were tried in open court. He was referred to as the spirit of the ancestors. The details of the procedure were not learned, except that a sheep or goat was sacrificed and eaten by the assembled elders. The heart and liver were given to the keeper of the mask.

Gbɔ gɛ (Gio) (pl. XII, *h*) could stop war. Whenever any Butulu section tired of war the warriors would send an old *zo* called *Glɔ* with a white chicken to ask this *gɛ* to come and stop it, saying, "Here is our heart." He would go to the *zo* people of the town, Tãwiɛ, and ask them to stop the war. They would send *Dɔ nu gɛ* to go and warn the fighters that *Gbɔ gɛ* was coming.

The messenger, *Dɔ nu gɛ*, said: "Excuse me, but *Gbɔ gɛ* is coming. Don't fight any more."

When *Gbɔ gɛ* arrived, he said, "Who makes all this noise here?"

Then both parties would say, "We were quarrelling but no palaver."

He would say: "The country does not belong to you. You have spoiled the law. Come now and fix the law. Just let me show you that I am what I am."

Then he would hold up his left arm and termites would fly out from under his arm. He would lift up his right arm and bats would fly out and catch the flying termites. The very bush where this *gɛ* sat would become bare a few days after, as though it had been burnt.[25]

He did not hear the palaver, but punished both sides equally for breach of peace. He fined the fighting bands four cows each. They brought the cows demanded. Then they each brought a slave, who was killed, and his blood rubbed on the face of the *gɛ*. All ate of the feast.

Dzyi gɛ (Konor) heard palavers between clans. If any man was found guilty of a serious offense he had to pay a cow. If he could not pay the same day he himself was likely to be killed, in which case his hair was woven into the beard of the *gɛ*.

Tche gɛ (Konor) settled town squabbles among women. He made them all sit down and called all the old women to settle the palaver. The fine was usually two or three sheep with enough rice, palm oil, and pepper to provide a feast for the entire town.

Ldoɛ gɛ (Konor) (pl. X, *h*) stopped fights in town. He commanded everybody to stop fighting and sit down. He had the power to shoot anyone who refused. After the furor subsided each side had to bring one cow. The cows were killed and eaten by all the people in all the towns of the section, as a pledge that the fight was over.

Nana gɛ (Pl. V, *c*) used to come to town in the daytime when there was a fight. No woman could see him. He adjusted the quarrel and whoever proved to be in the wrong had to pay two cows, one for the owner of the mask, one to be killed and eaten by the townspeople, who furnished rice to accompany the feast.

Some years ago this mask was worn by its owner to stop a war between the Gio and the Konor-Kpɛllɛ on the French side of the border. The *gɛ* was shot at by a Gio man and the right horn was broken and had to be repaired. In this case the Gio men were judged to be in the wrong. They paid eight cows and two slaves. The Kpɛllɛ contingent took the cows and divided them. Because the *gɛ* had been shot at they beheaded one slave. The victim was eaten by the Kpɛllɛ group and his blood rubbed on the mask. The Gio people had to beg pardon of the *gɛ*, with additional presents.

The second slave, who was a living sacrifice, married a woman who was thereafter called *Gɛ Na*, "the *gɛ's* wife." She was taboo to

---

[25] Undoubtedly with a little human help, secretly applied.

other men, and ritually a perpetual virgin. A mask was made in her honor (pl. I, c). (The woman was alive and living in the zo section when the mask was made.) After this the two masks, *Nana gɛ* and *Gɛ Na* would come to town together. If a small boy looked at the mask *Gɛ Na*, the wearer complained of it to *Nana gɛ* and he made a big palaver about it, accusing the boy of flirting with his wife. The culprit paid one cow, which was kept in town until a suitable time when he also had to pay over four hampers of rice. The town's zo people brought four hampers of cassava, which was made into *dumboi*.[26] The feast was eaten by all the people in town, both men and women.

POLICE

Masked officials were used as police by *Gɔ gɛ* in all parts of the country. A few typical examples follow:

Zuo wi nu (pl. V, f) was sent to collect a bad debt. If a man owed a cow and refused to pay, this *gɛ* would go to the town and threaten to break all the water pots unless the debt was paid before sunset. He would not sleep in town. If the man still refused to pay or had no cow the townspeople would pay rather than have all their pots broken. He took the cow back and demanded his fee, which was two dogs and one cloth shirt.[27]

The threat was not always the same. *Yidi bo gie* threatened to call down the wrath of the ancestors if he was not paid.

Mɔ gbɔ gɛ (pl. XI, b) started to take off his costume if payment was not prompt, whereupon all the women had to run indoors and no one could do any work. The men hastened to pay the debt.

Gbɛ gɛ, the "hamper" spirit (pl. VII, e), came to town to sit in front of the man whose name had been called by the chief's wife, meaning that he was guilty of adultery. (The woman was never punished except in private by her husband.) This *gɛ* brought a hamper about four feet long and a foot wide. This hamper had to be filled with "money," meaning cloth, rice, brass jewelry, and other things commonly used for barter.

When the *gɛ* was satisfied he said, "Now come and put on my whitewash."

The culprit then had to splash a mixture of white clay and water on the *gɛ's* forehead and ears. But before he could do this he had to pay the *gɛ's* commission of one homespun cotton gown such as chiefs wore.

Ya wi ("can't talk") also went and sat in front of the house of a man who was being forced to pay against his will. He could not talk, but pointed to whatever he wanted. His messenger, a "speaker," collected the things until the *gɛ* was satisfied. He ate out of two big wooden spoons and handled his meat with a wooden fork.

Nya gɛ, "the rice-bird" (pl. X, c), collected debts on the threat that he would eat the debtor out of house and home unless paid. He was also very noisy and would let no one sleep.

Ma va (gɛ va), from Maabɔ (Gio) (pl. V, e), was concerned if a man complained to the chief that his woman had run away. The chief then sent this *gɛ* to her people with a demand that she should return. He would accept the woman plus two sheep and two loads of rice for her husband. The *gɛ* demanded his commission of eight loads of rice, one chicken, twenty white cola nuts. This was divided between the *zo's* in the bush.

If the people refused to give the woman up they had to refund the dowry and return all presents that had been given them, besides paying the fees designated above. Every day the *gɛ* had to wait he had to be fed a chicken cooked with rice. It was a big palaver for a Gio woman to desert her husband.

Zai gɛ (Gio) called people at break of day to cut farm for the chief. All who had finished cutting their own farms had to respond. He went with them. When the chief's farm was finished the fee of one dog and two hampers of rice was paid to the *gɛ*, who divided it with the boys who had helped. The *gɛ* took the heart and blood of the dog.

---

[26] Cassava root, boiled and pounded into dough. It is eaten with "soup" made of oil, meat, pepper, etc.

[27] See Schwab, 1947, fig. 88, h.

Ga si gɛ (Kpɛllɛ and Gio) (pl. XII, *j*) called all the boys to help him clear a farm that did not burn well. Anyone not working well was fined a load of snail shells all filled with rice. This rice was cooked along with small snails and then eaten by the boys who *were* working well.

Gbi kɛla, from Dibison (Konor) or *Gba gɛ*, "dog" (Mano), with three helpers, broke up the party, with force if necessary, if people were dancing too much in the moonlight. He told them to go to sleep. His helpers beat people with sticks. He himself carried an axe.

Drɔ da yi mia, from Di plɛ (Gio) means "snail calls leaf his brother"; i.e., snail thinks it is hidden behind a leaf but it is easily caught. This *gɛ* had his system of spies and caught criminals who thought they were safe. He was a sort of detective-magistrate-policeman all in one.

MESSENGERS

Gɛ's as messengers were of two types. The more important ones were of high standing themselves, having the function of "speaker," or representative of still higher *gɛ's*. As such they could act in his stead or carry out his wishes. Less important ones announced Poro sessions, escorted the boys to and from town in Gio country (where the Bush was not really Poro but a circumcision school), or merely went ahead of the big *gɛ* to announce his coming. The *mã* of the Poro could also be sent ahead in a covered basket as "messenger of *Wai*."

Diɛ si, from Lepula (Gio) (pl. VII, *c*), was messenger to *Gɔ gɛ*. He was sent to stop ordinary fights. If he failed he threatened to call *Gɔ gɛ*. If *Gɔ gɛ* finally had to go, *Diɛ si* accompanied him and acted as his speaker and interpreter.

When the people wanted to open a Poro session they called *Diɛ si* and sent him to ask *Gɔ gɛ's* permission. If he said "no" they could not open Poro.

Maa va (pl. V, *a*) was a similar messenger serving the "big cow," *Nana gɛ*. He carried word that it was not good to fight and could impose a fine of one sheep for breach of peace. If serious fighting broke out he would warn the antagonists to stop, saying, "My father is coming next year."

If *Nana* came he would say: "Didn't you hear what my messenger said? Why did you fight in spite of his word?"

Then they would have to pay heavily.

Maa va also sat in council if called as "speaker" for *Nana*. As magistrate or lawgiver his fee was one cow. Here we see the function of *Gɔ gɛ* (Nana) shared with his speaker.

Ka gɛ, from Gbɔwiɛ (Gio) (pl. VII, *f*), was messenger for *Lɔla gɛ*. He was sent to stop fights in the market place or in town. If serious trouble broke out in a particular place, he called *Lɔla gɛ*.

The mask called *Gɔ glü* in *Notes on the Poro* [28] was more likely the messenger of *Gɔ gɛ*. He may very well have been called the same name, since *Gɔ gɛ* in Mano did not walk about, as *Gɔ gɛ* did in Gio country. When this mask is compared with the other messengers, e.g., *Maa va*, this classification seems certain.

Si bo nɔ gɛ, from Ziali (Gio), came in dry time about once every three years and said to the chief of a big town, "Why don't you send your sons to the Poro?" He abused the chief, telling him he was only a small boy himself. When the Poro was opened he would come again and collect his fee of a cloth and a white chicken and one load of rice from each "quarter" of the town; i.e., each kinship group, usually four or five huts.

Bɔ zulu gɛ, from Duopli (Gio), drove women from the waterside so that neophytes from the circumcision Bush could come and be washed, morning and noon, until the circumcision wounds healed.

Zo gɛ preceded Gio boys to town when they came out of the Bush and called their fathers to come and meet them. His fee was one brass bracelet and one chicken cooked with rice.

Dɔ nu gɛ was messenger to *Gbɔ gɛ* (p. 20).

---

[28] Harley, 1941b, pl. IX, *d*.

Gε'S PRESIDING AT PUBLIC FUNCTIONS

Gε's presided at various public functions, and those associated with crises in the life of the individual, such as birth, puberty rites, marriage, calamity, and death. Appropriate gε's did exist for all of these with the exception of marriage, which was probably too simple a procedure to attract the attention of the ancestral spirits.

They appeared also at the erection of important buildings and bridges, on the election of a new chief, on town holidays and feasts, at celebrations of victory in battle, at rain rites in time of drought, and at public witch trials — where a person suspected of witchcraft was tried, judged guilty or innocent, and executed if guilty, all by the simple procedure of forcing him to drink an infusion of sasswood (*Erythrophleum guineense*).

'Zi (pl. XIII, *i*) danced when an important new baby was presented in public. This happened when the child was four days old, if a boy; three days old, if a girl. The gε took a bowl of water, put the baby in it, washed it, and rubbed white clay on it.

He said to the baby: "Don't get sick. Stay well like I am."

The mother gave the gε rice, the father gave him a chicken.

Gba gε, from Ziali (Gio) (pl. XIII, *d*), danced when the mother presented a new child of a chief to the town.[29]

Gbini gε (Mano) (pl. XIV, *f*), as referred to above,[30] danced in town on the day after an important trial with execution of the criminal. This was perhaps to remove the memory of blood guilt, or to emphasize the new regulations designed to prevent such a thing from happening again.

Gbã gε (pl. X, *d*) seems to have been the Gio equivalent of Gbini gε and was undoubtedly intended to represent the ancestral spirits.

Pia sε, from Belewali (Krã) (pl. VI, *e*), danced for any town or "quarter" of a town at planting time. He could be sent for on any important occasion. He demanded a sheep to be killed and eaten by all the people. He chewed cola nuts at planting time, spewed them on the ground, rubbed up a paste, and rubbed it on the foreheads of all the important men, saying, "Good luck to you this year."

Lɔ gε was called the hungry one. Drought and famine were thought to be caused by the breaking of some Poro law, which was usually inferred from some accident in the Poro. In such an event the chief would send a messenger to the owner of the land, who would send Lɔ gε. He would demand a cow to be eaten by the elders of all the towns of the clan, assembled in the palaver house at night. Then the elders would beg the gε to give them food. He would explain how the Poro laws had been broken. Then they would beg him to "throw cold water for them," meaning that they realized they could never hope to propitiate their ancestors for such an offense, but would be pleased to beg for a little mercy.

He would then take water in his mouth, spew it on the ground while all assembled held their heads bowed down. He would say:

"At first my hand was on the ground so the crops would not grow. Now I take my hand off, since you have begged me." Then he would say, "So be it."

Tradition has it that it would thunder immediately and rain would fall the next day.

If the gε was not appeased sufficiently he spewed water on the ground and said crops would be better next year. It would thunder and rain just the same. This gε must have been a pretty good judge of the weather to time his ritual so nicely!

When a new blacksmith shop was to be built the area would be surrounded by a fence and the gε would stay in town all day. He went inside the fence and "talked" at intervals. Women were taboo in the shop.

When a suspension bridge was to be built or repaired,[31] the gε sent a messenger to tell all the people that the road would be closed for one month. Then the gε was supposed to supervise the work. In the adjacent towns his voice would be heard at intervals as if it came from the river or somewhere in the distance.

---

[29] See *Gu lda gε*, p. 34.
[30] See p. 14.

[31] See *Bla gε*, p. 26.

Gbala, from Zuamoni (Krā), supervised the building of the clay wall around a town, which was supplemented by palisades and gates and other barriers to keep out enemy raiders. His fee was one "white chicken" (a human being) and a hundred cola nuts.

Pei gɛ (Gio) could appear before dawn and say: "No one can go to farm today," thus declaring a town holiday. There would be a feast.

Gɛa — the lesser hornbill (Gio) (pl. XI, *e*) — would be invited by the chief to a palm wine festival. All the big people would gather. Palm wine had been prepared beforehand. Ten or fifteen calabashes would be set out. Only the men could drink. All sat down. If anyone drank standing, he would have to pay a fine of eight bowls of wine or eight empty bowls which he would pledge himself to fill "tomorrow." The culprit also furnished a little rice and palm oil. They would sit and drink all day. "In the evening we will talk." They would all joke about a man who was so thirsty he drank standing up. It got very funny about that time!

There is plenty of evidence that domestic animals were never killed primarily for food. They were killed primarily as sacrifices and eaten as such. If a chief wanted to make a feast he accordingly sent for the appropriate *gɛ* to preside. Each tribe had its own regulations as to how the butchering was done, but essentially it was a matter of cutting the animal's throat. The Mano *gɛ* always got his part.

Yɔ gɛ, from Bɛinwie, near Dananae, came to town when the chief wanted to kill a cow, and danced for all to see. His part was the lungs and heart. When he went away he thanked the chief and blessed all the people, predicting good crops and many babies.

Tiːn gbi (pl. XIII, *c*) was called to dance when a cow was killed in Krā country. He was given two bowls of rice with soup on it. Sometimes he went uninvited to a town to dance, accepting anything the people wanted to give him.

Zo gɛ, from Gbeli clan (Gio), was called when the elders killed a cow. A bowl of rice and two cola nuts were requisitioned from each house in town. The meat and rice was all brought to the *gɛ*, who divided the food among all the people, keeping the cola for himself.

Mɛ fei gɛ, from Gɔplɛ (Gio) (pl. I, *b*), had the face of a woman. She was called to town when the chief wanted to kill a cow for the ancestral spirits. She demanded a human sacrifice. Someone was caught at random, and a vein cut so that blood dripped on the ground. A cow was then killed instead of the person. Suitable prayer was made to the ancestors. This was done to rid the town of pestilence or ill fortune of any kind.

It is interesting to note that this *gɛ* with the face of a woman performed a function that would have fallen to *Gɔ gɛ* in the Mano country. In one Mano town the name *Gɔ gɛ* was given to a mask with a woman's face.[32]

Siɛ dɔ wana gɛ or "fire *gɛ*," from Diali (Krā) (pl. X, *g*), came to town uninvited when the chief wanted to kill a cow. He ran "like fire" all over the place. Then he came to the chief and said, "I am going now." The chief gave him a bowl of cooked rice, which he carried to the cult house and divided with his attendants.

Tɔ tɔ, from Gɔplɛ (Gio), was sent for when the elders decided that a man deserved to die for some offense. They told him the man must die and they brought him a bowl of cold water. He poured a little on the ground three times, then threw the rest on the ground, saying, "*Tiɛ dɛ̄*" ("Let the fire go out"). That was all he did. He stayed in town from sunrise to sunset. No one could walk in front of him. The culprit died in two days.

In accordance with information obtained in another connection, it is conjectured that poison was slipped into the man's food at some time during the interval. Such ritual poisoning was done secretly, but was within the rights and duties of high officials. It was usually administered by a woman, following instructions of the high officials.

Gli dɔ gɛ, or sasswood *gɛ*,[33] from Ziali (Gio) (pl. V, *d*), presided over the poison ordeal,[34] which was the public trial and execution of a person accused of witchcraft. If the culprit was found guilty, succumbing to the poison, the *gɛ* carried him off into the bush, where the

---

[32] Harley, 1941b, pl. IV, *c*.
[33] Schwab, 1947, fig. 88, *g*.

[34] Further details of this ordeal are given in Harley, 1941a, p. 153.

old men hacked him to pieces, cooked and ate him, even if he were not quite dead.

If the victim were a woman this *gɛ* did not sit in town, but in the bush where she would not see him. If she was found guilty her people carried her off. She was never seen again.

Gami dɔ zia gɛ, from Ziali (Gio), came into town whenever a big man died, and danced and sang, "We are carrying ——— away." Then he led the procession to the grave. Returning to the surviving family he said, "I have carried your bad thing away." They gave him cola nuts, held out in both hands.

Burial in this part of the country was usually made the fourth day after death, but when this *gɛ* came the body was given him right away.

Tɔ bu gɛ, the "chicken," from Tãwiɛ (Gio) (pl. XIV, *i*), was sent for whenever a big *zo's* death was announced. People were warned that no chicken could make a sound while he was there, because chickens were his children. They took all the chickens to the farms. The fine for a chicken that "talked" was a sheep or a goat.

The townspeople did not say the *zo* was dead, but "He has gone somewhere, we do not know where." There was no mourning for the dead man, people were merely very quiet and subdued. The feast for the dead would come a year later. They gave the *gɛ* a cow (or a slave), which he took home. All the *zo* people went with him to his home in the bush, where they killed and ate the cow (or slave) in secret.

In the Mano country the *gɛ* which was only a voice would "talk" in town when a big man died, but his death would be known only to the *Ki La mi*. No one else would know what it was all about. When the feast was made for the spirit of the dead a year later, there would be much celebration and *Gbini gɛ* would dance. This seemed to be done with the idea of sending the spirit to the realm of the ancestors, well pleased that his people remembered him. The size of the feast reflected the importance of the man so honored.

WAR LEADERS

In the *Notes on the Poro*[35] a Konor *gɛ* was spoken of as "god of war" (pl. VII, *b*). Perhaps *Blɔ gɛ* (pl. X, *f*) also deserves this title. He would not dance, but followed warriors into battle. They presented to him any captives or slain enemies. The slain were cooked and eaten on the spot if victory had been complete. Any parts left were carried back to the home town. There a cow was sacrificed to *Blɔ gɛ* in honor of the victory. It was eaten by all the fighting men. *Blɔ gɛ* was supposed to be immune against gunshot.

This feast was presided over by *Dɔ zɛ gɛ*, who probably functioned also as recruiting officer before the battle.

T'to gɛ, from near Dananae (Gio), was named after a famous warrior named T'to. In olden times a human sacrifice would be made to this *gɛ* the day before going to war. He would come to town, demanding a sacrifice. A slave would be killed by the head warrior. If he did not have a slave handy, he would take the child of a woman who had previously been captured and had married into the clan. This was cooked and eaten after dark. The *gɛ* got the heart and lungs. He did not go into battle. The warriors would raid and burn an enemy town that same night.

Zi bo biɛ ("road-making elephant") (pl. XI, *c*), when the clan went to war, would clear the way via an unexpected route so as to surprise the enemy town. He would take off his mask, hang it on his back, and with a long cutlass clear the way with his own hand. When he broke through near the town he stopped and signaled to the warriors to go ahead. All this happened at night.

Nyinɛ lɛ lai gã ("he looks up at the sun") was a Mano *gɛ* who, during a raid, would sit in town all day looking at the sun. When the warriors returned they escorted him to the "men's house" in the edge of the bush. This house was used by the young men only, who constituted the current age group of fighting men. From this house they paraded at night in a procession called *Gɛ yumbo*.[36]

---

[35] See Harley, 1941b, p. 26.

[36] See below, p. 27.

Siɛ da gɛ, from Bɛinwie (Gio), followed successful raiders into a town and set fire to it after they had plundered it. His share of the plunder was all the sheep and goats. Sometimes these animals were killed and eaten on return to the home town. Sometimes they were divided among the warriors, who could eat or keep them, as they chose.

A Mano informant said his uncle had a mask with a long nose like an elephant's. Wearing this mask he recruited fighters for a raid but did not go with them. Once, when the band returned successful, but having shed no blood or captured any persons, he was in a quandary; for his mask had a law which demanded blood sacrifice. His uncle was required by the law of the mask to furnish a human sacrifice, and he had only his favorite nephew. The nephew was brought, a cut made with a knife in his forehead, and some of his blood rubbed on the mask. Then a cow was killed as a substitute to be eaten. Otherwise the sacrifice would have been incomplete.

Di kɛla from Bɛlɛwali (Konor) (pl. XIV, c), danced for victorious warriors. This mask was kept in the same house as the image of *Wuliyɛ*, made in honor of a woman whose three sons were all great warriors. Her image was the object of sacrifice and prayer for victory before warriors went to battle.

Bla gɛ, "sheep gɛ" (Gio), was described as a god of war. He also officiated at the building of suspension bridges, and escorted the boys to and from the circumcision Bush. Evidently this clan did not believe in the necessity for a multitude of *gɛ*'s, and doubled up his functions.

Pā kɛ la (Konor) (pl. XII, a) was said to lead a victorious group in celebrating and settling a conquered territory, building houses, and planting rice. His cheerful face is certainly fitting for such an office.

INSTRUCTORS

Ka gɛ, from Bɔplɛ (Gio) (pl. XII, c and d), "the crab," was often prayed to for good luck in general, though he had other functions as well, showing the variability of function often seen in the Gio masks. For one chicken he would make medicine to aid a man to collect a debt.

Several masks with the distinctive features seen in plate XII, c and d, were collected from different localities. Most of them were called *Ka gɛ*.[37] In each case the functions described were beneficent, and would make one suspect that this *gɛ* was a sort of household god. In *Notes on the Poro*, page 22, he is the catcher of crawfish, to feed the boys in the Poro Bush. On page 23 he is the object of a monthly sacrifice in the household.

Du gɛ, with the face usually called *Ka gɛ*, was described as a clown, but with his clowning he taught respect to elders.

Diã[38] (half Mano, half Gio) also had the face of *Ka gɛ*. He was a "good gɛ." He said to the boys in the Poro Bush: "You must not make witch. You come here for a long stay. Behave yourselves so you can get well quickly and go back to your people." He also went out at night to collect food for the boys. He acted as a sort of godfather to them.

Ka da kɛ sɛ, from Kāplɛ (Gio) (pl. VII, a), was so highly revered he would be considered under the section devoted to *Gɔ gɛ* were it not that he had the face of *Ka gɛ*. When he went to town a messenger went ahead, telling the people to clear the road. When he came to town he talked about local customs, history, and tradition, and gave the people good advice. They gave him a cow to take with him and they showed him a kitchen loft full of rice, telling him to come and get as much as he wanted. In the old days they gave him a slave. No one could pass in front of him. No imported (foreign) article could be brought into the house where he retired to rest. He took the loft full of rice and divided it among all the people in town, whether residents or not. They cooked and ate what they wanted the same day. The cow he gave to the *zo* people to do as they pleased with it. They promptly killed it and gave the blood and liver to the *gɛ*.

[37] Harley, 1941b, pl. V, f and pl. VIII, f.

[38] Harley, 1941b, p. 20 and pl. VIII, e.

Za gɛ[39] took a group of boys to hear a palaver talked by the big men, from which they would otherwise have been excluded.

A *gɛ* from Bɛlɛwali (Konor) (pl. XI, *f*) danced before the old men and the big people. They killed a cow for him, then sat and listened while he advised them against certain things and told them how to conduct their affairs for the good of the people. Women were not allowed to see him.

Bla gɛ, "the runner," from Ganagli (Gio), came to town and led the boys in races. He could outrun them all. Sometimes he flogged the slow ones from behind. They ended the occasion by running up to a certain house, where the *gɛ* said: "Your boys have been running. Bring them something to eat." Then the chief brought a dog and a cat, with one hamper of cassava or some rice. They killed the animals and gave all the meat to the women to cook. When done they carried it to their own eating place in the bush. This was not done during Poro session. This was done to keep the boys in trim in anticipation of their becoming warriors who might have to run for their lives.

Gɛ yumbo (Mano) was not a mask but a kind of young men's cult.[40] The voice of this *gɛ* was heard near town at night. When all the women were inside the houses a procession entered town led by three young men in costume, but wearing no masks. The costumes were made of raffia, first a skirt, then a shawl or mantle, then a headpiece like voluminous hair. Each man held a pestle perpendicular in both hands, beating a rapid thumping rhythm on the ground as they glided along, winding between the houses. Each young man of that age group was supposed to fall in, carrying his weapons of war. If he came without them, he was severely fined. This was frankly a kind of military training.

Pɔ gɛ came to town at night after the women had all been sent inside. He begged palm wine, then told a story ending with a question which started discussion of some old custom or point in the history of the people. They sat around a fire in the moonlight.

Dŭ gɛ, "the coughing one" (Gio) (pl. IX, *e*), was a mask who came coughing and wheezing, walking feebly around in town in the daytime. Anyone ridiculing him or walking across in front of him would later have to pay a fine. The offender would not be reprimanded on the spot; but after the *gɛ* had disappeared he would be told by various people that he had insulted a spirit and would have to make sacrifice to the mask.

The chief, who had been present all the time, called for the mask; the wearer, who was in this case a woman, meanwhile having mingled with the other people. A messenger brought the mask and laid it on a white cloth with a cushion of soft leaves. The culprit paid a fine to the chief and was required to bring a sheep for sacrifice. The sheep was killed and some blood rubbed first on the mask then on the culprit's forehead. Then he was told to beg pardon. He would say: "Oh, my ancestors, I will not do so again. I did not know your law." Then rice was cooked with the meat and a little given to the mask first. Then all the people ate together. This procedure was designed for the purpose of teaching respect to the elders, to the mask, and to the ancestors.

This procedure was unusual in that the mask was worn by a woman, and in that the mask, as such, was exposed to public view. This would never have been done in Mano country, where not only the identity of the wearer, but the very fact that there was a *person* inside the concealing costume, were closely guarded secrets.

PORO Gɛ'S

Masks and masked figures were used in the Poro Bush school, called by the Mano, *Gɛ Bɔ*, or "spirit Bush," to discipline and educate the boys and inculcate them with a deep respect for the ancestral spirits. The *gɛ's* acting as Poro officials also exerted a similar influence upon the women and children, with the difference that they were kept forever "outside" and ignorant.

The session of *Gɛ Bɔ* alternated with those

---

[39] See p. 19.

[40] See Schwab, 1947, p. 272.

of the girls' Bush school. Neither school could be held if the clan were at war. They were preferably held when there was a surplus of food. Whenever *Gonola* and *Wai* decided the time was suitable, *Gɛ Na* would come to town at night and say that it had been a long time since he had seen anything to eat. Or in Gio country *Si bo nɔ gɛ* would appear in public and ask the chief why he didn't send his boys to the Bush.

The chief would go through the formality of sending to *Gonola* asking that the Bush be opened. *Gɛ Na* then came to town at night and said he would catch all the boys. *Zi kū gɛ* walked on the road when all was ready, saying, "The *gɛ* will catch men today."

The people in the meantime made sacrifices of food at the crossroads to the ancestral spirits, asking that all would go well in the Bush. The boys at play in the town would arm themselves with wooden weapons and pretend they were going to kill the *gɛ*, making great show of boldness to conceal their fear.

While the boys were thus preparing themselves the men were making ready the section of forest where the Bush school would be held. They closed all roads except one, and erected an outer and an inner portal through which all must pass. A house was built for *Gonola* and his consort, *Wai*. The boys would have to sleep in the open until they built their own houses.

Tɛa bli si (pl. VIII, *e*) stopped all traffic on roads leading to the Bush and flogged people caught on the forbidden paths after due warning had been given. He might also catch stray men and carry them into the Bush to be initiated.

Long before light on the morning of the day set *Dɛ bu gɛ* (pl. VIII, *f*) went ahead into the Bush carrying the sacred razor and a fetish to ward off harm. Following him came the other officials, some of them *gɛ's* with their masks and costumes and other properties for the rituals.

All day long a procession of people streamed out of town toward the entrance portal. The boys who were to enter were escorted by family groups all pretending to be happy and gay as they danced along the way. Some of the mothers, in rags and tatters, danced a ritual dance. There was an atmosphere of people setting out on a pilgrimage, as group by group they marched to the edge of the Bush within sight of the outer portal. In the Gio country one of the *gɛ's*, *Bɔ Ku gɛ*, might join in the procession, escorting the neophytes from the town to the Bush entrance.

Inside this, each boy had to fight and "overcome" three masked *gɛ's*. Then they went through the inner portal where *T'to bli gɛ* (pl. VIII, *a*) made them swear on the big *Mā* [41] that they would never tell any woman about the things they were about to see inside the Bush. He then spewed water on the ground, made a paste, and rubbed it on the boys' foreheads.

Yɔ pu gɛ in Gio country went to town on the first day of the Bush and asked for a bucket of whitewash (clay). It was set down in front of him. Each woman in town then saluted him. Before she spoke she was told to dip some of it and smear it around her eyes. This was symbolic of contact with the spirits and constituted a pledge of good faith and a prayer that all would go well.

Gɛlɛ wi gɛ (pl. VIII, *b*) went to town with the blacksmith's big sledge hammer to break off, from the anvil stone or some other convenient rock, three chunks of stone for the hearth. With suitable ritual these were set in the ground with the small end up, so as to support a big pot over the fire. When the stones were ready a human sacrifice was made to the fire, before kindling it with a brand from the eternal fire of the cult house.

Si kū gɛ, "smoke catcher" (pl. VIII, *c*), had ready a supply of firewood that would not smoke.

Gɔ gɛ commanded that a slave boy be brought for the sacrifice.

Bɔ ke tutu fed the victim herbs which made him dumb and blind and insensible to pain.

When he was unconscious *Bɔ zɛ gɛ* (pl. VIII,

---

[41] "The mother of all masks," the mask pictured in the frontispiece is said to be one artist's interpretation of their *ancestral spirit*, earth mother goddess. It is an old mask of uncertain history. Plate II, *a* is a recently carved interpretation by a Bassa artist. Plate II, *b* is a similar carving by a Krã artist. It was customary to have such masks carved by a "foreign" artist. Plate I, *c*, by a Konor artist, is in the same category of ultimate idealization of the female face.

g) cut out his liver with a sacred razor and *Bɔ kpo si* prepared other parts for magical purposes.

Then *Si kū gɛ* kindled a fire that did not smoke.

Bɔ bulu kpa gɛ finally cooked the meat as a sacrifice for all to eat.

The boys were again sworn on pain of death never to reveal what they had just seen, or run away, or contact any woman while in the Poro.

In the southern part of Mano country *Gɛa gɛ* had the townspeople catch a kingfisher alive, to be added to the human sacrifice.

During the days and months that followed the boys learned many things. *Bɛlɛ kpɔ gɛ* told them that white was the color of the spirit world and smeared them all over with white clay.

Gɛ Na came at night and said, "I see something to eat today I have not seen in a long time." He came again when the boys were to be circumcised. This was sometimes done in Mano country in a preliminary session not considered very important. This circumcision ritual was called *K'lɛ Bɔ* and constituted the entire ritual in the far Gio country. The Mano, like tribes to the west, had developed the true Poro, or *Gɛ Bɔ*, in which the boys were marked with scars supposed to be the marks of the *gɛ* that swallowed them and gave them rebirth.

Gbini gɛ (pl. XIV, f) presided over this scarification ritual, which took place toward the end of the session, long after the boys had been circumcised.[42]

Tɔ kū gɛ rounded up some chickens for this occasion and one of them was set aside for a "scapegoat" for the blood to go into, so the boys would have no serious hemorrhages.

Yumbo si gɛ caught any blood that dripped from the wounds in a basin, so that none would drip on the ground. This blood was eaten in the food of the big men, not by the boys.

If one of the boys was unduly scared, or a crybaby, *Zai bo lu* made a bit of horseplay, giving him some of his own blood on a kind of leaf to swallow. This made a lot of gas on his stomach and they then made fun of him, saying that *Zai bo lu* had made him pregnant. When he had had enough they gave him something to make him vomit.

Gɔ gɛ appeared four times during the session, wearing his mask, and saying, "*Dunuma*." At this word everyone present, including the big men, fell prone and stayed down until he touched each one on the back with a bundle of twigs held in his left hand. Anyone he wished to punish was left there.

Wai, unmasked as cult mother, supervised the cooking and heard the petty complaints of the boys. She had a real job, for it is certain some of the little fellows got homesick. She also had a spy and a fact-finder, because she had the responsibility to be sure than no boy ran away or contacted his mother, and tattling was taboo. This responsibility was terribly heavy, for running away was punished by death. *Wai* could also impose the death penalty on older members with *Gɔ gɛ's* approval. It was her hand that tapped the victim on the forehead with a tiny ceremonial axe as the signal to the executioner. If a victim escaped she "put his name in her *mã*." Then the entire Poro organization with all its intertribal ramifications was pledged to bring him back. There was little chance of escape.

The older men were coming and going all the time, and instructing the boys. These details, however, are outside the scope of this study of the *gɛ's* themselves.

There were three *gɛ's* who made medicine for the boys. This medicine was either herbal or magic.

There were in Mano at least seven different *gɛ's* who acted as foragers to round up food. In the Gio country their number increased to seventeen, in the Gɛh country twenty-two, each with his own special way of getting food. They would beg, steal, borrow, and extort from the outsiders in every conceivable way. There were catchers of frogs, snails, grasshoppers, snakes, chickens, ducks, or any small chop. They normally make the people help. Some tricked the people into paying fines, of sheep or goats, cats or dogs. Others were frankly beggars. No one could refuse them anything they asked. With so many boys out of circulation, and men often taking advantage of the opportunity to get an extra meal in the Poro, it was a serious drain on the resources of the

---

[42] For other functions of *Gbini gɛ*, see pp. 14 and 23.

community, and these foragers were a very necessary part of the Poro personnel.

Here are a few examples of the gɛ's who acted as foragers in Gio country. More than forty others are described in *Notes on the Poro*.

Mɔ gɛ, "the rat," from Meaplɛ (Gio), went to town at night and stole whatever food he could lay hands on. Anyone who objected had to pay a chicken or one hundred cola nuts. He had a man with him to carry the plunder back to the Bush.

Slu gɛ (Gio) ran up when women were beating out rice, grabbed some, put it in his basket, and ran off, saying, "*Sie kpana* (They force me to do this)."

Nɛ gɛ, "the bat," from Blɔntua (Gio), collected rice from the boys' mothers at night. The women could not come out of the houses, so he sent a messenger inside each house while he danced outside.

Blɛ bɔ gɛ, from Kăpa (Gio), danced during Poro, exacting a cloth from each house of a big man in lieu of "cold water" (preliminary sacrifice or payment), so that their sons might do well in their ordeals.

Near the end of the session *Gɔ gɛ* took the boys to the waterside, washed them, and gave them their new names. *Gbini gɛ* danced with no costume to show them the secret of the masked *gɛ*. *Gɛ Na* paraded openly before them, so they could see that this *gɛ* was only a voice and a means of making this voice.

In the circumcision Bush of the far Gio country, where the boys did not sleep in the Bush, they were escorted to town every night and back to the Bush every morning by a masked *gɛ* called *Bea dɔ su puɛ*, who cared for them in various ways, making medicine to keep trouble away from them and to help them get well quickly. After carrying the boys to the Bush in the morning he would return to town when the women were cooking, and begging a little from each one carry it back to the boys. He would come again at night when women were cooking the evening meal. No one dared refuse him. That is why they called him *Bea dɔ*, which means "beggar." They said, "He can't sleep," because he was constantly on duty for a month at a time. Perhaps more than one person could wear this mask in relays.

When he escorted the boys to the Bush he left them in charge of *Ya bɔa*, who took them to the waterside to wash their wounds. If a bird flew past he would say, "What is that?"

"A bird."

"Catch it for me."

The boys would beg off with cola nuts.

Shortly after the end of the session in Gio, *Dra ya bɔa* (pl. XII, *i*) went to town and called the names of all the boys in the Bush. When the people told him, one by one, that the boys were in the Bush, the *gɛ* pretended to cry, saying, "All my boys are gone!" Then he became serious and said: "Some of them will stay with me in the Bush; they will not come back." He named the ones who had died and told the people they would never see them again.

When graduation time approached *Bo gɛ* went to town and told the people to clean the roads and sweep the town. He watched at night and fined anyone caught soiling the ground, saying: "Don't waste it here, go farther away. Don't dirty the ground just because you had plenty to eat."

Bɔ kū gɛ came to town and took all the women's rings for the boys to wear on graduation day. *Nyū kū nɔ ngɔ* took all their beads and hung them around the necks of the boys. *Tu kū gɛ* gathered all the horns to be blown in the procession back to town.

Zo la kɛ gɛ, from Luãple (Gio), came to town the night before graduation to collect his fees from all the mothers. He demanded fine "brass things" — anklets, bracelets, or other ornaments — from each, telling them he had made magical medicine so that all the boys had been kept from getting sick. He had actually given each one of them a little iron hook wrapped with cotton string to hang over his shoulder. When the boys came home they returned the little iron hooks and each gave him a "dash" of a ring.

Flɔ gɛ (Mano) (pl. XI, *g*) had a similar function. He seemed to be a kind of guardian of the boys while in the Bush and made both magical and herbal remedies for them. When the Bush was not in session he sometimes acted as judge to try offences against the Poro laws.

Kpo Gɔ (Kpao, French Guinea) (pl. XI, *d*) was called to hear evidence and pass judgment when people broke the country law, or Poro law. He levied fines varying from three cloths to one cow.

Tɔ la gɛ (Mano, near Gio border) (pl. XI, *i*) came to town in the daytime when anyone

MEDICINE AND MAGIC

The practice of medicine among the people was a function of housewives, old women, midwives, and men who specialized either as herb doctors and bonesetters or as diviners who mixed their magical prescriptions with certain herbs.[46]

When an unknown pestilence came and the matter did not yield to the herb doctors and diviners the chief might seek higher aid by calling Zɔ gɛ (pl. V, b). All the women would be sent inside the houses by the gɛ's messenger. Then he would come to town and harangue the men, telling them to stop bewitching one another. If anyone sick at the time got well he was obligated to make a feast for the whole town. The gɛ was called for this feast. He carried his part of the food away into the bush.

Longwa, from Sɛaplɛ (Gio) (pl. XIII, f), came to town when there was an unusual amount of sickness. It was said that if he came on a sunny day the clouds would come and hide the sun. Any sick man watching him dance was supposed to be cured promptly.

The wearer of this mask was keeper of all the masks for that clan. He was therefore on a par with *Gbini gɛ* in Mano.

Dã ya bɔa, from Butulu (Gio) (pl. VIII, i), was guardian of the boys in the circumcision Bush and made medicine for their ills.[47]

Gu lda gɛ, from Zoli (Gio), was called to attend women in difficult labor. He spewed water on the ground and made a paste of mud. The midwife took some of the paste and rubbed it on the patient's forehead. What good this did is questionable, and limited, naturally, to the psychological effect. It is a fact that these women frequently stay in labor two or even three days and still have live babies. At any rate the gɛ would take the credit and visit the baby on the fourth day if a boy, the third, if a girl. On this occasion he presented the child to the town, naming it, and blessing it by spewing water on it from his mouth, and promising it good health.

Out of my collection of over five hundred masks there were five which had been made in memory of men with faces distorted by disease (pl. IX, a, b, c, d). Each of these was venerated as a petty god, and sacrifices made to it by indi-viduals suffering from the same disease, with prayers for recovery.

One of these masks represents gangosa, or destruction of the nose by yaws. Two others show one-sided facial paralysis. The fourth is a likeness of a man with a tumor of the lower jaw. The keeper of this last one posed as a doctor and tried to help sufferers by building a little fire on the tumor. It is interesting to note that this sort of medicine is rarely practised and that masks of deformed faces made little headway as gods of medicine. I was told of one other such mask. It was made in memory of a blind man.

Gbasa, from Du kling (Mano), was used in the initiation rites of the *Gbasa* society for suppression of witches. The head of this soci-ety also held it by the chin while dancing in town at night. He was accompanied by all members dancing backwards on their heels. They kept it up all night long, coming and go-ing at intervals. When there was any heavy work to be done "*Gbasa* would do it." This meant that all the young able-bodied men would do it just before dawn, working *en masse* and walking backwards on their heels. They could perform miracles of strength by working up a mass hysteria which trampled a wide path over ordinary obstacles.

Ga sua, also called *Gɔti, Tokali, Bɛlɛkɛ wea*, or *Gɛ* (Krã) (pl. XV, a), is not a mask but a solid sculptured clay head with grotesque hu-man features. Often it has four eyes like *Lu bo biɛ* (pl. VI, b). It is an object of sacrifice and prayer for protection against witches or for luck, new babies, fertility of the fields, or recovery from illness. Its keeper, like *Gonola*, is owner of the town. It is not, however, a clan symbol and not every town or clan had one.

Its owner is really more of a diviner than clan head. As priest of this great fetish he dances with it balanced on his head. Working himself into a frenzy he answers questions about past, present, and future. As an oracle the fetish is also featured in the catching and execution of supposed witches.

Sometimes a set is made (pl. XV, b), the big one having two smaller "helpers." When this is the case the priest with the big one on

[46] Harley, 1941a, pp. 37–43.

[47] See Harley, 1941b, pp. 16 and 21.

men, with whom they gradually came to enjoy more and more comradeship.

To the outsiders the *gɛ's*, of the *Gɛ Bɔ*, were a fearsome lot. They could not be denied or opposed. They had to be given whatever they demanded. They were immune from all laws and regulations except the ones which they themselves imposed. They existed for one purpose only, and that was to keep the *Gɛ Bɔ* functioning and protected. Since their own sons were inside, the women not only put up with it but even met the *gɛ's* half way working "day and night" to provide extra food. The life and tempo of the whole community was for the time being thus regulated by the *gɛ's* to the needs of the Bush school. Even war had to wait, and the final calamity of death sometimes had to be ignored. (The death of one of the initiates during a Poro session was not even announced until the close of the session, and then no mourning for him was allowed. They said, "He was a witch.")

When the girls were in the Sandɛ Bush school, *Dɪ Da Bɔ*, the women retaliated in principle, but neither in kind nor in amount, towards the men. There were no *gɛ's* to carry food. The women did that simply and quietly. Instruction of the girls was carried on in the same way by the women, without the use of masks. It was only at the time of the graduation of the girls that the *gɛ* exercised any function. At this time a mask [45] was worn by the head woman of the Sandɛ; but she did little more than escort the girls back to town and dance, at a distance from the men, more or less surrounded by other women.

EXTORTIONERS

When the *Ki La mi zo's* or other big men wanted to get together to talk things over they usually did so secretly in the seclusion of the bush. Between Poro sessions they used one of the *gɛ's* to round up something to eat. Here again we see the hand of *Gonola* at work, for the *gɛ's* could function only at his bidding.

Gbea gɛ, "crocodile," from Yiaple (Gio) (pl. XI, *a*), would sit down and talk where a party of men were fishing with nets. Each fisher must give him one fish. When he came to town he begged from each house for something to eat with his fish. Each woman cooked rice and one fish and put this in his basket. The *gɛ* took the food to the bush to be eaten by the assembled *zo's*.

N'ga dolo, "I can't agree with you," would demand and receive cloth and when that was given him he would ask for a loin cloth. Various items of clothing would be offered him, but he would refuse them until a black cat had been found for him. If a cat was not available he would accept a black cloth as a substitute.

Sa gɛ, from Kãplɛ (Gio), carried a small whip with which he would beat any small children he found in town. After he had flogged the children he would ask for chicken eggs. The mothers probably brought the eggs gladly to buy off the *gɛ* from further flogging of their children. He carried the eggs into the bush to be eaten by the *zo's*.

Tie bli si, from Butulu (Krã), was a bad *gɛ*. His nose was on upside down. On market day he used to sit on the road demanding tribute from everyone who passed. If a contribution was not forthcoming from someone, he would strip off whatever clothes the person was wearing and appropriate them.

Ya bu gɛ, "rice eater," would come when a chief made a feast and beg some of it and carry it away into the cult house where the *zo's* would eat it.

Gba ti dɛ, from Kãplɛ (Gio), danced in town and had to be given food. Whatever was given he would always complain that it was far too small. Rice would be brought in baskets, fanners, buckets, and so on, until he had gathered all he could extort. Then he would take it to the chief and beg him to cook it for him. He would also beg meat to go with it. Then he would take it all into the bush and divide it with his "gang." It was not known what organization was behind this *gɛ* or who ate the food.

Ya wɔ dɔ, from Kãplɛ (Gio), walked about or sat down when he came to town but said nothing. Children laughed at him but he didn't mind. He nodded his head at passers-by. People gave him small presents but he paid no attention to them. After three days of this the chief gave him a generous dash and sent him away.

[45] Harley, 1941b, pl. XII, *b*.

to secrecy and let them "wash my face" — with water in which the big *Mā* had first been washed.

I objected to this, thinking quickly that if I swore to secrecy I could never write this paper, which I had in mind even then. Then they agreed to proceed as though nothing had happened except that the *gε* had "retired." He had done his work anyhow.

The town crier then announced that the *gε* had "born" the boys again and the women could come out of their houses. There followed fully two minutes of absolute silence, which was exceedingly impressive, for the sunset light reflected from the clouds changed to an eery gray like early dawn. I am of the opinion that the men had been waiting for that lighting effect.

The town crier walked toward an open space in town where the boys were sitting on a long row of mats, each covered head and foot with a country cloth blanket, so arranged that he could peep out where the edges of the blanket were held around his face like a hood. Gradually little sounds came from the houses as one by one the women peeped out. Then they came slowly and the boys began to look out from under their blankets.

The chief of that quarter of town was introduced to me as mentor of the boys. He began to introduce them by their new names. They were treated as strangers even by their mothers. They said nothing.

Then began a strange pantomime of friends helping the boys to stand and teaching them to walk. Each was revealed covered with white clay. His friends showed him how to wrap his blanket around himself in lieu of clothing. Then they began showing him things, naming them, and teaching him to talk, carrying. out the idea that he was like a newborn baby.

The town belonged to the boys for two days, while nobody did anything except teach them — even how to eat. They were introduced to everybody, and a sort of open-house reception held in the house of the chief who was acting as their mentor. Needless to say, the boys learned very fast! At the end of two days they were men in full tribal standing, but for weeks afterward they were extended every courtesy usually reserved for visiting dignitaries.

The function of *gε's* in the Poro Bush school, or *Gε Bɔ*, must be considered from three ap-

proaches: first, that of the big men who regulated everything; second, that of the boys themselves; third, that of the women and children who, as a class, were outsiders.

To the big men the *gε's* were purely and simply masks. These masks were not only revered and worshiped, but at the same time used for very practical ends. They were used to control and instruct both the outsiders and the neophytes. In the old days when the *Gε Bɔ* was in session up to three years, instruction and discipline of the neophytes constituted a large proportion of the activities of the *gε's* toward the school. The other functions of the *gε's* in the school were essentially the same as their functions toward the community in general, including the making of medicine, both herbal and magical, protection against witchcraft or calamity, the administration of justice, and the conduct of rituals with or without sacrifice.

To the neophytes in the *Gε Bɔ* the *gε's* were all things. They were first of all to be feared as though they were living gods. Even as the boys came to know more and more about them, this fear was merely commuted into an attitude of worship. Concurrently, the fear of the masked figure with costume concealing the man was commuted to worship of the mask as such, at which stage the man or wearer simply joined in the worship.

This summary does not quite apply to the neophyte's attitude toward the small *mā* or the big *Mā* of the Poro. This attitude was always one of worship, but in the case of the small *mā* it was on a very familiar and personal basis. He could put it in his own pocket and carry it around with him. When he talked to it, it was more or less like talking to himself. He could even abuse it, provided he begged its pardon afterward.

The big *Mā* was less personal, since it represented the spirits of his ancestors, which he would never dare abuse or insult in any way. Above all other masks it was the one he revered most. On it he swore eternal secrecy with an oath that pledged his very life and set him against his own mother and all other women.

His attitude toward the *gε's*, however, was not always that of fear and trembling, because some of them were very busy, month in and month out, raiding the outsiders — begging, stealing, buying, or borrowing food and other good things for the boys themselves and for the

broke a sacred law of the Poro. Small boys could not look at him. Women could see him, but only at a distance as they went about their work. Anyone found guilty of telling an outsider, especially a woman, any of the secrets of the Poro would be sentenced to death. Anyone exposing sacred objects to public view would meet the same judgment. There was no possible ransom. This gɛ, accompanied by all the old men, would carry the offender into the bush, torture him to death, cook and eat him, with rice, salt, and spice.

He exercised a function here similar to that of Gɔ gɛ in the true Mano area.

In one way or another things were managed so that all the boys had new clothes. They gave the old ones to *Kunu gɛ*, "the owl," [43] who promised to keep them for them in case they wanted them later.

The Gio boys consequently returned to town with horns blowing and were met with singing and dancing. They were given anything they wanted for one day.

On the last day of the Bush school session *Wai* cooked several pots of stew so that each boy could enjoy his favorite meat and observe his family taboos. When the final feast was finished and all were ready *Gɛ Na* brought them into town.[44]

Yongolo to, from Luáple (Gio) (pl. II, *j*), was a mask that was not worn. It was one version of the big *Mã* of the Poro. At the end of the session it was carried in a basket called *Yumbo tiɛ* by the last boy to leave. With it in the basket were other properties, including the pottery whistles. All the gɛ's danced while this mask lay in state in front of the cult house. When their dance was finished the basket was carried inside the cult house and put away. It was said of this mask that if a woman ever saw it she would never menstruate again.

Bɔ la gɛ, from Luáple (Gio), came to town at the end of the Poro and said, "My man has eaten all the boys." This would tend to clear up the symbolism of Gɔ gɛ and *Wai*. To outsiders the musical voices of the gɛ who cannot be seen are attributed to the wife of the gɛ. Initiates also refer to the flute, the pottery whistles, and resonating pot (pl. III, *j–p*) as the voice of gɛ's woman. These "female" properties are kept along with the big *Mã* of the Poro

by *Wai*. The Gɔ gɛ mask is kept by *Gonola*, along with the powerful magical fetish, *dunuma*, whose name is the password of power in the Poro ritual. *Gonola* also kept the cult *lai* on which the ceremonial razor and hooks were sharpened. The *zo* who kept the razor and hooks was of secondary importance and should be considered as the operating surgeon, in spite of the fact that his work and his tools were the greatest secret of the Poro Bush school.

The ancestral spirits are, therefore, represented by male and female symbolism. Gɔ gɛ, with his deep voice like the growl of a leopard, is the symbol of the male ancestors. The big *Mã* and the voice of the gɛ that cannot be seen are the symbols of female ancestors.

The remark of *Bɔ la gɛ* that her husband has eaten all the boys, together with the tradition that the boys stay in his belly while in the Poro, to be reborn at the end of the session, can be explained only by considering that belly as sexless, or as the realm of the spirits without reference to sex.

It would follow that, since the boys could be reborn only from a female belly, they were therefore reborn by the female ancestral spirit. This idea is clearly substantiated by the fact that when the boys are actually presented to the town as newborn babies it is the voice of the gɛ that cannot be seen that brings them to town. I myself have seen this ceremony.

It was just at sunset with a pale pink light reflected everywhere. The town was absolutely quiet. I had been warned not to go to town, but I wanted to see what was happening. I met the group of men with their pottery whistles unexpectedly around a corner. In consternation they hurried into the compound of *Gonola*, dispersing, so that I could see clearly that no masked figure was among them. There was literally nothing to see.

The chief came toward me, saying, "You have scared the gɛ away."

I said, "Let us go to the old man's quarter, I want to shake hands with my friends."

On approaching the gate I was met by the big *zo* who kept the razor and hooks, the operating surgeon. He objected to my going in, admitting that I knew all the secrets, but pointing out that few of the people knew that I knew, and would not understand unless I swore

[43] See p. 39.

[44] See p. 28.

his head mutters and makes indistinguishable sounds. One of the others talks to the petitioner. The third one is an intermediate interpreter.

The fetish is greatly feared, and no rascal will willingly enter a town where one is located.

From Butulu in near-by Gio country comes the story of a wooden Janus figure with similar functions (pl. II, c). It is never seen in public. Its priest stays with it inside the house while one of the interpreters stands in the door and another talks to the people outside. It is a sort of court of high appeal for cases that cannot be settled in the ordinary way. It also issues decrees and announces taboos and "laws."

MASKS WITH ANIMAL FEATURES

The grotesque exaggeration of features of the "male" masks often include likenesses of animals and birds. Some are deliberately hideous and so much more animal than human that they deserve the name *demon*. It must be admitted that frightfulness is part of the technique of keeping women and children in awe of the spirits, but the awe of the wearer himself is just as real. No man could fail to respect a mask to which he had sacrificed his own son, as did the "priest" of *Gɔ gɛ* on succession to his office.[48] There must, therefore, be more than frightfulness to explain the grotesque animal masks.

The explanation lies in the native veneration of force or power inherent in anything whether animate or inanimate. The *mana* of the forest animals is very powerful. The tendency to worship animals for this reason has been combined with the conviction that ancestral spirits are the most powerful of all forces. The consideration of animals as totems and helpers represents a stage of that combination, and gradually the spirits of animals became linked with those of ancestors. The combination of human and animal features in these masks is visible expression of the attempt to recognize spirit power as having both human and animal attributes. Animals on earth were able to do some things that human beings on earth could not do. The all-powerful spirits are thought of as able to effect both types of activity.

By combining human and animal features with frightful exaggeration an impression was created which tended to match the further idea that there were certain unexplained phenomena and calamities pointing to a force more potent than either human beings or animals. By combining the symbols of the most powerful things they knew they sought to create symbols of the all-powerful unseen force of their universe. To that symbol no sacrifice was too sacred, no price too much to pay for its *mana*.

Gɔ gɛ (pl. VII, d) in some parts of Gio country is identified with the leopard. In Gbande country the great mask was a crocodile, *dandai*.[49] In Gio the elephant, or a conglomerate forest demon, *Lu bo biɛ* (pl. VI, b), seemed to hold a very high place. His high cheekbones and his four eyes tend to connect him with the gorilla masks of the Cameroon. The Gio have an important mask called *Klua gɛ*, which is the chimpanzee (pl. IX, j). One Gio mask of high standing was called the "python." In the Konor country toward the pastoral savanna the big mask is distinctly a cow, but it has the chimpanzee cheekbones and the same protuberant eyes as all the other *Gɔ gɛ's*. Finally, there is the peculiar four-eyed clay demon head, *Ga sua*, which as we have seen,[50] serves several of the functions of *Gɔ gɛ* in the Grebo country.

Many of the lesser animals were represented by masks. Sometimes they had human faces only slightly modified to suggest animal characteristics. Sometimes the animal features were predominant, especially the mouths.

The hornbills and the crested hawk illustrate this very well. When anyone killed a great hornbill the "owner" of the hornbills put on his mask (see below) and demanded why the

---

[48] If a *lai* (celt-adz) whetstone (pl. III, b) accompanied the *Gɔ gɛ* mask, another human sacrifice consecrated the transfer of this sacred tool to a new home. The same ceremony was necessary when *Gonola* or *Wai* obtained a horn of magical substance called *Dunuma* which gave power over all other *gɛ's*.

When a new costume was made for any of the *gɛ's*, human sacrifice was again demanded. See Harley, 1941a, p. 131.
[49] Harley, 1941b, p. 27 and fig. 2, p. 28.
[50] See p. 34.

bird had not been brought to him. He was usually satisfied if he was given some of the meat, but, if he wished, he could impose the fine of a goat.

Kpala (pl. XI, *e*), the lesser hornbill, sometimes went to judge petty palavers. When they saw him coming they settled the matter hurriedly because they knew he would judge harshly.[51] *Za*, the crested hawk,[52] would put on his mask and lead the whole town to the house of the man who had killed a hawk without reporting it, singing, "*Za, wing bi Za*," and collect five hampers of seed rice to be divided among the women who had sons in the Poro. They planted the rice.

The beliefs of the people left plenty of room for the animals in their traditions. As pointed out above, the owners of the forest were also owners of the forest animals. Sometimes the ownership was connected with specific clan totem animals but there is much confusion on this point and nothing very clear can be said — except that it was taboo to kill or eat a totem animal, and that if one were killed for meat or as a dangerous beast it had to be brought to the clan "owner." Sometimes such an owner had his own personal animal familiar. It was finally believed that such an owner could not only influence the totem animal to do his bidding, but could actually change himself into his animal familiar and walk about alone or lead the animal herd in person.

An old bull elephant separated from the herd and on the rampage was certainly a person, and the people thought they knew who it was. They said, "Bumbli is vexed about something." The idea of were-animals and of animal helpers was widespread. Anybody's dream soul was believed capable of entering an animal and getting into all sorts of mischief. If an animal pressed by hunters took refuge in a village it was certainly a person and suitable ritual was necessary to readjust matters if the animal was killed, e.g., its tail had to be cut off to keep it from "disappearing." Sometimes it was allowed to go unscathed.[53]

PETTY GODS

Most important of the petty gods were those supposed to bring fertility to childless women. The first two here described had the same face and may have been carved by the same artist, though they came from different parts of the Gio country.

Zei, from Luãple (pl. XIII, *e*), was called to town by a group of men, some of whose wives had failed to conceive. He told the men in public that it was God's will that they had no children, but that he would give them his blessings and then their women would all have babies.

He took some water in his mouth, spewed it on the ground, made paste, and rubbed it on the abdomen of each childless woman. "That is a fine baby I leave in your belly." Then he danced and the women cooked rice for him. The husbands furnished a goat and all the town feasted. The *gɛ* took his part to carry with him. He put his hand in the bowls of rice and said: "That is a fine baby I put into the rice. Let it go into your belly."

Women sometimes came from other towns to get the blessing. The blessed rice was shared by the husbands who had called the *gɛ*. Then the *gɛ* danced again and went away.

The *Zei* mask from Bɔplɛ, a variation of the one above, was worn by a man who came to town when requested. He took dried powdered leaves of Kãi (*Maesobotyra sparsiflora*), a tree which bears much fruit on limbs and trunk, and put them in a pan with water. Childless women washed with the water and prayed to the *gɛ* for babies. All the women in town brought rice, which the *gɛ* took into the bush and shared with the *zo* people. His fee was one cloth.

Three other masks with the same face have already been described. One [54] came to town to present a new baby to the public. The two others [55] were called when a cow was to be killed as a sacrifice to the ancestors at planting time. In time this face would probably have come to be widely worshiped as a goddess of fertility.

Along with one lot of masks there was brought to me an unusual sacred piece of pottery — really two bowls joined together (pl.

---

[51] See also *Gɛa*, p. 24.
[52] Harley, 1941b, p. 22, pl. VII, *e*.
[53] Schwab, 1947, pp. 321 and 355.

[54] See p. 23.
[55] See p. 24.

XV, c). The story told me by the man who brought it was that it had been made about fifty years before by a woman named Madia, who lived in the town of Loli, Zo clan, Gio.

Madia was herself a twin, and was the mother of three pairs of twins. This remarkable family seems to have given rise to a sort of "cult of twins" in that clan.

One of Madia's daughters gave birth to four pairs of twins. Her husband, whose name was Gbli mia, "pot cover," had a mask made for himself as a patron of twins, and called the mask *Kpɛ gɛ*. Whenever his wife gave birth to twins the man put on his mask and danced in town. *Kpɛ gɛ* was a "good" *gɛ*. When he danced all the people brought him small presents and congratulated him.

When the twins were old enough to walk, Gbli mia killed a chicken as a sacrifice to the mask, and each twin was given a leg of the chicken to eat. This would "make their legs strong." In that locality twins were considered good luck, an opinion which is very unusual in the country as a whole.

The twin pots were made for the twins to eat from. In this example, the pot at one end was larger than the other. This variation was explained by the fact that this set of pots was made for a pair of mixed twins, and the larger pot was for the boy twin, the smaller for the girl.

At the time the twin pots were brought to me, I was told that the grandmother, Madia, was still living, and that the grandchildren were already adults. The owner of the mask, Gbli mia had died. I believe his mask was brought to me and is somewhere in the collection, but I cannot now identify it.

Vlɔ ya gɛ, from Duoplɛ (Gio), chewed certain leaves and spewed them on the door sill of a childless woman, first rubbed some of the paste on his forehead, then on the woman's forehead as she sat just inside the door. He promised that she would have a baby. If she did he visited her again and named the baby *Pea sɛ*, "good face." Then he demanded a sacrifice of a sheep or a goat. A cloth was acceptable as a substitute.

Z'na gɛ, from Maabɔ (Gio), was a mask that was not worn. The *zo* who was its keeper was called by childless women. He took the mask to their town, washed it in water, then told the women to wash themselves with the same water. Their husbands watched the procedure. Five or ten women might wash in the same water. Each one of them then brought some rice. One of them brought a chicken and presented it to the mask, saying: "We have no children. We have called *Z'na gɛ*. He will make us get children." Then they presented the rice to the mask. The *zo* then killed the chicken and rubbed some blood on the mask. The women cooked the chicken with rice. The *zo* offered a bit to the mask and called all the people of the town to eat. Everyone, including the *zo*, ate some.

Another mask from the Gio country was described in *Notes on the Poro*.[56] It was prayed to by the midwife and the pregnant women for fine babies and easy delivery. Here again the mask was washed and the women washed with the same water. They made a thank offering to this mask after the baby was born. This mask had a woman's face with two breasts carved on the forehead.[57]

Zena, meaning "God" (Gio) (pl. XIII, a), blessed people and predicted good fortune. This mask had the face of a woman but it was worn by a man. He promised babies. Women cut off bits of their hair and worked it into the headdress of the mask. He went to the waterside, got a pan of water, and took it to the center of town without looking back. Childless women then dipped their hands in it, rubbed it on their bodies, and prayed: "Let me have a baby." A baby born to one of them was named *Zena*. Then they brought rice, which was cooked by a *zo* woman. Everyone in town had to eat some of it. No one was allowed to leave town on the day *Zena* was expected.

Gba gɛ, "dog spirit," from Tāwiɛ (Gio), was kept by the owner of the land and was probably similar to *Gɔ gɛ* in Mano country. He decreed, "No one may take a cutlass to cut farm until you bring my rice." The people brought him ten hampers of rice and a goat, which was sacrificed so that no one would cut himself or anyone else during the farm cutting. The *gɛ* told them no one would get hurt. Then they brought a white chicken and a hamper of white

---

[56] Harley, 1941b, p. 29.

[57] Harley, 1941b, pl. XI, d.

cola nuts to thank him in advance for protecting them.

When they had finished cutting all their farms the women brought five hampers of rice, one goat, and one white chicken. The *gɛ* sacrificed the animals for good crops, then told the women to go plant their rice, promising them good crops.[58]

Sie da gɛ, from Bɔplɛ (Gio), also functioned at farm-cutting time. When a man was ready to burn his farm he went to this *gɛ* and told him. The *gɛ* gave him a leaf to chew, with oil, and spew out on the spot where he planned to start the fire. Then the *gɛ* said, "Take the fire away from my heart." The man had to promise to make a pot of palm kernel oil for the *gɛ* after he burned his farm.

Kluɛ gɛ, from Luāple (Gio) (pl. X, *b*), was supposed to come to town and sing before anyone could harvest and eat new rice. The people had to bring him some first. Then they all ate a little and after that everyone could eat of the new crop.[59]

Blɛ gɛ also demanded new rice in return for having helped drive away the rice birds which were a pest everywhere.

Gbɛa, "wild goose," from Ziali (Gio), was a patron of fishermen and made medicine for them to put in the water. He went with them to the catch. Some men worked under water with elongated dip nets held under one arm. Others drove fish toward the nets, diving and splashing about. They gave the *gɛ* one fish out of every ten. The medicine stupified the fish so they were easily caught.

Gbu, from Bɛinwie, near Dananae, was not worn but carried and put on some leaves near the river where men went to catch fish. Any fish caught was shown to the mask. All were cleaned on the spot and the "belly" parts put in a pot for the keeper of the mask. When the men returned to town the women cooked the fish, furnishing some rice "for the mask." The keeper and his son ate this rice cooked with the fish livers and cleanings.

Sɔ̄gɛ, from Bɔplɛ (Gio), was the hunters' patron. Its keeper washed the mask with water containing certain leaves, then washed the hunter's dog with the water. The dog was thereby protected from snakebite or other bad luck.

If the hunter made a kill he gave the heart to the keeper of the mask.

Sometimes the hunters would also pray to this mask, spewing water out of their mouths onto it and asking for good luck.

Yi lo gɛ, "running water" (Gio), made "medicine water" for various people — for hunters, trappers, and fishermen — to give them good luck. When a chief was about to go on a journey this *gɛ* gave him medicine water to rub on his body, saying, "If any man makes witch for me let his own witch kill him." When a man was ready to cut farm the *gɛ* would make medicine water, take it and sprinkle it on the spot where farm was to be cut so the crop would be good. This medicine water was called *Gbɔ gbea*. Fees to be paid were the blood and heart of any animal killed by the hunter, a hamper of new rice from the farmer, a sheep or a goat from the chief who went on a journey. All these fees were divided among the *zo*'s of the town and eaten in the bush.

A Gio man once brought a mask which had belonged to his grandfather, who was chief of the hunters in his clan. The man did not know its name. The hunters used to bring it out when they went after a Bongo antelope. They put it on some leaves and danced around it. Then its keeper "threw cola" to find out whether or not they were likely to see a Bongo. If the cola fell right, each hunter would then chew one of the cola nuts and spew it onto the mask. Then they went out to hunt.

The Bongo is a very wary animal and hard to kill. A successful hunter must tell all the assembled hunters afterwards every detail of the kill, exactly how he stalked it. This was done as they gathered around the carcass. If he left out any detail they would never kill another one, because the spirit of the animal must be convinced that it had been outwitted.

The carcass belonged to the chief. No common man could claim such meat. The chief divided it according to definite rules.

Di wi was the gate-keeper of the diviners' Bush (see below). The entrance fee was one chicken.

Dɛ gɛ, from Diali (Gio) (pl. VI, *f*), the diviners' patron, tested the wits of the boys in the Poro school. When the diviners met in a

---

[58] See *Bɔ*, Harley, 1941b, p. 25.

[59] See Harley, 1941b, p. 26.

certain place in the Poro Bush, the "drum" beaten was a human skull. The masked and costumed figure sat over one end of a concealed tunnel or hollow log through which ran a long string. A neophyte would bring this gε a white chicken, which he put under his foot while he tied the string to its legs. Then the chicken disappeared, drawn into the tunnel by a man concealed at the other end of the string. This man killed the chicken and threw it over the bushes to fall at the feet of the gε. The conundrum was put to the neophyte: "Who killed my chicken?" The boy had to discover the answer for himself or pay six bracelets.

This gε also danced in town when the diviner had reason to rejoice over the good fortune supposed to have resulted from following his advice. When he was through dancing, the diviner gave him a brass anklet.

Kunu gε, "the owl," from Bεwi (Krã), was a bad gε, the patron of witches. When his voice was heard at night, the members of the witch cult assembled to "play" and dance. Members were said to specialize in charms for catching or harming enemies or in actual poisoning. This was the only really bad gε in the whole collection. This cult was unknown in the Mano country.

PORTRAIT MASKS

As stated at the beginning of this discussion, masks were often portraits. Here are a few of the portraits with definite histories to illustrate how portrait masks became petty gods as "recent ancestors." At least, the people represented were still remembered as human beings and had not yet become merely masks (pl. XII).

To be slightly inconsistent, I want to refer first to the mask, Gɔ gε, supposed to be the founder of the Poro. It has been conventionalized until its fearsome characteristics outshine its human features, but the tradition is that the mummy still exists in Loma country to the northwest of the Mano people. The ritual of initiation of a wearer of the mask in that country includes the laying of the mummy's hands on the head of the new "priest." [60]

The great warrior whose mask became a sort of god of war has already been mentioned, as well as the mother of three great fighters who was similarly venerated.[61]

Ma die (pl. XII, e) was remembered by the Gεh people. "She was a woman of so generous a reputation that she was immortalized by a mask. The wearer danced at the time of farm cutting while the women cooked for the men cutting the farm. The wearer sang of the fame of Ma die, who cooked a pot of rice that never got empty. This was to please the spirit of Ma die so all would have plenty to eat and the farm would be fruitful." [62]

Nya wɔ was a very popular young woman. When she was about to die, she begged that a mask should be made for her so her friends would not forget her. This was done before she died. She saw it and was satisfied (pl. XIII, b).

Gɔ gbi gε [63] was a mask made in honor of a man famous for the amount of cola nuts he consumed. His mask became a collector of cola nuts for the Poro boys.

Sie gε [64] (pl. VIII, j) was the name of a mask made in honor of a man who was both greedy and generous. He collected huge supplies for the Poro. When he died the people made this mask. They prayed to it when they went to plant rice, asking for fertility and plenty.

Mε ma gε [65] was a mask made in honor of a boy artist, famous for his skill in carving masks. He was teacher of the art, and since this mask carved by one of his pupils is of very fine quality, it is unfortunate that his art cannot be carried on today.

Other portraits include the fine masks of mutilated faces which became petty gods of medicine.

Gε Na was the name given to the mask (pl. I, c) made in honor of a young woman who became the wife of a slave brought as a living sacrifice to Nana gε. Here we have a beautiful mask which was the "wife" of a very powerful gε. Both these masks are on display in the Peabody Museum.

[60] Harley, 1941b, p. 27.
[61] See p. 3.
[62] Harley, 1941b, pp. 22-23.
[63] Harley, 1941b, p. 21.
[64] Harley, 1941b, p. 23, pl. VII, a.
[65] Harley, 1941b, p. 26, pl. IX, b.

The little *mā's* have already been described as partly portraits of their owners. There were also small replicas of big masks, made when a big one became worm-eaten or was destroyed by fire. It was always a miniature of the big one, and was in a way a portrait of *it*; for it was made so that the dispossessed spirit of the big one would have a resting place where it would feel at home.

Ma bɔa, "what thing do I lack?" was immortalized by her portrait carved on the front of the handle of a ceremonial spoon made about 1860 in Glai in the Krã country. On the back of the handle is the portrait of *Nying gli*, "dry your tears," the favorite girl first to be called by *Ma bɔa* when she needed help to prepare a feast for all the people. This Janus spoon [66] was carved at the request of *Ma bɔa's* husband by a young man named Mɛa wɔ̃. As a carver of masks his cult name was *Zena* (God).

The spoon was used at public feasts. The head woman would announce the feast: "My name is *Ma bɔa*. *Nying gli* is here to help me. No one will go hungry today."

Another ceremonial spoon, *Wɛ ya*,[67] 28 inches long, was made about 1830 in memory of *Wɛ ya*. It was first used by Mɛ yi kɔ who died about 1850. She used to say: "My name is *Wɛ ya*. Anyone who has no food will come out of his house and eat with me today. When we have a feast it is not good for anyone to go hungry." She gave a brass ring to the chief and salt to all the poor people, then cooked the rice.

When the feast was prepared she took first some of the food in the spoon and offered it to the spirits, then passed the spoon around to all the people, who pretended to take and eat with the ancestral spirits, but actually they took none. After that, all could eat. One old man and one old woman spoke for the crowd, thanking *Wɛ ya*. The chief gave Mɛ yi kɔ a cloth, which she "gave to the spoon."

These portraits on spoon handles were not quite masks but were very similar in function. They were ancestral soul-pieces used in public ritual.

DANCERS, MINSTRELS, AND CLOWNS

People speak of fine *gɛ's* who dance and sing on public occasions. Other *gɛ's* who dance include good *gɛ's* who share their gifts with all the people and bad *gɛ's* who are never satisfied and beat people. Most of these dancers have female faces, but the bad ones have faces of demons or animals.

Occasionally, two of them appear together, one acting as speaker or interpreter for the other. There has been little development, however, of *gɛ's* as dramatic actors. The costumes are too cumbersome, and it was strictly taboo for the actors to reveal themselves as human beings.

Zɔ gɛ, "the stutterer," and his speaker appeared together, both masked (pl. IX, g and h). The stutterer tried and tried to say what he wanted, then finally the speaker said it for him and he came out with, "Yes, that is what I was trying to say." They made it so funny that they got more than they asked for.

At harvest time another pair played in town. One represented a sleeping rice-bird, the other a spirit driving the flies away from the sleeping rice-bird, he himself falling asleep frequently.

Bea gɛ visited a new grandfather, asking his woman to give him the crusts of scorched rice left in the pots from the feast celebrating the arrival of a new baby. The woman ridiculed him and even cursed with impunity. He took it good naturedly, laughed, and joined in the fun.

Kupa ya gɛ was the portrait of a flirtatious young woman, worn by a man who went about complaining in a woman's voice: "My fashion is bad. My husband beats me. I can't stay in any place long. Palm wine makes me vexed. Rice makes me mad." People drove him from place to place, laughing.

Di va had a big mouth, which was his name. He was a noted teller of tall tales and made much out of nothing. Sometimes he came to town when people were quarreling. His exaggerations of the case were so ludicrous that the quarrel was forgotten. If there were any weapons involved, he took them with him.

---

[66] A similar spoon is figured in *Notes on the Poro*, pl. XIII, *a*, and Schwab, 1947, fig. 71, *b* and *c*.

[67] Schwab, fig. 70, *c* and *d*.

Mini sɔ gɛ sang for women beating rice to the rhythm of his singing, and in this way so lightened the work, keeping them amused with his song.

Zã gɛ, from Butulu (Gio), sang for women to dance. This mask had the face of a man and was worn by a man. He sang in front of each house in turn and expected a small gift from each householder.

Gbing gɛ, from Maabɔ (Gbeali, Gio), went from town to town, and sang inside the houses, accompanied by various musical instruments. The door was shut and presents were collected for him by an assistant outside the door.

Zo gɛ, from Bɔplɛ (Gio), danced in town, thanked the old men for their wisdom, and urged them to take good care of the young women. Then he thanked all husbands for taking such good care of their wives. He expected three chickens and one bucket of rice. The food was cooked and eaten by all husbands. Some of the chicken's blood was rubbed on the mask. The *gɛ* was given a fee of one hundred cola nuts.

Nɔ a nya, from Butulu (Krã), a fine dancer, asked for a dash from each person; but if a man had nothing to give, the *gɛ* would give him something. Finally he danced before the chief, asking for something to eat. This he divided among all those present. He was called a "good *gɛ*."

Zi mia gã, "traveler can't see," from Bauldi (Gio), was so-called because a traveler would become so intrigued by this *gɛ's* dancing and singing that he would forget about his journey, no longer be a traveler, but stay to see and talk about what he had seen.

There are several masks who all danced and played at festive occasions [68] (pl. XIV, *b*).

Gbɔlɔ gɛ, from Kãplɛ (Gio), danced and played with boys not yet initiated. He received a dash of fresh palm kernels. The son of a big man would sometimes kill a chicken or a sheep for all the boys to eat. Blood was put on the mask.[69]

A boy would sometimes dress himself all over with plantain leaves and dance to amuse his elders.[70]

Dɔ mia, "chief" (Mano), was a clown who carried a piece of rope and pretended to beat people who could not sing well. Everybody laughed at his antics. He tried to show them how to sing, but he couldn't sing at all well himself. Anyone who did not give him a dash had to sing to the tempo of the *gɛ's* whip, pay money, or take a flogging. There was a lot of horseplay. This *gɛ* was for the young men.

Klua gɛ, "the chimpanzee" (pl. IX, *j*), from Bòelu (Krã), came to town dancing boisterously. He carried a whip or stick with two iron prongs, threw things around, and beat people. His rough clowning amused some people very much. He might even take up a mortar and throw it through the door of a house. If he hurt anyone, or even drew blood with his iron hooks no one complained. He was easily vexed and went off in a rage, even chasing people into their houses. People barred the door if there was a baby inside. Finally the chief bribed him to go away. He was something to talk about for days afterwards.

This *gɛ* also taught manners in the Poro school by always doing the wrong thing.

The "long *gɛ*"[71] was not masked but had his face covered with a black net so he could see well while no one could see his face. Like masked *gɛ's*, he was completely covered by his costume. He danced on stilts so long that he sat on the roof of a house to rest. He was called by the chief purely as an entertainer to honor a distinguished guest or amuse people on a holiday. He was surprisingly agile and acrobatic.

SUMMARY

The *gɛ's* had many faces and almost as many functions, but there were certain fundamental qualities shared by all. They were inanimate masks manipulated by human beings, who were in turn manipulated by the spirits supposed to dwell within the inanimate masks. Some were portraits of recent or distant dead, others were characterizations. The characterizations were partly human, partly animal — deliberately representing the combined *mana* or essential

---

[68] See also Harley, 1941b, p. 22 and pl. V, *g*.
[69] Schwab, 1947, p. 364.
[70] Schwab, 1947, fig. 86, *a–d*.

[71] Schwab, 1947, fig. 86, *e*; also, Harley, 1941b, pl. XIV, *c* and *d*.

power of both. The essential power was thought of as emanating from the ancestral spirits, both human and animal; for tradition included animal ancestors, animals as brothers, and men who could actually change themselves into animals of the forest at will.

In use the *gɛ's* exercised all the functions necessary for control of society on the religious, the executive, and the judicial levels, reinforcing their authority by oracular responses. The human manipulation of these inanimate objects was so regulated by custom that abuse of power was kept at a minimum. The "owner" or high priest-judge could send *gɛ's* as his messengers, police, magistrates, extortioners, or entertainers; but he himself was subject to the will of the people through the council of elders.

If the wearer of a mask died, his place was taken by another and the mask continued to function without interruption. Thus the equilibrium of the community suffered a minimum disturbance, being that occasioned by the loss of an individual not especially important as such, rather than the loss of an important official whose individual character could not be replaced, whose successor might be activated by policies divergent from those already established. The mask thus provided continuity of authority, regardless of the personal attributes of the current wearer.

Even the individual loss was minimized by keeping the man's death secret for some time, probably until all necessary adjustments had been effected. The tendency was for the community to carry on as though nothing had happened.

The fixed functions of the *gɛ's* extended, with some local variation, across the borders of the clan or tribe, and even across language barriers. They even exerted control over warfare. This was carried to such an extent that arbitration through the great *gɛ's* was more final than the results of war. This regulation of war, reaching beyond the limits of clan or tribe, marked the beginning of intertribal unity.

Since Gɔ, the Creator, was chief of the town of the dead, the great ancestral masks became linked with the name, Gɔ, and called Gɔ gɛ, "God spirit." As an oracle it was supreme judge, but it needed a good deal of human help. The mask and its keeper were, however, inseparably united in spirit by mutual responsibility to the people on the one hand and to the ancestors on the other, both by custom and by tradition of the Poro and Sandɛ. The sense of their responsibility, in the minds of the people, was kept alive by the unknown mysteries of sickness and calamity, by the sense of unknown danger lurking in the forest. This sense of danger was accentuated deliberately by the masked *gɛ's* (who were supposed to live in the forest), by the seclusion in the forest of boys and girls in Poro and Sandɛ, and by trial and execution of criminals in the secret place of the forest.

Such a mask passed from father to son, or to nephew, with a human sacrifice to let the ancestor know that a new priest was in office.

The differences in function of the masks in the various tribes was partly due to the variation in the development of the Poro. The Gio people did not have the Poro as such, only a circumcision Bush. The Gɛh people were basically Gio, but had partly accepted the true Poro from the adjacent Mano people. The Krã were really Half-Grebo with an entirely different system of initiation rites. The Konor were half Mandingo, half Kpɛllɛ, and had a modified form of the Poro. All, however, had *gɛ's*, and these masks were everywhere used to enforce law and order, to intimidate women and children, and to furnish the central figure at any important event or crisis.

The *gɛ's* were seldom, if ever, bad spirits. An occasional clown or prankster appeared and upset things in general; but sickness, calamity, and witchcraft were universally blamed on people — preferably living people. Sometimes poor crops and other such general calamities were blamed on the ancestral spirits and propitiation was directed towards them. There was no evil demon whose character it was to bring calamity unless appeased. Therefore, none of these masks should be called "devils." Yet that is exactly what they are called by English-speaking Liberians. To distinguish them from Satan they are called "country devils." This is another example of the old gods being replaced and becoming "devils," which originally meant "little gods." To the natives, "heathens" were the ones who could not see the *gɛ* — the uninitiated.

CONCLUSION

The mask as a portrait of an individual still living was demonstrated in the case of *Nya wɔ*, who requested that a mask be made in her memory, and saw it before she died. The symbolic *Gɛ Na* from Konor country, while not a portrait, was made to immortalize an incident in which the subject of the mask was still living, as the wife of a living sacrifice or consecrated slave, whose fellow had been eaten as a true sacrifice of propitiation. The small *mā's* were essentially portraits of their owners.

A death mask was regularly made of a great man before he was buried. Some of these became petty gods. The *Gɔ gɛ's* and other masks of similar rank were conventionalized representations of the first grandmaster of the society, though they sometimes represented him as half totem animal or forest demigod. Thus it has been shown that masks of the living as well as those representing the recently dead became objects of worship along with those of traditional heroes.

Masks in the likeness of animals and birds always had features partly human. These undoubtedly came to represent the dual power of the owner of the land and forest animals, and of the animals themselves, totem or otherwise. Masks, whether they were human or half animal, could therefore represent ancestral spirits, and all the evidence collected points to the belief that they possessed this essential soul-substance.

There was also the feeling that a mask was an entity in its own right, and in this sense it was a true fetish according to the present definition.[72]

It was, in practice, a human fetish with a character of its own. The wearer could not act out of character and although he could use his own mind while wearing the mask he was *en rapport* with the spirit of the mask and subconsciously was inspired by his concept of what the mask represented. If he should act out of character, he was liable to swift and final punishment at the hands of the *Ki Gbuo La mi*, who took all these things very seriously.

In the final analysis the ruling force was custom, and as Marett has put it: "Our custom, our whole custom, and nothing but our custom."[73]

Yet there was room for gradual change of this custom. New masks were added to the hierarchy, and so interpretation of custom by a living person was added to the whole, provided that interpretation received sufficient popular approval to perpetuate the individual as a hero or heroine. The function of a mask might also be modified by the interpretation or even the forgetfulness of the owner-priest, or conceivably by the assembly of the elders; but on the whole a mask had a remarkably well determined character, which was often intertribal in distribution.

While public opinion, acting through the elders, did not hesitate to deal the death penalty to anyone who blatantly overstepped the bounds of custom there was, nevertheless, considerable leeway in everyday matters, which enabled the "owner" or *gonola* to be almost a law unto himself.

There was a certain amount of rivalry between these clan leaders,[74] and petty warfare was almost constant so long as it did not interfere with local Poro and Sandɛ sessions.

So strong, however, was the tendency to conform to custom that the rugged individualist was very likely to be eliminated and his "estate" divided among the surviving peers.

So long as he worked within limits prescribed by custom and the inspiration of the ancestral memories that clung to the masks, the "owner" was a grand old man who accepted approaching death complacently, feeling that he, too, would be preserved in the memory of his descendants by having a mask made to him, and that any contribution he had made to the culture of his people would be thereby perpetuated.

With this in mind it is possible to appreciate the tragedy of my old friends, dying off with the feeling that no mask would be made, and turning over their sacred relics to me in the hope that I would provide for them a final and suitable haven — in the Museum!

I can only hope that in this paper I have, to some extent, interpreted the gist of the matter, and that these old masks will lie in the vaults of the Museum enveloped by a suitable aura of appreciation.

---

[72] See Harley, 1941a, pp. 142, 181–83.
[73] Marett, 1932, p. 142.
[74] See poisoning of rival *zo's*, Harley, 1941a, p. 147.

REFERENCES

HARLEY, GEORGE W.
- 1941a. Native African Medicine. Harvard University Press. Cambridge.
- 1941b. Notes on the Poro in Liberia, *Peabody Museum of Harvard University, Papers*, vol. XIX, no. 2. Cambridge.

MARETT, ROBERT R.
- 1932. Faith, Hope and Charity in Primitive Religion. The Macmillan Co. New York.

SCHWAB, GEORGE
- 1947. Tribes of the Liberian Hinterland. *Peabody Museum of Harvard University, Papers*, vol. XXXI. Cambridge.

PEABODY MUSEUM CATALOGUE NUMBERS FOR SPECIMENS ILLUSTRATED IN PLATES

Frontispiece
(Dr. Harley's property)

Plate I
a, (Dr. Harley's property)
b, 48-36-50/7345
c, 48-36-50/7382
e, 40-34-50/4600
f, 37-77-50/2851
g, 40-34-50/4601
h, 40-34-50/4603

Plate II
a, (Dr. Harley's property)
b, (Dr. Harley's property)
c, 48-36-50/7370
d, (Dr. Harley's property)
e, 48-36-50/7340
f, (Dr. Harley's property)
g, (Dr. Harley's property)
h, (Dr. Harley's property)
i, From arrow clockwise: 48-36-50/7308, 7327, 7332, 7338, 7334, 7330, 7336, 7328, 7335, 7329, 7331, 7337, 7333, 7339
j, 48-36-50/7289
k, 48-36-50/7326, 7325, 7364, 7365, 7321, 7324, 7322, 7320, 7323

Plate III
a, 48-36-50/7287
b, 48-36-50/7295
c, 48-36-50/7293
d, 48-36-50/7313
e, (Dr. Harley's property)
f, 48-36-50/7301
g, 48-36-50/7299
h, 48-36-50/7310
i, 48-36-50/7294
j, 48-36-50/7316
k, 48-36-50/7302
l, 48-36-50/7304
m, 48-36-50/7305
n, 48-36-50/7304
o, 48-36-50/7306
p, 48-36-50/7307

Plate IV
a, 48-36-50/7315
b, 37-77-50/3013
c, 37-77-50/2993
d, 48-36-50/7290
e, 37-77-50/2824
f, 40-34-50/4584

Plate V
a, 48-36-50/7381
b, 40-34-50/4588
c, 48-36-50/7379
d, 40-34-50/4580
e, 48-36-50/7344
f, 40-34-50/4583

Plate VI
a, 48-36-50/7353
b, 37-77-50/2744
c, (Dr. Harley's property)
d, 48-36-50/7372
e, 48-36-50/7373
f, 48-36-50/7385

Plate VII
a, 48-36-50/7351
b, 37-77-50/3024
c, 48-36-50/7360
d, 37-77-50/3017
e, 40-34-50/4586
f, 48-36-50/7343

Plate VIII
a, 37-77-50/3000
b, 37-77-50/2876
c, 37-77-50/2820
d, 37-77-50/3008
e, 37-77-50/2653
f, 37-77-50/2657
g, 37-77-50/2798
h, 37-77-50/2966
i, 37-77-50/2788
j, 37-77-50/2818
k, 37-77-50/2797
l, 37-77-50/3020

Plate IX
a, 37-77-50/2699
b, 48-36-50/7349
c, 37-77-50/2649
d, 37-77-50/2991
e, 37-77-50/2760
f, 37-77-50/2799
g, 37-77-50/2708
h, 37-77-50/2707
i, 37-77-50/2989
j, 37-77-50/2969
k, 37-77-50/2881
l, 37-77-50/2647

Plate X
a, 48-36-50/7352
b, 48-36-50/7359
c, 48-36-50/7341
d, 48-36-50/7363
e, 48-36-50/7346
f, 48-36-50/7319
g, 48-36-50/7387
h, 48-36-50/7376
i, 48-36-50/7362

Plate XI
a, 48-36-50/7350
b, 48-36-50/7318
c, 48-36-50/7389
d, 48-36-50/7384
e, 37-77-50/2982
f, 48-36-50/7378
g, 48-36-50/7383
h, (Dr. Harley's property)
i, 48-36-50/7317

Plate XII
a, (Dr. Harley's property)
b, (Dr. Harley's property)
c, 37-77-50/2756
d, 37-77-50/2654
e, 37-77-50/2784
f, 37-77-50/3019
g, 37-77-50/2858
h, 48-36-50/7354
i, 48-36-50/7371
j, 48-36-50/7348

Plate XIII
a, 40-34-50/4582
b, 37-77-50/3005
c, 48-36-50/7388
d, 48-36-50/7386
e, 48-36-50/7357
f, 48-36-50/7347
g, 37-77-50/2672
h, (Dr. Harley's property)
i, 48-36-50/7390

Plate XIV
a, (Dr. Harley's property)
b, 37-77-50/2755
c, 48-36-50/7377
d, (Dr. Harley's property)
e, (Dr. Harley's property)
f, 48-36-50/7288
g, (Dr. Harley's property)
h, 48-36-50/7358
i, 48-36-50/7356

Plate XV
a, 48-36-50/7374
b, 48-36-50/7375
c, 48-36-50/7391

PEABODY MUSEUM PAPERS   VOL. XXXII, No. 2, PLATE I

a, Entertainer who may be seen by all, Gompa (p. 3). *b*, Mɛ fei gɛ, ancestral mask with headdress (p. 24). *c*, Gɛ Na, portrait mask (p. 20). *d*, Boys' gɛ, wearing mask, in Half-Grebo where masks are not so greatly feared. *e*, Headdress, Gio. *f*, Mano dancer's mask and headdress. *g*, Headpiece with cowrie shells. *h*, Matching belt, both part of gɛ's costume.

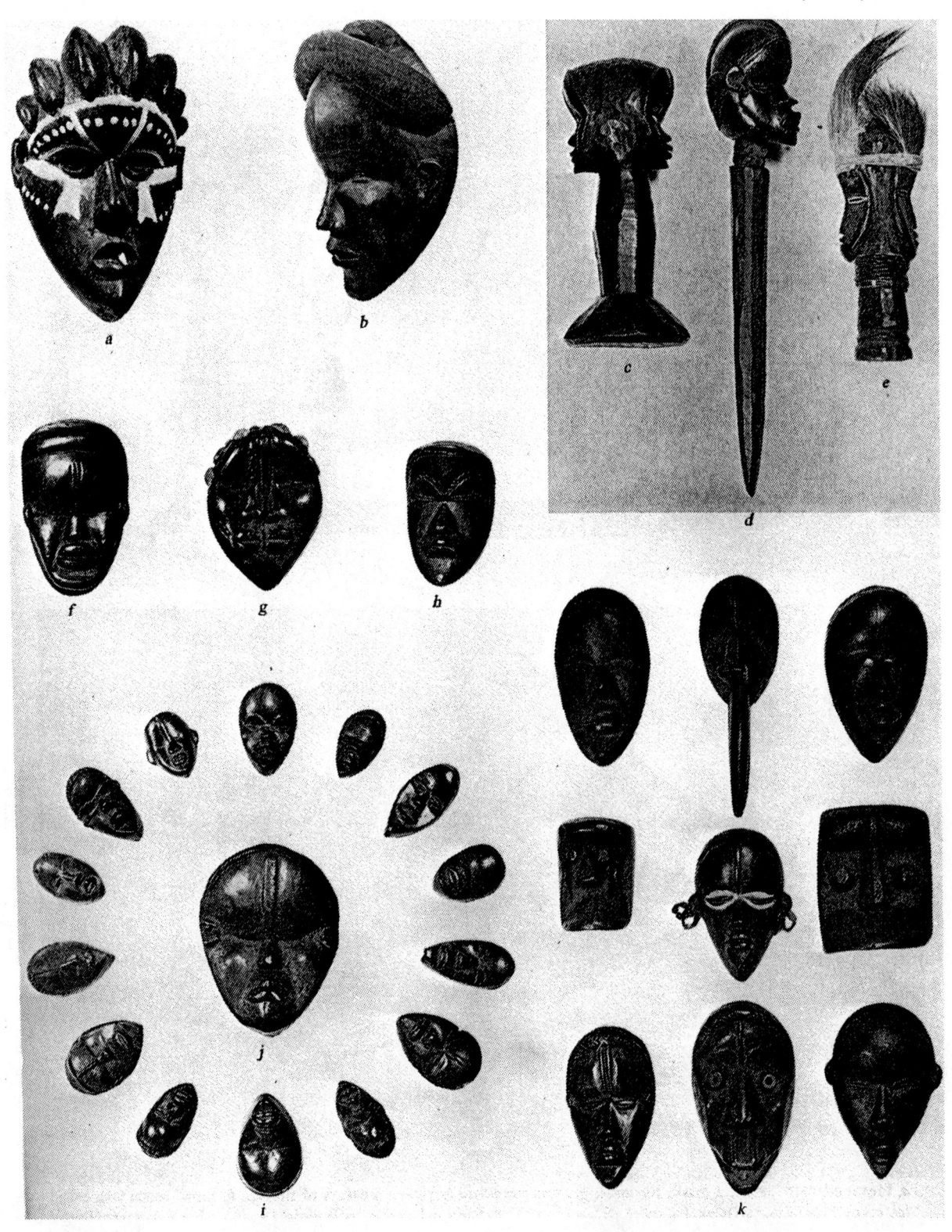

a, Conventionalized portrait mask, Bassa (footnote 41, p. 28). *b*, Conventionalized portrait mask, Krā (footnote 41, p. 28). *c*, Janus handpiece (p. 35). *d*, Mace, carried by *Gɔ gɛ*. *e*, Handpiece belonging to *Wai* (p. 9). *f, h*, and *k*, Replicas of big masks (p. 8). *g*, Twin *mā* (p. 10). *i*, Collection of small *mā's* (p. 10). *j* (in center of *i*), *Yongolo to*, carried from the Poro session by last boy (p. 31), there is some confusion about this mask which may be identical with the great *Mā*.

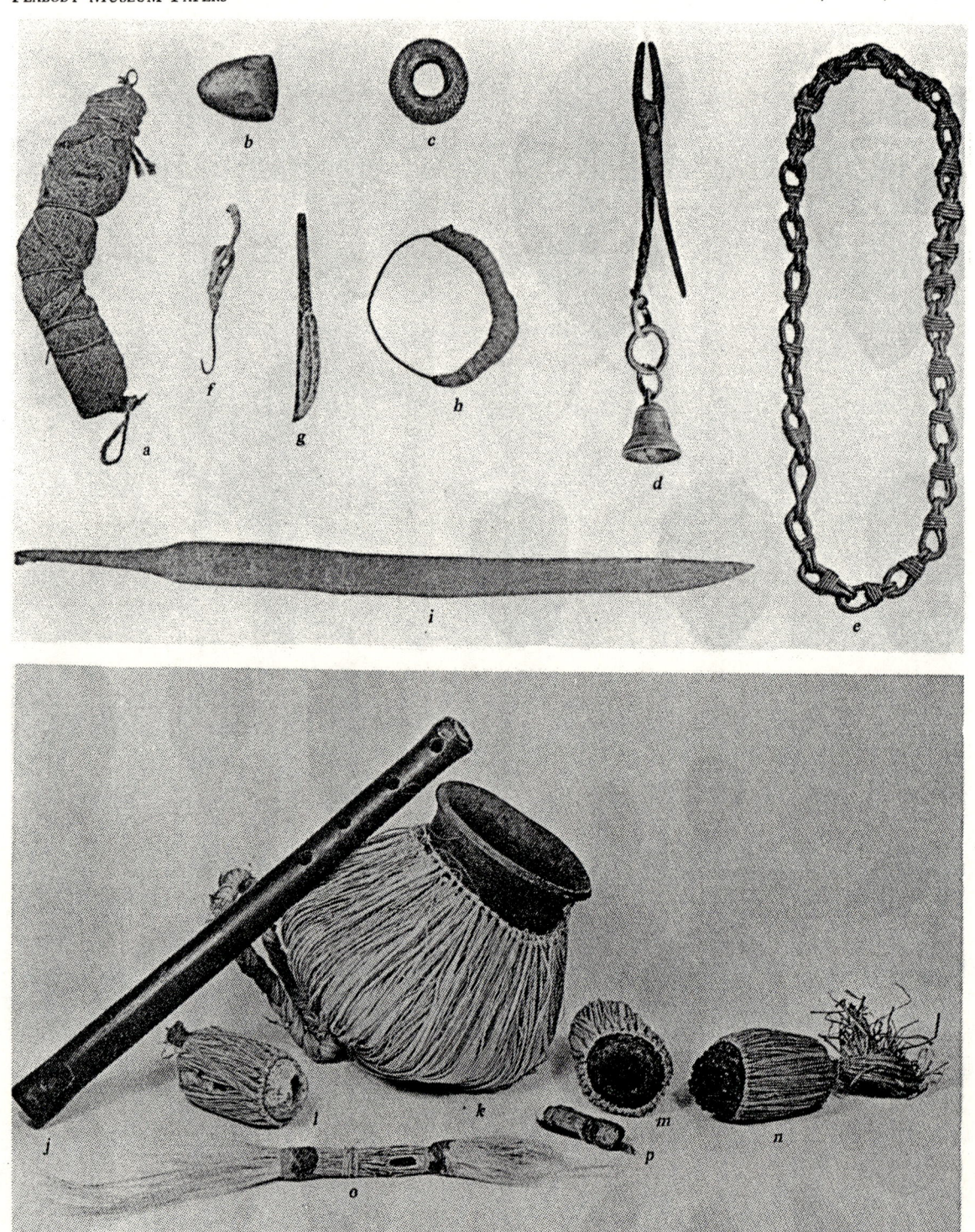

a, Headpad worn under a mask; its name, *gɛ*, was password between wearers of masks. *b*, Small stone adz, called *lai*, owned by *Gonola* (p. 35, footnote 48, and p. 15). *c*, Ring belonging to Zawolo (p. 16). *d*, Messenger-talisman of Zawolo (p. 16). *e*, Brass chain of Zawolo (p. 16). *f*, *g*, Scarifying hook and razor, belonging to Zawolo. *h*, Zawolo's ceremonial armlet (p. 16). *i*, Knife, messenger-talisman of Nya (p. 15). *j-p*, Flute and whistles used to create the voice of the *gɛ* (pp. 14 and 31).

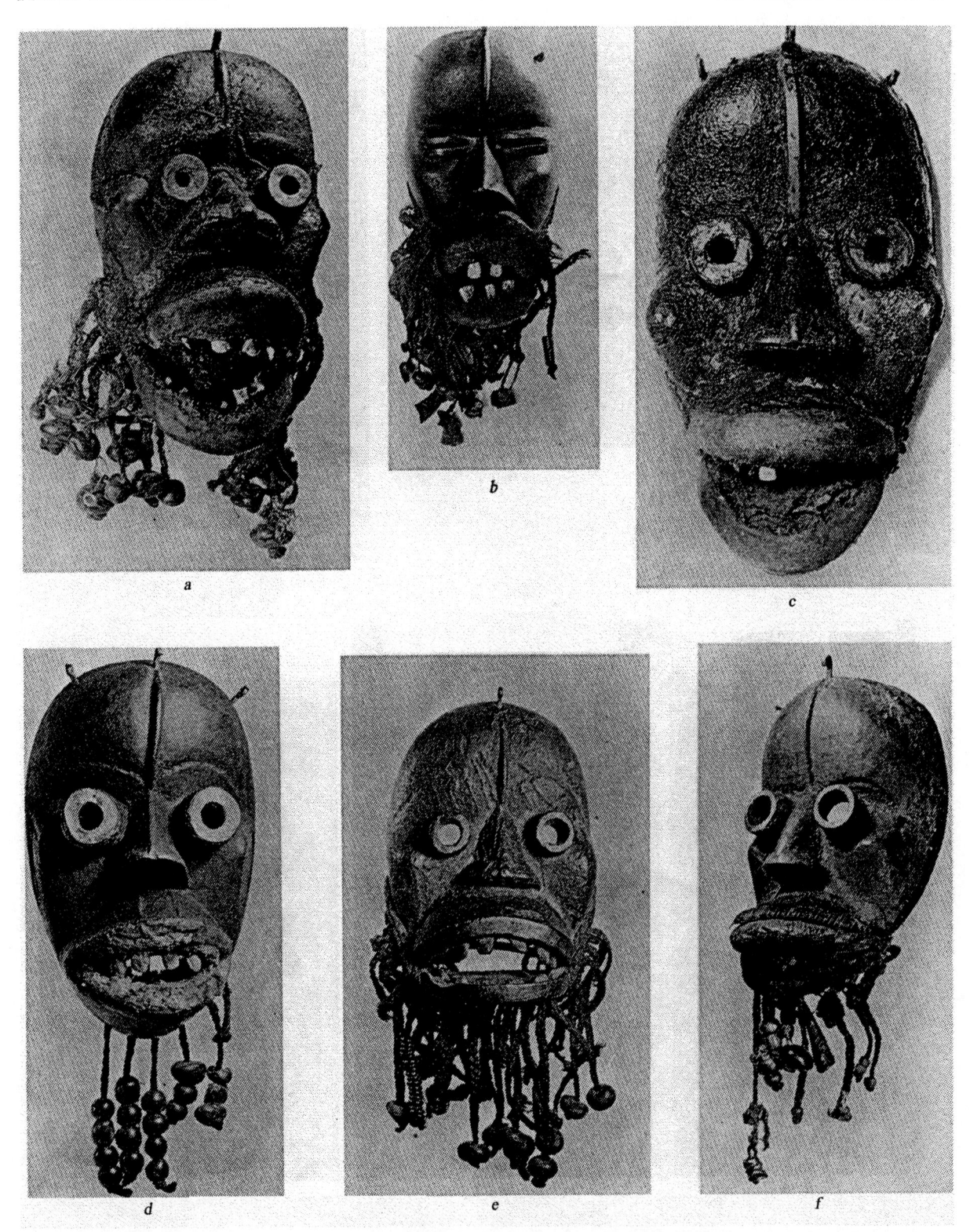

a, *Gɔ gɛ*, mask of Gbana (p. 17). *b*, *Zo zɛ gɛ* (Harley, 1941b, p. 10). *c*, *Blɔ zɛ gɛ* (Harley, 1941b, p. 15). *d*, *Gɔ gɛ*, mask of Nya (p. 14). *e*, *Du gli*, "cow-eater" (Harley, 1941b, p. 23). *f*, Mask of the *Gɔ gɛ* type, history not known.

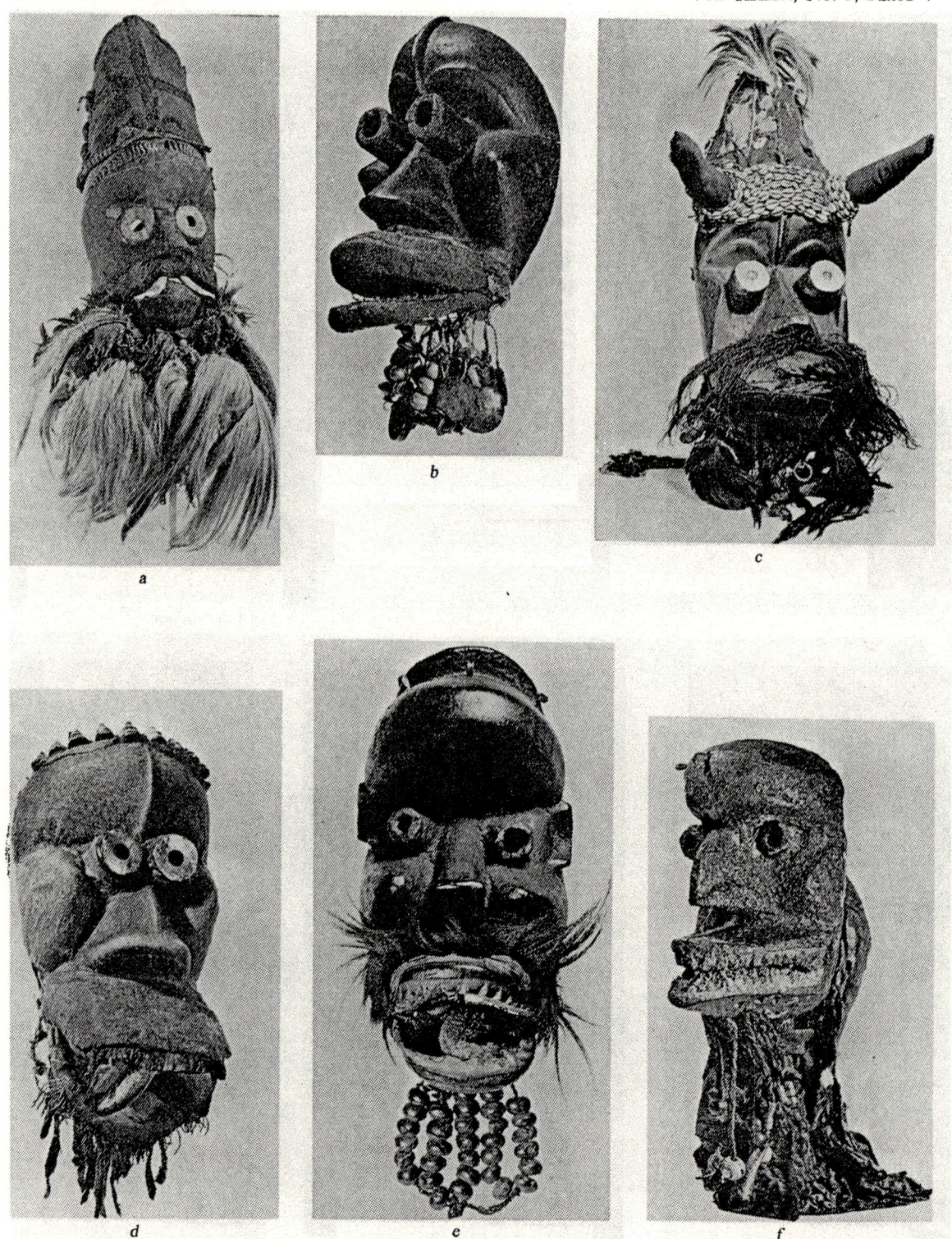

a, Maa va, red felt-covered face and headdress, "speaker" of *Nana gɛ* (p. 22). *b, Zɔ gɛ*, who came to town to stop pestilence (p. 34). *c, Nana gɛ*, a Konor mask with horns and headdress, covered with red felt; the equivalent of *Gɔ gɛ* (p. 20). *d, Gli dɔ gɛ*, judge of the sasswood ordeal, face covered with red cloth (p. 24). *e, Ma va (gɛ va)*, a mask with police functions (p. 21). *f, Zuo wi nu*, broke pots in town for punishment (p. 21).

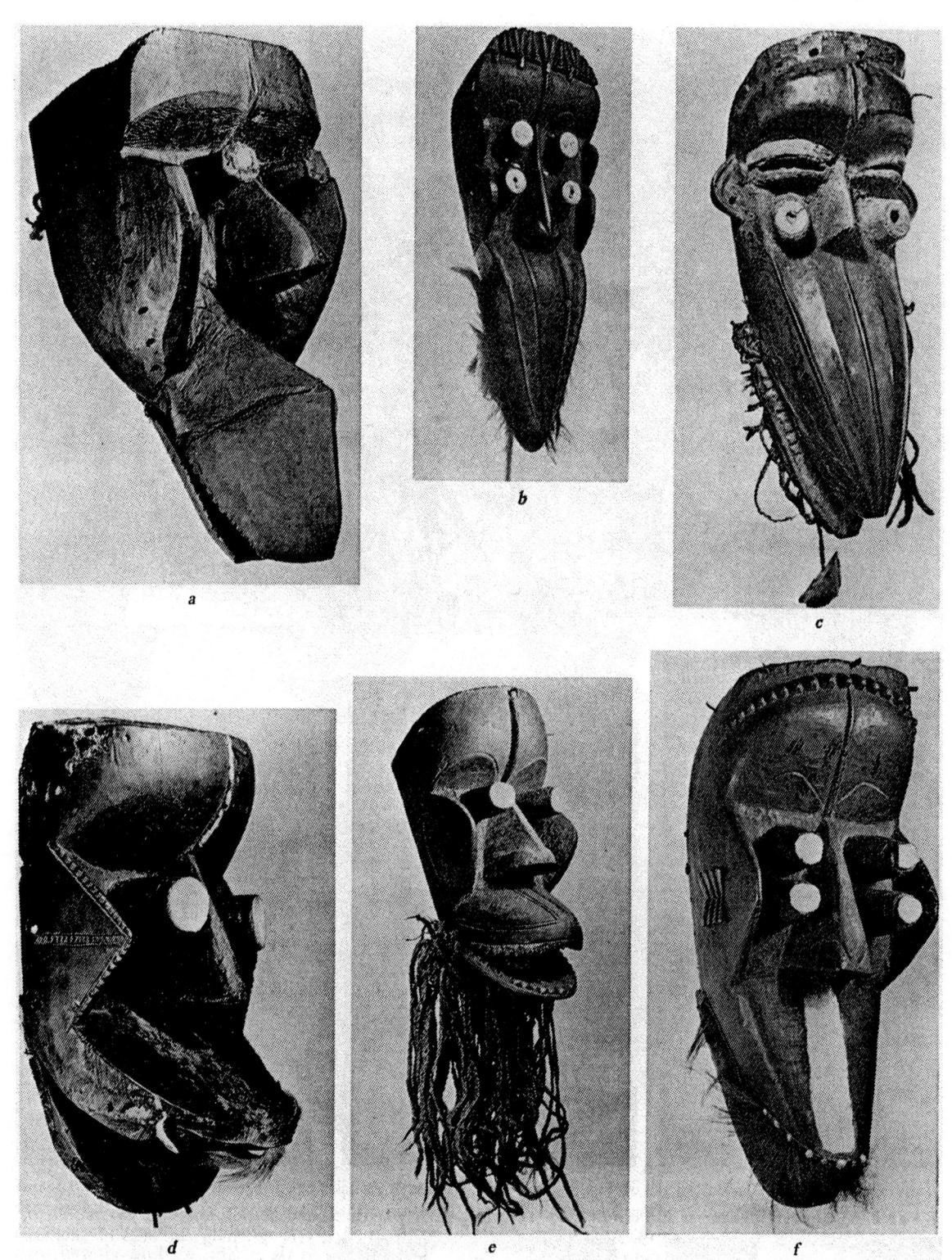

a, Lu gbo biɛ, a judge between lesser *gɛ's* (p. 19). *b, Lu bo biɛ* (p. 35 and Harley, 1941b, p. 19). *c*, Crocodile mask, name and function not known. *d, Kma gɛ*, judge in major disputes (p. 19). *e, Pia sɛ*, danced at planting time (p. 23). *f, Dɛ gɛ*, diviner and judge (p. 38).

a, *Ka da kɛ sɛ*, a powerful teacher and lawgiver (p. 26). *b*, God of war (p. 25 and Harley, 1941b, p. 26). *c*, *Diɛ si*, messenger and "speaker" for *Gɔ gɛ* (p. 22). *d*, *Gɔ gɛ*, "leopard" (p. 35). *e*, *Gbɛ gɛ*, judge in cases of adultery (p. 21). *f*, *Ka gɛ*, "crab," messenger for *Lɔla gɛ* (p. 22).

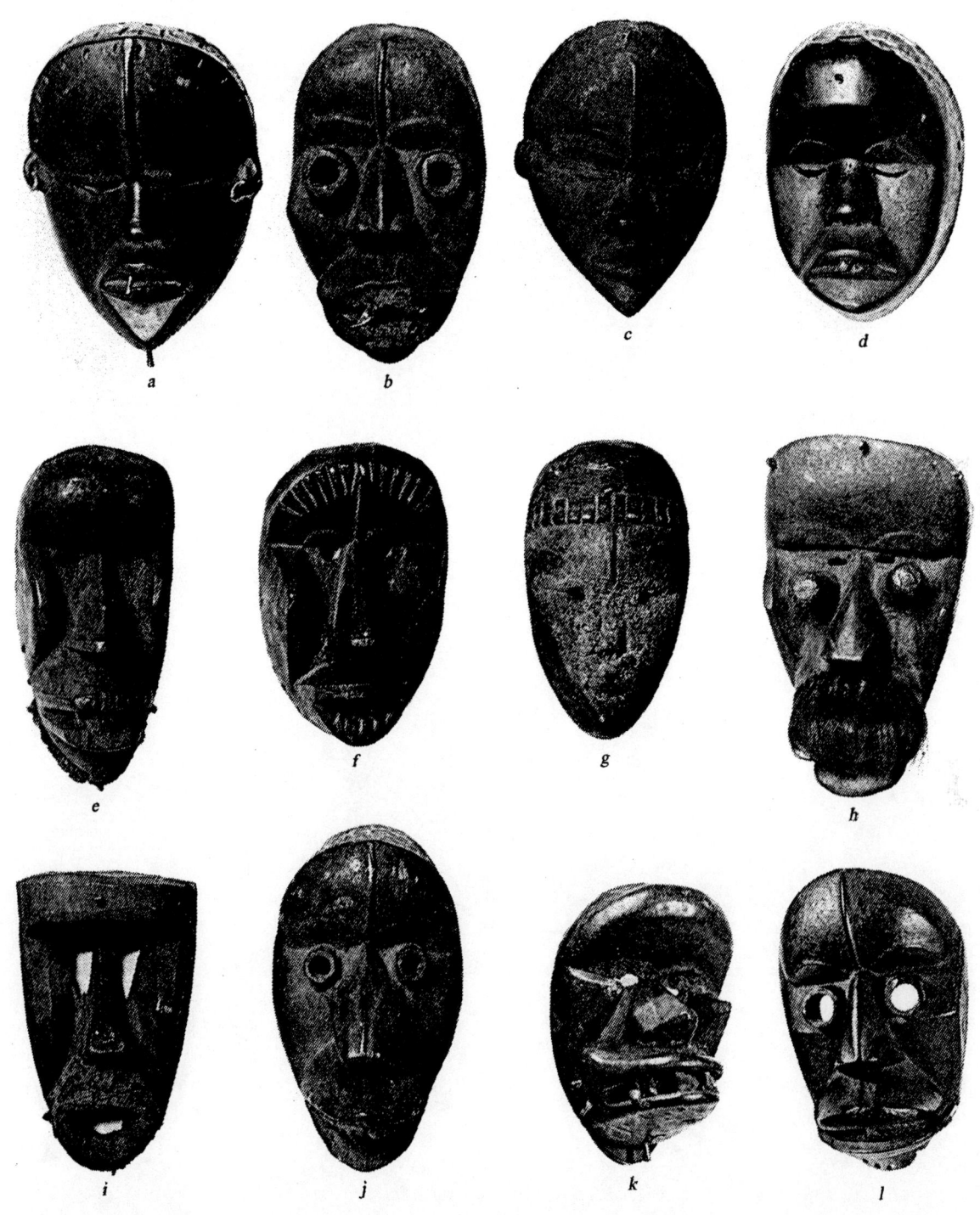

MASKS OF VARIOUS Gɛ's OF THE PORO (pp. 28 ff and Harley, 1941b). *a*, *T'to bli gɛ*, swore boys to secrecy (p. 28). *b*, *Gɛlɛ wi gɛ*, broke stones for Poro fire (p. 28). *c*, *Si kū gɛ*, "smoke catcher," made fire (p. 28). *d*, *Sa yi gɛ*, received boys into the Bush. *e*, *Tɛa bli si*, closed off roads to the Poro (p. 28). *f*, *Dɛ bu gɛ*, carried sacred razor into the Bush (p. 28). *g*, *Bɔ zɛ gɛ*, cut out liver of the sacrifice (p. 28). *h*, *Mi gli gɛ*, Poro executioner. *i*, *Dā ya bɔa*, dressed the boys' wounds (p. 34 and Harley, 1941b, p. 16). *j*, *Sie gɛ*, collected supplies for the Poro session (p. 39). *k*, *Tiɛ bli sai*, attacked and plundered passers-by (Schwab, 1947, p. 90, *b*). *l*, *Gblɔ zɛ gɛ*, "executioner" of boys who broke the most sacred law of the Poro, forbidding contact with women during the period of seclusion (Schwab, 1947, pl. 90, *i*).

PEITY GODS AND PATRONS: *a, b*, Masks commemorating man with facial paralysis, prayed to (p. 34). *c*, Mask prayed to for cure of gangosa (p. 34). *d*, Patron of victims of jaw tumor (p. 34). *e, Dū gɛ*, "coughing spirit," entertainer and instructor (p. 27 and Harley, 1941b, p. 22). *f, Yo gɛ*, patron of rubbing-chalk for rheumatism (Harley, 1941b, p. 23). *g, h*, The stutterer and his "speaker" (p. 40). *i, Dinga*, "duck," settled domestic quarrels (Harley, 1941b, pp. 23–24). *j, Klua gɛ*, patron of chimpanzees (pp. 35, 41, and Harley, 1941b, p. 26). *k*, "The hungry one," collected food for the Poro (Harley, 1941b, p. 17). *l, I yɛ gɛ*, diviner in war (Harley, 1941b, p. 23).

a, Di gɛ, judged palavers between sections (p. 19). *b, Kluɛ gɛ,* "chimp," ate of new rice (p. 38). *c, Nya gɛ,* "rice-bird," a collector of debts (p. 21). *d, Gbā gɛ,* danced at sacrifice to ancestral spirits (p. 23). *e, Ni bli bu gɛ,* "baby-eater," judicial consultant (p. 19). *f, Blɔ gɛ,* god of war, immune against gunshot (p. 25). *g, Siɛ dɔ wana gɛ,* "fire," attended killing of a cow (p. 24). *h, Ldoɛ gɛ,* a judge who stopped fights (p. 20). *i, Bā gɛ,* patron of blacksmiths and judge (p. 19).

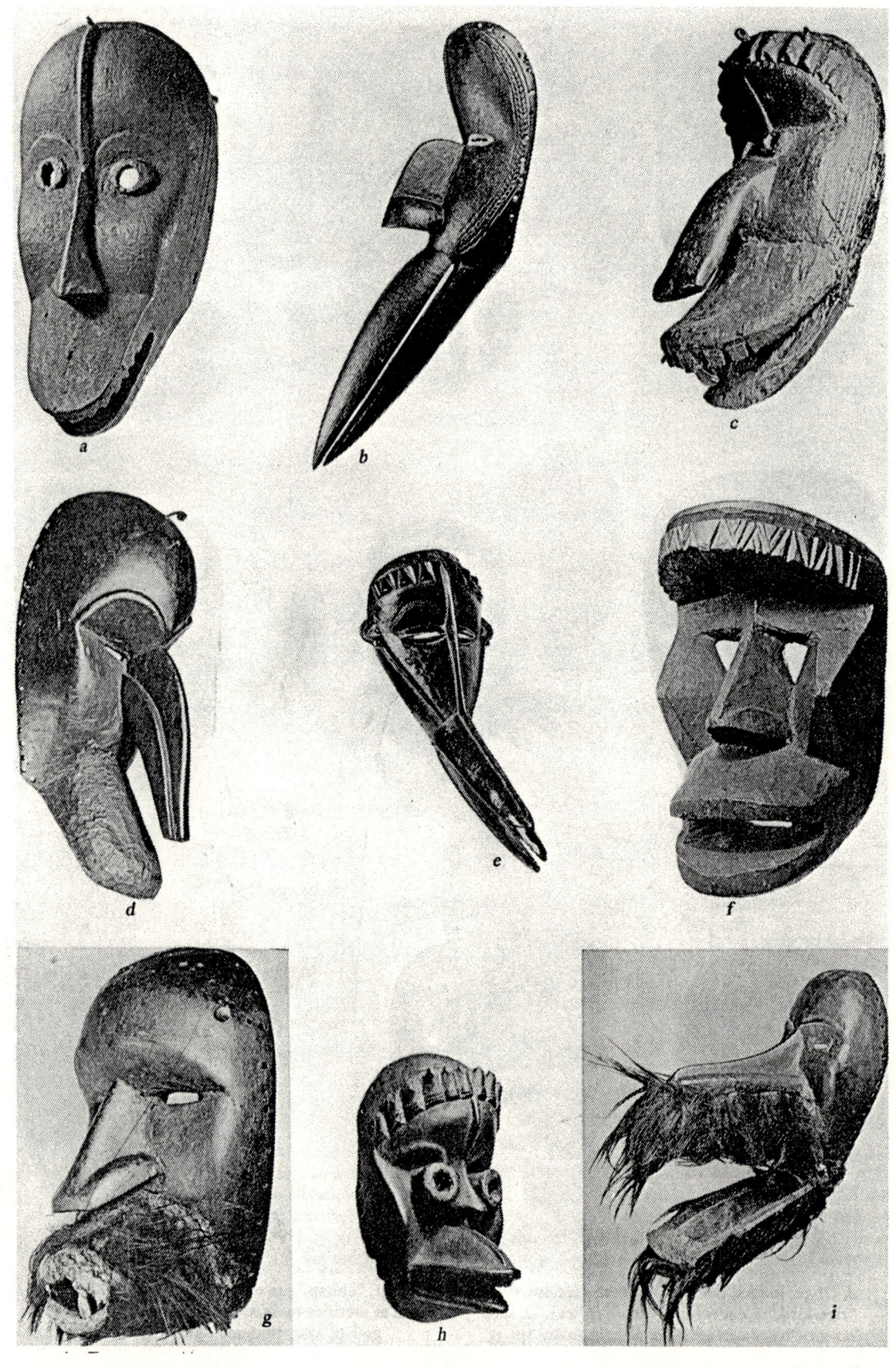

a, *Gbea gɛ*, "crocodile," patron of fisherman (p. 33). *b*, *Mɔ gbɔ gɛ*, collected debts (p. 21). *c*, *Zi bo biɛ*, "road-making elephant" (p. 25). *d*, *Kpo Gɔ*, Poro judge, much respected (p. 30). *e*, Kpala, "lesser hornbill," a judge (p. 36). *f*, A judge from the Konor tribe (p. 27). *g*, *Flɔ gɛ*, made medicine for boys in the Poro (p. 30). *h*, Function unknown. *i*, *Tɔ la gɛ*, executioner for offences against the Poro (p. 30).

a, Pã kɛ la (p. 26). *b*, No information available. *c, d*, Ka gɛ, "crab," household god (p. 26). *e, Ma die*, patron of rice planting (p. 39). *f, g*, Portrait masks (pp. 39–40). *h, Gbɔ gɛ*, could stop war (p. 20). *i, Dra ya bɔa*, cared for boys in the Poro (p. 30 and Harley 1941b, p. 21). *j, Ga si gɛ*, helped clear farm (p. 22).

a, *Zena*, prayed to by childless women (p. 37). *b*, *Nya wɔ*, portrait mask of a popular young woman (p.). *c*, *Ti:n gbi*, ancestral spirit (p. 24). *d*, *Gba gɛ*, danced for a new baby (p. 23). *e*, *Zei*, goddess of fertility 36). *f*, *Longwa*, medicine dancer (p. 34). *g*, "Dancer," true function not known. *h*, Figured for artistic terest, no information available. *i*, *'Zi*, patron of babies (p. 23).

a, No information available. *b*, Goddess of the dance (p. 41). *c*, *Di kɛla*, goddess of victory (p. 26). *d, e*, No information available. *f*, *Gbini gɛ*, ancestral spirit (p. 23). *g, h*, No information available. *i*, *Tɔ bu gɛ*, patron of chickens, officiated at burials (p. 25).

PEABODY MUSEUM PAPERS VOL. XXXII, No. 2, PLATE XV

a, Great clay head (p. 34). *b*, Small clay head (p. 34). *c*, Twinned pots (pp. 36–37).